JOURNEY
TO ARDMORE

JOURNEY TO

HODDER AND STOUGHTON
LONDON · SYDNEY · AUCKLAND · TORONTO

ARDMORE

JOHN
RIDGWAY

Contents

*For Marie Christine without whom
there would have been nothing*

Illustrations

CREDITS

[1] Associated Newspapers Ltd.
[2] Thomas Hanley (Photography) Ltd.
[3] Bureau of Commercial Fisheries, US Dept of Interior.
[4] Syndication International.
[5] *Sun.*
[6] Channel Sun Publications, Jersey.
[7] Keystone Press Agency.
[8] Press Association Photo.
[9] *The People.*
[10] *Sunday Mirror.*
[11] British Travel Association.

1

How We Found Ardmore

'FOOTPATH TO ARDMORE – 3 MILES', the fingerpost on the narrow moorland road pointed towards the wild Atlantic coast. It was the first day of May 1964, and raining hard. Marie Christine was in London, nearly 700 miles away, at her brother's wedding. We had been married for just two months ourselves, and during that time had tried, in vain, to find somewhere to live and work on the north-west coast of Scotland, in wildest Sutherland.

We both had temporary jobs at Kinlochbervie, a tiny fishing village, seven miles north along the winding coast road from the Ardmore signpost, Marie Christine as a secretary on the pier, and I as an assistant to the crew of the salmon coble, while they set their bag nets in the spring of the year. In the evenings I supplemented my eight-pound weekly wage by loading the fish lorries for a pound a night. We lived in a caravan near the pier and earned a total of fifteen pounds a week; by this means we managed to save fifty pounds within two months, with the help of free fish from the pier. All the same it seemed rather a loss when compared to the twenty-five pounds a week I had been earning as a lieutenant in the Parachute Regiment, after eight years in the army.

We very much wanted a croft house, but seemed to have

exhausted every possibility from Ullapool to Cape Wrath, I had heard of remote Ardmore, from the salmon crew.

'Aye, it's very bonny in the summer,' they said, 'but desolate in the winter. You'd need to be hardy to live out there, right enough.'

As I turned my green mini-van down the 'footpath', I thought it was really rather a fine-looking drive. However, after about a mile I rounded a bend and my drive became just an old footpath, barely wide enough for the track of the van. There didn't seem to be any turning places, and the hills became steeper and the bends sharper. After a further mile I lost my nerve and decided to turn the van on a firm-looking piece of ground, which seemed as if it had once been used for stacking peat.

After several cautious manoeuvres the back wheels slid off the track into the ditch, and there I was, stuck across the path, two miles from the road and fifty miles from the nearest breakdown service. The rain drummed on the roof. I sat and thought, but that wasn't much help.

I got out to jack up the rear wheels when a strange figure happened along through the rain, from the direction of Ardmore. She was dressed in Wellington boots, stockings very baggy at the knees and an old green coat fastened at the waist by a piece of stout white cord from which dangled an old iron key. Her long, tangled auburn hair framed a deeply lined face, and there was a rather wild look in her eyes.

I had already abandoned the idea of visiting Ardmore on that afternoon, as it was now half past four, but I asked this strange person if there were any vacant houses out there.

'Oh, Johnny Macpherson's house is empty,' she said, pointing back along the track which runs high above the sheltered sea loch, then dips down across a narrow gorge, before petering into a zig-zag goat track up a cliff and finally disappears into the most northerly wood on the west coast of Scotland, which is Ardmore.

Winnie, as I later discovered was her name, said she had to go to the post office at Achlyness some three miles along the foot-path and down the road, 'To fetch some stores,' she said, showing me the folded sack in her right hand. With that she set off at a cracking pace, into the rain. I gazed after her, feeling rather puzzled, then, about a couple of hundred yards away, she suddenly broke into a wild dance, spinning round and round and throwing her hands up in the air. I redoubled my efforts to right the van.

After half an hour or so, I was cautiously edging the vehicle back along the path, when I saw, far below by the edge of the sea, a small grey-stone croft house. Leaving the van squarely on the track I scrambled through the heather and down the hill, climbed the dry-stone wall of the croft and ran the remaining hundred yards or so across the short-cropped grass and round the house to the blue front door, which faces the sea.

Soon I was sitting beside a glowing peat fire, as the brothers Donald and Peter Corbett, two bachelor shepherds in their sixties, explained the situation over at Ardmore. Ruby, their cheerful niece, laid the table by the small window overlooking the loch, for the inevitable highland tea of crowdie cheese and a great assortment of buns and cakes.

They told me that old John Macpherson had suffered a heart attack, and consequently had been taken out of Ardmore to be nearer a doctor. He was now staying with relatives, some forty miles away in Strathnaver, and was keen to sell up.

They described Ardmore to me over tea, the two Gaelic words 'Ard', hill, and 'more', big. It consists of Upper and Lower Ardmore at the eastern end of a hilly peninsula some one and a half miles from east to west and half a mile from north to south. Both places, the houses and the wood between, are on the side of a steep hill, which protects them from the fierce south-westerly gales which are a main feature of each winter.

Upper Ardmore is three miles off the road, along the path which runs down steeply across the narrow neck of land at sea level. This connecting strip, with its rickety fence, keeps the sheep on the peninsula in winter, and out on the common grazing in summer. A short, almost vertical climb through the wood, up a rough goat track (which becomes a waterfall after heavy rain) takes you to the green of the two crofts, No. 81 and No. 80 which are Upper Ardmore. Croft No. 81 is of stone and visited only rarely by the Browns, who have a hotel some seventeen miles away at Durness on the north coast. John Macpherson had lived at No. 80, a little house with stone gable ends, and of corrugated iron construction lined with wood. It faces east, across a small dry-stone wall and stands between two rowan trees, planted when the house was built at the beginning of the century – they are just as important as a front door or a chimney for they guard the house from evil spirits. The house looks over the wood, 150 feet down to the narrow sheltered sea loch A Chadh-fi (loch of the spindrift), which cuts inland for a further mile to Skerricha, another croft served by a small winding strip of tarmac road, off the coast road itself. Beyond that rises the majestic ridge of Foinavon, up nearly 3,000 feet above the sea. This view, with its ever-changing light and cloud, has kept me alive on more than one occasion.

The path carries on half a mile through the wood, and in the middle, crossing a small burn, it passes the little felt-roofed stone cottage where Winnie lives on her own during each summer. At Lower Ardmore, farther along, there are two good stone croft houses with green grass running before them a hundred feet down to the sea. This is near where Loch A Chadh-fi runs into Loch Laxford, which in turn boards the southern side of the Ardmore peninsula, and opens into the Atlantic. Of the two houses the nearer one, No. 76, had been empty for five years, since the death of Angus McLeod. The other one, No. 77, is the home of the Ross family, Robina in her seventies, and four of her eight children, Mary and Bessie, Hector and Hughie.

The houses on Ardmore, are known only by their numbers, which are those on the roll of the parish of Eddrachilles. There are few houses, but more fresh water lochs on Eddrachilles than any other parish in Britain.

In the sheltered natural harbour, below crofts No. 76 and No. 77 the wooden 'yaulies' are kept, for nearly all communication with the mainland is made by boat from Ardmore. 'Willy the Post' has the path almost to himself, for his daily walk out with the mails in the late afternoon.

According to Donald Corbett, over tea on that wet afternoon, in his croft at Portlevorchy, facing across the water to Ardmore, it appeared that my only chance was to call on John Macpherson at Strathnaver. As I made my way back to our caravan I was filled with hope once more.

Next week Marie Christine and I visited Mr. Macpherson; he said he was willing to assign his croft to us, but he was keen to include his flock of sheep in the bargain. We were not too sure of this, and so we decided to try and take advice about the idea of our keeping sheep.

Next day we drove over to Ardmore and walked the path with two local experts from Stoer, about thirty miles to the south. Gregor and Duncan both had sheep of their own and welcomed the idea of an outing. Liberal drams of whisky made the day pass the more pleasantly. After some discussion we thought we would be unwise to start with such a large flock of sheep, and therefore John Macpherson and I agreed to the assignation of No. 80 Ardmore without the sheep, for £150, pending the agreement of both the Crofters Commission and the proprietor. With time, this all came to be agreed and I found myself a crofter. At last we had somewhere in the world that was truly our home.

Perhaps for me, the most significant happening during that summer of 1964 was the publication of a book. We had many wet Sundays in our little caravan, and as this was our only day of rest, we read the newspapers avidly. I remember how anxiously I would wait for the private car which came each Sunday afternoon, selling papers all the way from the railhead at Lairg, fifty miles away. I enjoy contemporary autobiographies because they always seem to be written by people who have known success of one kind or another. I seemed to burn with the need to succeed in some field, but I didn't know quite which. Surely the key to a successful man's determination and drive must appear somewhere in his autobiography?

I enjoy searching through a book to pick out the simple statements of fact and faith which ring true. Compared with this, I find that of all the speeches I have heard, at prizegivings and the like, during my school days and since, I am able to recall only three statements. First, that Lord Mountbatten said at a Founder's Day at the Nautical College Pangbourne in the early 1950s, 'Britain will need a Royal Navy into the foreseeable future.' Second, Field-Marshal Lord Templer said at Sandhurst in 1950, 'I have tried to keep up my reading throughout my army career.' And third, General 'Tiger' Urquhart said, again at Sandhurst, 'A belief in God has been a great source of comfort to me, and a pillar of strength.' While I have remembered these three quotations, I am sorry that I have been unable to remember any of the other speakers, most of whom were probably keen to help their young audience. Perhaps this forgetfulness is reflected in my somewhat weak academic achievement.

One Sunday afternoon in the caravan, I read a review of *The Lonely Sea and the Sky*, the autobiography of Francis Chichester. I wrote immediately to Hatchard's bookshop in Piccadilly, and asked them to send me a copy, a major expenditure on our meagre pay. I was particularly impressed by the Introduction in which J. R. L. Anderson highlighted the success of Chichester as an individual or 'single hander' in a world of mass production and mass effort.

I believe I felt from that day, that opportunity was not the prerogative of the rich but that it would come my way. I felt that I must keep looking for my chance, with my life well balanced, in other words 'holding my elbows close to my body ready to step forward'.

Meanwhile I was employed at the salmon nets each day. Once they were firmly set, at right-angles to the rocky shore and the salmon began to run, hugging the coastline in their quest for the rivers of their birth, the catches began to improve. It is all quite simple. The fish swim close to the surface, and within a stone's throw of the shoreline, until they are faced with a long floating net, meshed too small for them to force even their heads through. They swim inshore along the net until they reach the rocks, and then back out to try and find another way round. Some hundred yards offshore, they unknowingly swim into an arrowhead of net, at the end of which is a bag net with a narrow entrance. Once inside they swim round and round, but cannot find a way out.

Twice a day except on Sundays, the heavy grey coble motors out with its crew of four. As the bag is hauled the dark blue-grey backs of the salmon are drawn nearer and nearer through the clear, pale green water. Soon the bars of silver are gasping on their sides, and then lifted into the coble; a sharp smack on the head with a billet of wood, into the box, and it's all over. Frequently the bag is empty, when the boat calls, and a tell-tale hole in the side shows how a visiting seal or otter has caught himself a meal and let the rest of the catch escape. Occasionally a graceful porpoise becomes entangled and, unable to surface for air, dies and then stiffens with rigor mortis. If the salmon can be killed without much struggle, then rigor mortis takes longer to set in, and consequently longer to wear off; this is an important factor in the marketing of the fish. A salmon still in rigor mortis is clearly freshly killed, and the more valuable for it.

For me the season ended early; once the nets were out and the fishing well under way, there was no need for me, the fifth member of the coble crew. I was relegated to pier hand during the day – this meant odd jobs such as the repairing of boxes for the cod, haddock, whiting and other fish the neat little seine-net boats brought in from Monday to Thursday. At nights after the auction, we often had to load as much as thirty tons of boxes on to the lorries, so that they might reach the markets in Glasgow, Edinburgh and Aberdeen early the next morning. My co-lifter and superior was a slim sixteen-year-old boy, of surprising strength.

As the summer drew near, the potatoes were planted at Ardmore, but we were no nearer to moving from our caravan to the croft; the formalities seemed interminable. Gradually I came to feel as if I had retired at the early age of twenty-five; clearly there was no scope for employment beyond our work on the pier. If we moved to Ardmore, however, the pier would be so far away that certainly Marie Christine would be unable to work there; and a crofting life alone did not seem to justify the expense and time spent on my education and the subsequent training at Sandhurst. Inevitably we realised that we must return to the more normal rush of life, as it is carried on in cities. For me, this meant trying to return to the Parachute Regiment. I had been envious of their active service in the Yemen in South Arabia, while I was working on the pier.

After a desolate couple of months working on a traffic survey in London, I was accepted back with little loss in seniority. We were determined to return to the croft, improving it as best we could, during all available periods of leave. At the same time we had to plan a way of life based on the croft which would enable us to live and work there when I retired from the Army, with a small pension, perhaps at the age of thirty-seven in another twelve years' time. This was a considerable problem.

The challenge was clear. Many people had smiled knowingly when we said we were going to try to make a life in the north-west of Scotland once we were married. Most of them believed that it was a wild-goose chase, and they were right, almost. We had returned south, defeated, and soon enough. However we had gained a foothold. We should return to try again.

Marie Christine and that little croft house, clinging to the side of the hill, above the wood and the sea, were to be the sheet anchor in the dangerous times ahead.

Two lessons had been learnt. Firstly, any attempt to make a living on the north-west coast would have to come entirely from outside – the small local population is not much interested in progress. Secondly, God helps those who help themselves.

2

The First Croft

'THE house has a beautiful view, Johnny, but I don't think it's suitable for a short visit; it is rather a long way from the road,' said Colin Thomson over dinner at our home in Farnham near Aldershot.

All the same it seemed that he had enjoyed his weekend at Ardmore in January 1965. He was twenty-five then and a captain in the Parachute Regiment, and had decided that a couple of days alone would be something to remember during his impending spell in Cyprus, as part of the United Nations Force.

After careful preparation, he had caught the Royal Highlander at Euston, on the evening of Friday, 15th January. As befits the economic station of a modern young officer, he slept in his light-weight sleeping bag in the guard's van, as the famous train thundered 600 miles through the night, north to Inverness. With a characteristic dash of extravagance, this tall lean bastion of Western defence had hired a car for his last weekend in the United Kingdom. During the 100-mile drive to the North-West Highlands, the weather was fine, and the Captain hummed the Marsellaise in his usual monotonous fashion.

Three miles north of Laxford Bridge on the Durness road, he saw the footpath sign. Turning the Morris Traveller off the road, he cautiously advanced along the track. Soon he became anxious for the hired car; the bends and hills became sharper as the path dwindled, and the light began to fail in the late January afternoon. Soon the shiny vehicle was in the ditch with its rear wheels axle-deep in the soggy peat. It was beginning to spot with rain, but a paratrooper is trained to ignore such things, and the borrowed oilskins were left in the car. After proceeding half a mile or so along the track on foot, the rain turned to sleet and there began a deluge in the classical Highland style. British grit demanded that the Captain should go on. On the steep hill down to the Ardmore sheep fence, the inferior brown-paper carrier bag, of foreign origin, failed. The weekend's supply of food bounced off the streaming gravel and stuck in the heather by the edge of the path. Thomson's determined mouth tightened yet firmer. At least his load was reduced, but by this time he was soaked right through his cavalry twill trousers, sports jacket and underwear, to the skin.

Closing the fish-box gate in the rickety sheep fence behind him, he strode up the waterfall into the darkness. A little better than half-way up, his inferior imitation brown leather suitcase, also of foreign origin, fell open, and he was able to watch his remaining possessions cascade down into the night. On gaining the crofts at the top, he could just make out the dim shape of the ramshackle black corrugated-iron cottage on the side of the hill. Of course the door was locked, and he had no key.

Groping his way through the thick wood he couldn't help thinking of the warm Cyprus sun on his back. When he reached the croft house at the far end, he allowed his iron self-discipline to falter, and accepted a cup of tea and a chance to warm himself by the peat fire. The Ross family will remember that night for ever.

Key in hand, the Captain returned to let himself into No. 80, where he spent a rather uncomfortable night, for the house was bare, and there was no light, no food and no fire.

The next day, Sunday, was spent digging the car out of the peat and turning it on the path. On the Monday, refreshed by his holiday, the Captain returned south to make his assessment of Ardmore.

The rebuilding of No. 80 was to be something of a problem.

That March I managed a weekend visit myself, using the same means of transport as Colin, whose sun drenched letters arrived spasmodically from 'the front'. On this occasion there was a light

B

dusting of snow on the crofts. The brittle wintry sun shone from an ice-blue sky as I rowed the mile or so down the narrow sea loch, flanked by the pink-hued rock of the hills, which rise steep from the waters' edge.

I had borrowed the boat from Bill Ross who lives at Skerricha where the bumpy side road twists down to his little house beside the inland end of the loch. Now in his seventies the hard times of Bill's youth are hard to imagine, in the warmth of the Welfare State. During the First World War he joined the Machine Gun Corps, and carried a Vickers tripod through the horrors of many of the main engagements. He was there at the Somme, on the day when 60,000 allied soldiers died before breakfast. On more than one occasion during those years, he had looked round to find the rest of the gun crew dead. One of his proudest possessions is a small pair of binoculars which he cut from the body of a dead German officer, during one of these many times when he went 'over the top'. Trench foot suffered all those years ago still causes him pain during the frosts of each winter. He has lived at Skerricha ever since the First World War, and now he is often alone in that little house at the end of the loch; for his burly son, Donald Hugh, himself wounded as a Commando in the Second World War, often drives fish lorries to the markets in the distant cities of Edinburgh and Glasgow. Bill still works a long day on the hill whenever necessary. Erect, white-haired and slightly built he is always followed around the croft by his dogs, Dan and Chief. The sense of humour which has helped him through many lonely times, with neither television nor telephone, but increasing deafness, is as sharp as ever. The broad grin and ready crack, encourages visitors to 'Be gone – and get on with your work'.

In return for the loan of the rowing boat I agreed to buy a second-hand Seagull outboard engine for our joint use. Bill and Donald Hugh use the boat to put the rams, or 'tups' as they are called, on to an island in Loch Laxford at the end of August. Then, in November, they are brought back to run with the ewes.

Over that weekend Hughie Ross, from No. 77, agreed to undertake the 'improvements' at No. 80. The first priority was a new roof, as the zinc-dipped corrugated iron, although painted with pitch, had become badly corroded. As John Macpherson had grown older he had found the more difficult maintenance, such as working on the roof, beyond his strength. The relentless wind soon deals with makeshift repairs.

Hughie thought the most suitable new roof would be asbestos sheeting, and as the next gale could easily strip the old roof, action was needed immediately.

On the Monday morning of my departure, Bill and I spent two hours coaxing the hired car up the steep hill away from Skerricha. Every inch of the first 200 yards had to be covered with gravel. . . . We brought it down from the tip at the top of the hill in a rickety old wheelbarrow, and then shovelled it into the wheel tracks once we had scraped away the snow. In future, I always came on the daily mail bus which meets the train at Lairg. This set me down, fifty miles later, at the little wooden mail box on the junction with the side road to Skerricha. The half-mile walk down to Bill's croft, even in vile weather, was no problem when compared to digging that car up the hill with a train to catch.

The asbestos sheets were ordered from Inverness, and Rod Liddon, an old friend, and also a captain in the Parachute Regiment, agreed to travel the guard's van and mail bus way to Ardmore, only three weeks later. He was to collect the roofing materials by boat from Laxford Pier, where they were supposed to be stockpiled on delivery by a fish lorry, returning through Inverness. His journey was in vain; for the first time we encountered the 'Highland Delivery Systems', perhaps the main factor in any building project on the north-west coast. We have since learned to order materials months in advance, and to concentrate on a cheerful mental acceptance of late delivery as an inevitable fact of life. This is an achievement without which we might have gone mad long ago.

From that brief, although disappointing first visit, it was clear that Rod would like to live at Ardmore. He had married Jeannie, a pretty dark-haired girl, who had spent much of her childhood riding on the wild Devonshire moors. Their wedding had been just a month before ours in the spring of the previous year.

The four of us planned to spend the whole month of August at the croft, if we could arrange our leave and holidays for Jeannie and Marie Christine, who were doing secretarial work in Aldershot.

Another month passed, and when I was absolutely certain the ninety sheets of asbestos were stacked on Laxford pier, I managed to persuade Richard Pirie, the fittest officer I knew, to take a long weekend and help me with the roof. The plan was to ship the material four miles from the pier, in two trips, using Bill's boat and the newly acquired outboard. Then we would carry the ton or so of asbestos 150 feet straight up the hill through the wood to the house. Next we would remove the old roof and, with Hughie's help, replace it with the new one. The whole operation was to be completed in four days.

It was a dreadful weekend for April, with sleet and rain blowing continuously and almost horizontally from the north-west, straight from Greenland. We were nearly drowned on the second trip from the pier, when with only a couple of hundred yards to make the comparative shelter of Loch A Chadh-fi from the main Loch Laxford, we were caught in a sudden blinding squall. All at once the water was coming faster over the bows than Richard could bale with the bucket.

'The outlook is grim,' I shouted, ramming the outboard hard over, to run before the wind for the shelter of a small heathery island, uninhabited even by sheep. The little boat was so laden with the asbestos sheets, that it seemed like a saucer more than half full of water. But we gained the sheltered side of the islet and went ashore.

'No good can come of anything attempted on the Sabbath', is a well-known saying in the remote north-west. We were soaked through and our teeth chattered, we had no food and no matches and no shelter. It looked as if we were in for a thin time of it unless there was a change in the weather.

After about half an hour, however, we were relieved to find the weather improving. It was, after all, just a rather long squall and not the start of yet another gale.

Once we had all of the ninety asbestos sheets off-loaded on the shore below the house, we began the long climb up through the wood. Richard and I found that the best method was for one of us to carry the upper end of two sheets on his shoulders, and for the other to hold the lower end at about waist level. In this manner we made forty-five trips up and down the hill, and so had all the roofing materials on the site within two days. The weather ensured that we were so wet and cold that we had to keep moving.

Hughie took two days off from his work to help us. As an interior decorator with his brother Robert, who lives two miles away by boat, or twelve by road, on the other side of Loch Laxford at Foindle, he often travels as far as 150 miles for work.

We were pretty tired after the lift up the hill, but Hughie soon had us going again. There is surprising strength in his wiry frame. A lifetime of moving sheep up and down the nearly vertical hills on Ardmore, and many years of using a paint brush have given him, now in his mid-thirties, an exceptional load-carrying ability and a remarkable grip. In the unlikely event of thieves taking his Seagull outboard, they wouldn't get far, because no normal grip could undo the screw-top air-vent on the petrol tank!

Without Hughie's help and encouragement we never could have come to Ardmore. Locally he is reckoned to be very 'knacky'. What extraordinary luck we had to find such a highly skilled painter, plumber, joiner and intensely kind person all in one, living so close at hand. I don't suppose he has ever been known to have one cross word with anyone, in his whole life.

Stripping the old roof took only a couple of hours, although in the high wind it was rather dangerous; flying corrugated-iron sheets have been known to take a man's head off. By the end of the day the front side of the roof had been recovered with the new sheeting.

Lying in my sleeping bag on the living-room floor that night, I wondered what would happen if another gale should spring up. Although the house is tucked right under the hill, away from the weight of the usual south-westerly gales, it takes quite a shaking from the rare but devastating north-westerly storms.

We were lucky. Next morning, after a simple breakfast of raw oatmeal blocks and black coffee, we went on with the work. The job was done by late afternoon. This was for me another milestone. Now the house would stand, my anchor would hold firm.

That evening, Richard cooked a celebration meal of army dehydrated curry and rice. A South African girl friend had sent him a small bottle of Pirie Pirie powder, and this made it a real feast.

In the guttering light of an old oil lamp, which I had rescued from a rubbish heap, the peat and driftwood fire seemed to be telling me that I must continue the struggle with the elements at Ardmore. It was a struggle that had almost been lost in the most unexpected fashion; for it was easier times that had nearly finished Ardmore, not the weather and isolation.

Spread out around 'the loch of the Spindrift', on the single crofts at Skerricha and Portlevorchy, together with the pair at Upper Ardmore and the three at Lower Ardmore, seven families had succeeded in winning a livelihood from the poor soil and surrounding sea. The very fireplace into which I now gazed had come from the school at Ardmore; which had been closed nearly twenty years before. Hughie had been the last pupil.

With the coming of the Welfare State hard times had become a memory. But gone, too, was the ring of childish laughter, from the houses which had each been homes for families of nine or ten. It was now unthinkable to walk the sheep to the Lairg sales, cars replaced bicycles. Only recently television, that breaker of community spirit, had reached Achlyness, the nearest village, some five miles across the hills. The youth of all the families had left the shores of the loch, and only the older generation remained. The crofts fell into disrepair, coarse rushes crept back along the choked land drains, and obliterated the green of the grass.

I smiled into the glowing fire. How easy to fall into the trap of over-sentimentality, which has killed the good intentions of so many who have come from outside to build a new life in the Highlands! The rock which is Ardmore has stood for 2,000 million years. It doesn't do to be oversentimental.

This wild, deserted, beautiful place – somehow I would live here. I could think of no young person who had succeeded in staying. . . . What an interesting challenge! I realised from the previous year that it would have to be something new and completely self-contained; it would have to be a very good idea.

Next morning, Richard and I left on the mail bus for the distant train south.

At the end of May, Mike Howe drove up from Aldershot, with Silver his Welsh collie. In the back of his grey mini-van he carried the beginnings of comfort for the croft; a gas cooker, which Rod and I bought for two pounds ten in a saleroom, and had converted to Calor Gas for a further thirty shillings. It was the first of several visits Mike made with Silver to Ardmore. As an Olympic pentathlete he had much time for training and could choose his leave as he wished, to suit his arduous training schedule.

Another stroke of good fortune came our way in July. Rod and I had managed to arrange our leave during August. Jeannie and Marie Christine were both declared redundant by the firm for which they worked in Aldershot; this meant some financial compensation, which was particularly welcome at the time of Hughie's improvements to the croft.

Our summer holiday came. Rod and I drove up in triumphant

procession, Rod leading in his 150,000-mile veteran Volkswagen 'Beetle', and I in the tired green mini-van. It is about 700 miles from Aldershot and although we have done it in sixteen hours' continuous driving, the journey is best spread over two days. On this occasion, as Rod and I were driving alone (the girls' holidays didn't start for another week), we decided to sleep by the roadside when we felt tired. As it turned out, Jedburgh was as far as we could go, after a late start on the first day. The cars were crammed with furniture and odds and ends for the croft, so we unrolled our sleeping bags in the dark, at about midnight, beside the road almost two miles short of the old border town.

Some little time later I awoke in best silent paratrooper style, I was certain that something was up. It was pitch dark, and the road unlit and empty. Rod snored steadily a few yards farther along. I glanced over in his direction and could just make out the shape of a big black dog lifting its leg on his sleeping bag. I shouted, the dog ran off, Rod sat up, and it started to rain – 'all in one moment' as the army would say. There was nothing for it but to try and snatch a few hours' sleep hunched over the steering wheel.

We arrived at Ardmore late in the day, and the long-awaited holiday began. Two more friends from the Parachute Regiment joined us for the first week. One was Richard Brinton, whose mother stayed at the Garbet Hotel at Kinlochbervie, which burnt down, the day after they left for home. Ian Mcleod drove up for a few days from Wales and was a great help in repairing half a dozen old lobster creels we found on the beach.

The weather was at its best, and the days and nights passed in a haze of fishing.

We fished for lobsters in the pearly light of early morning under the cliffs of Paddy's Isle; so called because two Irish smugglers were buried there in the last century, after falling through the ice one winter's day on a hill loch near by.

Baited with fish the willow creels are sunk to the bottom, at the edge of the tangle. It is best near cairns of rock formed by small avalanches from the cliffs above, on whose ledges the ravens nest and a pair of shaggy wild goats can sometimes be seen. Hauling in the line below the cork buoy, the creel comes gradually into sight through the pale green water. Eyes strain to see if we have bright blue lobsters, for they are red only after they're cooked. Sometimes it was lobsters, sometimes crabs. We kept them in an old fish box, claws tied, deep down under the wood below the croft. By the end of the week we had quite a few of both, but there was a massacre in the box. A couple of lobsters cut through the twine securing their claws and set about the execution of all the crabs. Too late we realised why many of the local fishermen cut the claw tendon of their lobsters, before putting them in the store box.

During the day we often fished for brown trout, which abound in the fifty or so small hill lochs within the common grazing of the croft. The trout are usually small but easily caught on the fly. Donald Corbett of Portlevorchy has had fish of up to six pounds on the worm, and Hughie too has caught several over three pounds. It seems that the best method of improving size is to take a pail of small fish from one of the overpopulated lochs, and then free them in other lochs which may have no fish in them, owing to a lack of spawning ground.

A tour of half a dozen small lochs, each with its own individual character and beauty, can usually provide a good basket of trout. The favourite cast of three flies is Black Pennell, Red Palmer and Invicta, in size ten. These are easily tied at home during the long winter evenings.

Without our wives to cook for us, Rod and I relied on smoking the trout in just eight minutes in a Scandinavian tin smoker.

In the evenings, when Hughie returned, in his little blue 'yawlie', across Loch Laxford from Foindle, we would often go out to Ardmore Point with him after the mackerel, pollack and coley. Trolling feathers, and sand eels which I had made out of polythene tube painted with Marie Christine's nail varnish, we ran the Seagull outboard just fast enough to keep the water cooling system going. Skirting close to the rocky islands, seventy fish in an hour was not uncommon, late in the evening on a rising tide. Hughie had fished there all his life, and knew the best places.

When the girls arrived the following week, tired out after a twenty-four-hour journey by rail and bus, we took them straight out in the boat on a glorious evening. Their tiredness quickly changed to excitement as they caught pollack up to four or five pounds on each run across the Point. Excitement is a good anti-dote for fatigue.

Domesticity meant that our easy-going routine had to change; Rod and I found we were heading for a mutiny unless the fishing was severely curtailed. Picnics became the order of things, much to our disgust. While days were spent on deserted little beaches or searching for seals round the outer islands. Never was it so clear that marriage means give and take.

A good holiday arrangement, Rod and I thought, would be sea-trout fishing trips to Loch Hope, on the north coast about forty miles away. We reasoned that the beautiful drive, the picnic on the boat, and finally the delicious taste of smoked sea-trout would win the day with the girls.

Douglas Mair, the keeper at Loch Hope, was most helpful. He not only hired us a boat but also offered the use of a deserted croft house near by, where we could cook and spend the night. It was really too far for a one-day trip from Ardmore.

Our first visit was the best we ever made. The loch, running due south off the north coast, is almost six miles long and averages about half a mile in width. There is a small river, running perhaps three-quarters of a mile down to the sea; this is such a good salmon river as to be almost unknown, so jealously is it guarded. On that first day, it was quite windy from the south, and this kept the worst of the rain away. We fished, one with the wetfly and one with dapping rod, while Jeannie and Marie Christine either rowed the boat or prepared our favourite snacks of cheddar cheese and Branston pickle. What an admirable situation!

Dapping takes very little time to learn, unlike casting a fly. The sixteen-foot-long rod has a twelve-foot length of silk floss blow-line eighteen inches up from the huge furry fly, which is about the size of a ping-pong ball. A good breeze is necessary to blow the line and fly, which is then systematically played across the line of the drifting boat. The fly dances about, just kissing the water and then moving on. After a while a sort of hypnosis sets in as the angler watches the fly, then the sea-trout comes up with a splash like a dog. Nine times out of ten, the astonished novice will jerk the rod in surprise, and the fish, which has only come up to drown the fly on the first rise, has no chance of turning to gulp it down.

We had beginner's luck, and after countless misses learnt the knack of not reacting to the splash. The result was three 'bars of silver' four, three and two pounds.

It was cold on our second visit to the loch and we caught nothing. Canny Douglas confirmed our excuses that it was too cold, the water too high, the wind too changeable, that we should have been there the day before, and all the other fishing faults.

It was not a good time to spend our first night at the deserted croft; we should have driven home. A roof was all Rod and I wanted, but the girls cried most of the night, the floorboards were too hard, the bare rooms too dusty, the house too cold – fishing trips to Loch Hope were over.

As we drove home next day there were periods of silence. The holiday needed drastic surgery, if it was not to prove disastrous. The basic difficulty was the complete lack of comfort, which it seems girls are not brought up to accept.

We spent the remaining two weeks working on improvements to the comfort of the house. Hughie had already repainted it blue outside and white in, and had made a start on the joinery involved in transforming the little kitchen into a bathroom. Cutting a window in the back of the house had greatly improved the light in the new kitchen, and the living-room was beginning to take shape as well, but it couldn't be called comfortable.

Rod is a great man for 'earthworks', and we soon dug the hole for the septic tank, and the trench for the fireclay pipes from the back of the house down to the tank. We also tried to improve the water supply, which was simply a small well under a cliff near the Atlantic end of the house. This well had a reputation for drying up in the heat of the summer, which meant the Macphersons had had to walk half a mile through the wood to the other well, which serves No. 76 and No. 77.

After extensive digging operations, which produced only a muddy puddle, instead of our projected deeper well, we decided that the most practical scheme would be to dam a small burn some 300 yards away on the hillside behind the house. The main attraction of this scheme was the added water pressure needed to work the Calor Gas water heater, which we were saving up for at that time. The site for the dam was selected in a narrow defile, but digging could not be started as the time had come for us to leave Ardmore and return south, to the army.

There are times when Ardmore seems truly magical. Shortly before we left, the weather was showery, and around teatime one day, as we looked out of the kitchen window, we saw a rainbow. I suppose sooner or later just about everyone must see a rainbow with one of its ends close enough to set the mind dreaming of that fabled pot of gold. Our rainbow was brilliantly coloured and it formed a high and yet very narrow arch, to bridge the sea loch below the wood. Either end was clearly visible as it drilled into the hillside. Above, another larger, paler, rainbow seemed to be standing guard. A photograph would have appeared unreal. It was a vision to be carried in the mind for a lifetime.

The only intruders during our stay came by way of the sea, in a rather large yacht. She anchored out in Loch Laxford, while the owner's party came ashore for a picnic lunch. Certainly they travelled in style, the fine jolly-boat was crewed by men in proper sailor's uniform. The boat-hooks looked as if they had real brass fittings, as they clattered on to the rocks just across from the croft. The wicker hampers looked splendid. As the party of eight spread their rugs on the grass in the warm sunlight, I considered the idea of going across and telling them, 'Get off my land.' The reaction would have been interesting, if nothing else, for the yacht was called *Brittania* and the owner was the Queen!

Life seemed rather dull in Aldershot, but in late October I managed another long weekend, and Mike Howe met me off the train at Inverness. As he had ten days' leave he had travelled by car.

The Saturday morning dawned clear and still, so we decided to go up Foinavon with Hughie. After climbing for two and half hours, we were at the top, nearly 3,000 feet above the sea, among clouds of ptarmigan, all dressed in their winter feathers of white. Since that day I often think of those birds when the January blizzards shriek in from the Arctic to tear great plumes of snow from that lofty ridge. Little wonder those warm feathers extend right down the leg to the very claws of their feet.

From the top, a knife-edge ridge runs south-east into the heart of the Plat Reidh, where over a thousand red deer live in safety, many miles from the road. This is the home of the Golden Eagle, so rarely seen. Swooping down with his slashing talons he can bowl over a young deer calf, should it stray too far from its mother. Each spring, on the hilltops around Ardmore, rough scarecrows are fashioned of sticks and old clothes, to keep these great birds from the lambs, for they range far and wide in search of prey. Occasionally they used to be caught in the gin-traps laid for the foxes which infest this wilderness of rock and heather.

These traps were set at tiny hill lochans in a particularly deadly fashion. Foxes are liable to bite off a foot in order to escape, so the baited trap would be placed on a rock just out from the bank, and a narrow path of stones built across the deep water to it. On reaching the bait the fox would step in the trap, and a delicately balanced boulder would drag both trap and fox under the water. One crofter caught a badger, an otter and two golden eagles last spring, before the gin-trap was made illegal in Scotland.

As each lamb is worth five or six pounds at the Lairg sales, sentiment is quickly replaced by anger as the valuable spring crop is daily reduced.

On this particular Saturday on Foinavon, the heat shimmered above the flat grey stones along the ridge. To the north and the west lay the deep blue of the sea, and at our feet spread a moonscape of some of the oldest rocks on the surface of the earth. Facing south, the view was of endless mountains, interspersed with innumerable rings of bright water, each reflecting the sun. Clinging to the side of one of the many fiord-like sea lochs which reach far inland, the isolated cottages of Ardmore were just discernible far below us. How brief is one man's life when compared to this timelessness.

As we started to make our way down through the gaunt boulders, the roaring of a peat blackened stag floated up two thousand feet or more from the corries on the precipitous northeast face. The ptarmigans exploded into flight only if we came within perhaps half a dozen paces of them; they seemed like tame doves. Farther down a mountain hare bolted in panic before us, racing headlong down the slope and out of sight. Soon we were drinking from the first of the burns which run fresh from springs on the mountainside. The tiny alpine flowers and bare rocks gave way to the heather and bogland as we descended. Within the hour we were at Skerricha.

Round the log fire that night, we talked of many things. I remember discussing a new thirty-foot masthead sloop which had just been introduced by the Westerly boat-building firm, from Portsmouth. For £5,000 we could sail out of Ardmore to anywhere in the world, and back again. Sadly we had rather less than no money to buy such a fine craft. We settled for a *Daily Mirror* class dinghy kit which I would buy and send up to Ardmore. Hughie would build it and we would own half shares in the vessel.

The month of November brought to a head the legal proceedings concerning the croft. I travelled up by train one Thursday night to Inverness from Euston, settled the business, and caught the Friday night train to London, feeling jubilant.

On both journeys a whole dining car and a sleeping car had

been added to the Royal Highlander. This was to carry the Press to and from the opening of the Rank Organisation's opulent Coylum Bridge Hotel at Aviemore. I feel sure I was the happiest person on the train returning to London. That little house, perched, dark and empty, on its remote hillside, meant more to me than a hundred hotels. I didn't need their champagne; when I treated myself to a celebration dinner that night, I felt tremendously warm and content. The thunder of wheels over rails filled another pocket in my memory.

The Sutherland County Council gave permission for the house to be improved to Standard Improvement Grant level. I ordered the materials immediately and planned our first Christmas at Ardmore – to carry the concrete blocks, and all the thousand and one items required by Hughie, across the water from Skerricha and up the hill through the wood to the house.

Marie Christine and I set out from Farnham in the indomitable green mini-van, at three o'clock on the afternoon of Thursday, 22nd December. With us, we had the full benefits of having joined a grocer's 'Christmas Club' in August, with this very plan in mind.

On the long night drive we found the battery unable to provide power enough for the lights, heater and windscreen wipers in heavy rain on the A1. We finally crept to a halt just short of the new Forth road bridge, north of Edinburgh, at two o'clock in the morning. We slept for a couple of rather cold hours. With Marie Christine showing signs of 'flu, we had to push the van to start it. Then we motored on to Pitlochry, where we slept another hour at dawn.

Hughie was waiting at Skerricha when we arrived in the middle of a raw December afternoon. The skinning north-westerly wind drove lines of pure white spindrift along the slate-grey face of the loch, matching the white of the snow-covered land. Hughie's little blue yawlie soon had us ashore under the wood. We clambered up the hill, had a quick meal and crawled into bed.

Next morning we woke up to find the top blanket wringing wet with dew, and Marie Christine's cold rather worse. After breakfast Hughie came along, through the wood from his house. Together we managed to lift the ninety-six forty-pound concrete blocks the two hundred yards down to the shore, from the shelter of Bill's cowshed at Skerricha. Trusty army socks of grey angora wool made fine mittens in the bitter cold, and by lunchtime we had half the blocks over the loch and stacked on the green below the wood. The dinghy kit had also come, and we stored it away in Hughie's little shed, on the foreshore at the foot of his croft. Although everything was rather grim in the little house when we first arrived, Marie Christine whizzed about and soon had it warm and cosy.

Christmas morning dawned bright and clear, and we had cake and sherry over at the Rosses' croft. I slipped and nearly fell off the snowy path coming back through the wood. Although there was enough snow, and Marie Christine had brought her skis, her cold prevented the long-awaited exhibition.

Hughie and I managed to lift all the remaining blocks across in his boat, and then we tried a little fishing out at Ardmore Point, but with no success.

The oven was known to be rather slow, so we decided to have the turkey at seven in the evening. Hughie came over all dressed up. Marie Christine wore her long red dress and I played the gallant host in my dinner jacket. Hughie and I sat at either end of the table, which had been the front door at some earlier date. Marie Christine sat on one side, facing the open log fire in the old iron fireplace from Hughie's schoolroom. The roast turkey sat on the table, huge and brown in the flickering candle-light. Dinner lasted five hours, and we dozed off to sleep in between courses. Our little world was a warm and very happy place. Even if the powdery snow did blow in under the front door, old blankets above the other doors kept the cold at bay. This was home.

Sunday was spent in the house, playing Scrabble and eating in front of the fire. Over the crackling wireless, Peter Ustinov described his experiences as platoon runner for the point platoon, of the point company of the point battalion, of a demonstration force on Salisbury Plain during the Second World War. Outside the snow showers continued from the north-west, and trips to the byre to saw logs were made as brief as possible.

On Boxing Day I made thirteen trips up the hill to the house, carrying two forty-pound blocks of concrete for the septic tank on each climb. In the afternoon M.C. joined Hughie and me in his boat, when we went to collect a dozen sacks of sand from the beaches at the head of Loch Laxford. The scurrying snow showers often obscured the shore. In the little boat I thought of Captain Hudson, cast adrift by his mutinous crew in the bay which was later named after him.

Over the next three days we managed to carry up to the house everything that had been delivered; even the six-foot cast-iron bath came up without too much difficulty. We would do a lift of two concrete blocks each, and then on the way down move the bath ten paces up the hill. The whole scheme was good for one's moral fibre. It had been a good Christmas.

I made a weekend visit in February with Tim Churcher, again of the Parachute Regiment, to carry seven hundredweight of cement, half a ton of sand and all the fireclay pipes up the hill – this on a fine diet of winkle pie from the beach.

James Emson drove us up at Easter in his Alfa Romeo, 700 miles in fourteen hours. It was a two-seater car and so Marie Christine took a sleeping pill to overcome the discomfort of the journey. It wasn't much fun for her sitting in the middle.

While fleeing from a nurse in Aden Military Hospital many months before, James had had to let himself drop from an open window. The subsequent twenty-foot fall in bare feet on to the concrete had shattered both his heels. Walking was still difficult, in fact barely possible, but typically he didn't complain.

As he couldn't walk far, we concentrated on the new game Scalectrix, which we had bought for rainy days. James is a great competitor, and the game soon turned into a tremendous struggle for supremacy. One car was clearly faster than the other, so we decided on alternate single car races against the clock on three circuits of the track, which was laid out on the rug in front of the fire. The fastest time switched from person to person. James was livid when, just as I had regained the title, the batteries began to fail. Try as he might the car would not go fast enough, even with his thumb permanently held on the accelerator button of the control box.

Hughie had performed miracles of plumbing and the only problem was the water system itself. I had sent up a temporary polythene swimming pool for fifty pounds. We set it up just below the level of the well, and siphoned the water in down a small pipe, hoping that it would fill overnight. Sadly, there was rather a wind during the night, before the pool filled. Next morning the whole apparatus looked rather like a crashed Zeppelin; another scheme had failed. The next one would have to succeed or I would be dead before the summer was out.

3

Childhood

MEMORIES of my childhood are centred around old Percy
Dann's jetty on the Thames at Datchet some three or four miles
down-river from Windsor, in those days (just after the war) a
sleepy little village.

Fishing alone at the end of that small wooden jetty, in the
early mist of a summer's morning, with the smell of the weeping
willows and the gentle cooing of the woodpigeons, my world was
complete. Percy was kind to me; he didn't allow other children
on his property for fear of damage to his boats, but he knew that I
only wished to fish.

I was born in 1938 on the 8th July. My family always seemed
on the move around the South of England – my father is a civil
engineer, and we moved house as his work dictated. For me the
war was simply an occasional 'dogfight' in the night sky above
a little cottage in Devonshire.

I was eight when we settled into the rambling Victorian riverside house which was to be home for the next fifteen years. My
bedroom was right at the top and from my window I looked
straight up the River Thames. On the right bank lay Percy
Dann's boathouse, with its collection of cabin cruisers moored
along the waterfront. Beyond the moorings a curtain of graceful

willow trees shrouded several river gardens, and then, farther still, there stretched the tangled undergrowth bordering the green watermeadows of Steven's Farm. On the other side of the river, which is crown land, neat rows of trees and well-kept fields lead up to the distant walls of Windsor Castle.

Nearly every day of every holiday was spent on the jetty. At first it was jam jars, and then bottle traps, for minnows and little gudgeon. Soon it was a cane and string, with a bent pin and bread paste for dace. Eventually a cheap lance wood rod with reel to match, a little float and a real sixpenny hook to gut. The bait was maggots and worms, for everything that lived in the river.

My younger brother Michael and I held our father in considerable awe. He remained in the background during our childhood, much preoccupied with the business of earning enough to keep us at school. All orders from and questions to him were relayed through our mother, a generous-hearted if rather zany Irish figure who always regretted not taking up an operatic career. Instead she devoted her considerable imagination to smoothing over schoolboy pranks when Pa came back each night. This imagination was fired daily by an unvarying diet of espionage paperbacks and bars of Fry's Chocolate Mint; this combination assured us of an original viewpoint on every subject under the sun. Looking back, I can now see that much of my own fierce wish to stand alone springs from my mother's individuality. For this I am deeply grateful.

School years at prep school in Slough and later at the Nautical College, Pangbourne, near Reading, passed in the usual dull fashion of the times. Exams were failed, reports were bad and the rugby and cricket teams always hard to get into. Sadly for me, games occupied a much higher priority than academic work.

My real life in those years was lived alone by the river during the holidays. A dip of the red quill float, or a tug at the tip of the legering rod – this was the stuff of life; a ceaseless battle with small fish, which were always returned to the water at the end of the day from the keep net. During the Easter holidays, usually four weeks which fell in the close season for coarse fish, I adapted a rod for fly fishing. I stalked the fast-rising dace in the shallow runs over the clean gravel. If questioned I would always reply that I was after the wily Thames trout, although I never saw nor even heard of one being caught in our part of the river.

When I was sixteen, I saved up enough pocket money to buy a

c

cheap medium-action-built cane fly rod from a firm in Edinburgh. That same summer my parents kindly bought me a little rowing boat, which I painted green and named *Chinook* after the Canadian Pacific salmon. I then took to fly fishing for chub on the hot summer days. Each afternoon I would row upriver to Eton College, casting a black Zulu, or brown Soldier Palmer fly whenever I saw the thin black line of a chub's back, lying motionless in the shadows under the overhanging bushes which lined the banks. The fly would plop down, as if falling from the branches, on to the water some eighteen inches upstream from the waiting fish. As it drifted down the chub would rise lazily to meet it, sometimes turning away at the last moment, but usually opening the white ring of its mouth to suck in the fly from the surface. In the summer holidays of 1955 I caught 130 chub on the fly, thirty four of which were over one pound in weight. This represented hours and hours of patience and harmony with nature.

I wrote to the fishing-tackle firm in Edinburgh, delighted with my fly rod. When they published my letter in their next catalogue it was one of the great thrills of my life.

If the weather was warm, I would swim downriver for two or three miles, pulling the boat along with a line round my waist. The quest for physical fitness to make up for my lack of athletic ability was making me stronger.

My parents were becoming increasingly worried about my studies and were summoned by my house tutor when the results of my first attempt at G.C.E. 'O' levels, became known. I had tried six subjects and passed only one, History. My housemaster was D. M. Holland; he taught history and he stands out as a rock in my life; his nickname was the 'Brute'. I hated him at school and yet grudgingly I admired and yearned for his integrity. He was the son of a bishop and his teaching career was delayed by the Second World War, until he was twenty-seven. He was a tall rangy man with thin greying hair and a large scarred nose. He frequently had to leave the field to be sick at the end of a training session with the First XV, so hard did he drive himself. In the classroom his history lessons lived; we could identify him with the great figures of the eighteenth and nineteenth centuries. Somehow he seemed the embodiment of all the determination which placed Britain on top of the world by the end of the nineteenth century. He would stand on the dais with his huge hands stretched before him, fingers splayed and curving backwards as he rammed a point home. Most of us passed history first go as I did.

D. M. Holland was an epileptic. During my time at Pangbourne he suffered polio, but recovered quickly to continue his duties as housemaster. I was a senior cadet when he married a kindly lady with red hair; tragically their children died soon after birth.

A convinced rebel against authority, I had many battles with Mr. Holland, and invariably lost. I had to write long essays on 'Manners makyth Man' and 'In Peace there's nothing so becomes a man as modest stillness and humility'.

Shortly after I left Pangbourne, Mr. Holland was involved in a road accident. His wife died in the crash, and he was in hospital for many months. Then he left Pangbourne and went to teach at Millfield School.

Ten years later, on the occasion of my marriage to Marie Christine, he wrote to me and included a quotation from Lavengro, 'Follow your calling, for however various your talents may be, ye can have but one calling; . . . bound along if you can; if not, on hands and knees follow it, perish in it if needful; but you need not fear that.' He knew we were going to try and make a life in his beloved North-West Highlands, and he sent a Tilley lamp for a wedding present.

While rowing across the Atlantic his example inspired me when the going was roughest, and when spirits were lowest. Afterwards, when I wrote and told him how he had helped me, I was shocked by his letter of reply. Tragedy had stuck at him again, he was now convalescing after an operation for cancer. He thanked me for my letter, and said that he too saw the flowers and clouds through new eyes.

We were too busy after the rowing for me to visit Mr. Holland. It was three months before I was able to visit Pangbourne and address the college.

'Sad about Don Holland, wasn't it?' said one of the housemasters after my talk.

'Yes, I hope he's better now, I must go and see him,' I replied.

'Oh no, he died. I went to the funeral last Friday. His brother, a bishop, came over from New Zealand. He read out one of your letters to Don.'

I didn't reply. I could feel the tears welling to my eyes as I turned away.

In a world of shabby compromise, the memory of Mr. Holland stands as a rock – a humble yet proud figure, who knew right from wrong.

One Saturday afternoon in December, the First XV were at Douai School; their pitch was like running on corrugated iron it was in the grip of such a fierce frost. The game had nearly been cancelled. Douai had a good team and we were likely to lose. My parents had come to watch for the first and last time; my father never really believed that with feet like mine, I could ever be much good. By half-time we were six points down and still in with a fighting chance. Their captain played at full back and he was good.

I played at open side wing forward and specialised in crash tackles; my job was to break from the set scrum or line-out at the earliest opportunity and catch the fly-half in possession before he could pass the ball out to the swift running three-quarters. I was durable but not very flexible. My aim was always to dominate the fly-half from the outset, by hitting him at the earliest opportunity with everything I had; this often ruined his confidence and resulted in fumbled passes for the rest of the match. Sadly I was not difficult to outwit, and a few clever side-steps would tire me.

In this particular match the fly-half had not been crushed, but I was fit and the frozen ground meant the game was fast and open; it also meant that when a man went down and hit the ground, it was not very much softer than tarmac.

Early in the second half we were pinned in our twenty-five when our captain kicked the ball high in the air down the centre of the field. The Douai full-back and captain was well positioned to catch the ball and open an attack on our line. There was no wind, the ball was still light and dry. It flew high as I raced down on their full-back, and the long time of flight enabled me to close on him while he was still in possession. He fielded the ball with some elegance, and moved a couple of paces to gain sufficient momentum for one of his precise kicks for touch.

The ball was just leaving his hands and his trailing right leg swinging forward to kick, when I hit him at full speed, my red, white and blue jersey parallel with the ground like a dart. My skull smashed into his braced left thigh just above the knee. He stayed down, surrounded by his team, after the ball had been fly-hacked into touch. I trotted back to my team, in a daze. The stretcher was brought on and the prostrate full-back carried off, destined for six months in bed with internal bruising of the muscle. My parents were horrified at my lack of sportsmanship and never came again. I was too stunned to worry about the poor fellow.

As the time drew near for me to decide on a career, it was clear to me that I should never pass the Civil Service Commissioner's exam for entry into the Royal Naval College at Dartmouth. Quietly I decided that at this early stage in life, I must not start with a failure. I decided that I must go into the Merchant Navy as there were no examinations, only an interview to be passed. I felt I could talk my way into a shipping line. Unfortunately, I had neglected my nautical studies and this became only too evident at my interview with the Peninsular and Orient Steam Navigation Company in London. I was unable to answer a simple question on lifeboat drill and when asked for my views on the abolition of hanging I said, I thought in a very mature fashion, that I was too young to feel strongly either way. When I was sent downstairs for a medical examination, I was able to produce a sample of urine only with much aid from the running of taps. Meanwhile my mind raced with possible new solutions to the lifeboat question. I asked permission to give a fresh answer, this request was granted, and I gave another wrong solution.

Several days later I was summoned by the executive officer of the college; he told me that, having failed to P. and O., the only hope now was Clan Line, or Bibby Line. Always keen on Scotland I opted for Clan Line; they must have been desperate, for I passed. My final sum of 'O' level passes was six: one first time, two the second, one the third and two on the fourth attempt. Rather weak at seventeen and a half years of age. No matter how hard I try I have always had a sort of mental block in concentration when involved in academic study.

Early in January 1956 I presented myself at the East India Docks in London, to the *Clan Kennedy*. She was a rusty 'liberty class' ship, built by Kaiser in the United States during the war, in welded prefabricated sections. When she crossed the Atlantic for the first time with a full cargo it was accepted that she had paid for herself; now, some fifteen years later, she was a slow and corroded gold mine for her owners. At her maximum speed of eight knots, she was sometimes forced to a standstill in a heavy gale of wind dead on the bow.

With a crew of eleven Europeans living amidships, and perhaps fifty Indians quartered in the stern part of the ship, we were to load in London and Rotterdam, and then several other British ports. The voyage was to South and East Africa; discharge, reload and return home.

On our first night at sea, we were hove-to in a blizzard in the Thames Estuary. I felt sea-sick even on duty on the bridge, where I made tea for the officer of the watch. Already I had some doubts about my new career; why hadn't I stuck Pangbourne for another year, and at least tried my exam for the Royal Navy? However the storm passed, and soon we arrived in Rotterdam, through the ice floes in the river. I noticed how much faster the Dutch dockers worked than their counterparts in London. We were turned round in twenty-four hours.

My fellow-cadet was named Tugwell; he was on his last trip before taking his Third Mate's ticket. We hated each other. I knew nothing of the job, and he despised me for having gained a year's remission in sea time by attending school at Pangbourne. We shared a small cabin directly above the engine room; I slept in the top bunk. The deck was painted dark green, and the bulk-heads white. I thought Tugwell none too clean, and being a couple of inches taller I believed that when it came to the inevitable fight, I should smash him. He always made me collect the officers' newspapers when we were in port, as I was the junior cadet, and the shop was inevitably some distance from our berth. On a rainy winter morning the docks don't look very picturesque.

At sea, when sailing round the coast, Tugwell and I served three hours on and three hours off the bridge. I found the three hours as look-out interminable, and yet somehow there is a great romance about ships and docks and the sea. Another of my tasks as junior cadet was to take the temperature of the various holds in the ship, both morning and afternoon. Secretly I felt that Tugwell should do his share, but I never pushed this to a con-frontation.

I did not like the docks of Cardiff, Swansea, Newport, Liverpool or Birkenhead, but I found Glasgow the most gloomy. We loaded whisky into a special locker amidships, and I was ordered to supervise this with a stick in my right hand which gave me little confidence. Luckily no one ever attacked me, and I was confident that none of the cases had been tampered with. When we reached Capetown it was discovered that many bottles had been stolen; those Glaswegian dockers were skilful: they always seemed to take a dram instead of tea during their breaks.

We sailed from Avonmouth fully laden, and within two weeks we called at Dakar to refuel. I wondered why the crew wore so many clothes when they went ashore in the sweltering heat. The third mate told me that they bought second-hand clothing in Liverpool, then sold it at Dakar. They returned aboard very lightly dressed, and maybe just a little richer. Every Saturday morning the captain held an inspection of the ship, and one of the cadets had to hold the D.D.T. spray as he surveyed the crew's quarters. Cockroaches thrived in all parts of the ship.

On the ocean passages, Tugwell and I were employed in an endless war against rust. First we donned goggles and scaled the metal with light chipping hammers, and then we painted the clean area with red lead paint, finally we brushed on either the white or black top coat, depending on what part of the ship we were painting. The noise of the hammer was inclined to give me a headache in tropical waters. It was there I learnt the value of the salt tablets which I was destined to eat in many hot parts of the world in the years to come. A steamer heading north or south in the Atlantic soon passes from one climate to another and the body has little time to acclimatise if there is heavy physical work on deck each day. I felt tired all the time until I took the salt regularly, and thus made up the deficiency incurred through sweating.

One day after lunch, on the outward passage, Tugwell and I were chatting with a couple of engineers before starting work. We were sitting on the bollards just forward of the No. 4 hatch on the starboard side; I was leaning over the rail. I stretched to point out a lazy Portuguese Man o' War jellyfish as it passed; this effort dislodged the Parker 51 fountain pen from my shirt pocket and it curved in a gentle arc down to the indigo water. We were a hundred miles off the west coast of Africa; later I checked my pen's resting place on the chart. Unless swallowed by a fish on its descent, it should be two miles down below the surface, among the oceanic mud and ooze on the bottom of that part of the Atlantic. This was the first of four Parker 51 pens, all of which came to an interesting end. Eventually Ma gave me a maroon Sheaffer which I have found much harder to lose.

When we reached Capetown I was delighted with the scenery and climate although I found that the anglers to whom I talked on the breakwater all seemed to have different political views. It seemed so sad that in such a wonderful part of the world there could be no peaceful living but only a kind of seething political volcano. How is it that with all the creative talents possessed by man he has been unable to make happiness?

I soon found that Merchant Navy men did not enjoy a very high social standing in ports of South Africa. I had only to mention that I was off a ship and my new friends would desert me. Perhaps I should have done better if I had accompanied Tugwell, but we found the uneasy peace between us could best be maintained if we stayed apart while the ship was in port. Anyway, one of us was usually required on duty so there was little opportunity to go ashore together.

In Port Elizabeth I attended a rugby match between two clubs which I found rather better entertainment than a similar Saturday afternoon in England. The ground was harder and drier than at home, and the clubs played consecutively all four or five of their sides against their opposite teams. This meant the spectacle started at around noon, continued all afternoon, and culminated in the clash between the first teams. The players were big and fast, and the game beautifully open. I suppose that neither the light nor the pitches in Britain would prove satisfactory for that kind of contest. Sadly, the coloured population did not play, but were segregated into a special stand at one end of the pitch.

On reaching Beira, we had to wait for a berth and so we lay at anchor for a while, out in the river. Tugwell and I had to paint the depth marks in white, on the bow and stern of the ship. I can never see a merchant ship now without looking for the depth marks on her stern, and remembering the urgent flow of the muddy brown river water of Beira. I remember swinging in the bosun's chair with one hand, trying ineffectively to dodge the erratic dribble of urine from the crew's latrine directly above my head, while I jabbed at the marks savagely with the paint brush held in the other hand.

Once at a berth we loaded copper from Rhodesia, and I was impressed by the poetic strength and rhythmic chanting of the African gang as they manhandled the heavy ingots. Down in the hold these glistening giants would come up and pull at my clothes, inquiring sharply, 'Buckshee?' I puzzled at the difference between these fast and efficient men and some of the lazy gangs at home.

On the homeward leg we called in at Durban and I went ashore alone. I decided to try the famous beach which boasted the best surfing in Africa. Luckily it was a calm day as I struggled into the brief royal blue trunks with the kingfisher embroidered on the left side, which I had bought at school to give more speed in my efforts to gain the honour of second string, senior backstroke in the swimming team. I was putting on weight and the trunks felt too small.

Despite the calm sea it was not long before I had had quite enough salt water up my nose, and wanted nothing more than to lie in the sun. But there was no sun, so I shivered as I rinsed off the salt under a fresh-water tap I found farther up the beach. As I couldn't afford one of the rickshaws, drawn by huge Zulus in full ceremonial feather costume, I plodded slowly down the promenade and felt the symptoms of an approaching cold. There was little to do but go to the pictures.

In the cinema I watched a centre three-quarter shimmer through the defence, then streak over the line to score, in a rugby international on the newsreel. I felt goose pimples breaking out on my skin; in my bones I knew that the Merchant Navy was too steady a life for me.

When I came out of the cinema it was dark. I made for the famous Playhouse, and what I imagine was called a beer garden downstairs. On eleven pounds per month I was not going to drink much beer, and I hated the stuff anyway. There I sat, alone with one glass of beer and a half-empty bottle, dressed in sports jacket and trousers, at a round metal table. I don't know what I expected to happen, or how I should be amused. I really believed that nothing would happen, and this of course is usually when the unexpected occurs.

After a quarter of an hour, as I neared the end of the beer, a pale and sickly looking man came towards me. He clasped a Tyrolean hat, complete with feather, in one hand, a bottle and glass in the other.

'Mind if I join you?' he said.

'No, certainly,' said I, full of politeness.

'Johnson, Peter Johnson, Sydney,' he said. I told him my own name, as he beckoned the waiter and called for two more beers.

It seemed that Peter had come across from Australia to look for work in the copper mines of Rhodesia. On the voyage over in the *Southern Cross* his duodenal ulcer had burst, and he had had a rather serious operation on board ship. He was preceding his family, who were to be called to join him as soon as he found work, but the operation had seriously delayed his plans. Stuck in Durban, awaiting a doctor's note of clearance, he had rapidly run through his money. It now was clear he had decided to spend his remaining funds on one last drunken spree. How was I to know that alcohol was bad for a burst duodenal ulcer? Peter looked at least fifteen years my senior and I automatically assumed he knew better than I how to look after himself. Indeed I was not a little flattered that such a mature man had deigned to pass the time with a youngster like me.

While Peter poured out his troubles I noticed another character come into the bar. He stumbled towards us, a huge unshaven figure in a dirty chequered lumberjacket which matched the ginger of his hair.

'H'lo,' he mumbled, crashing on to a frail wicker chair at our table. I thought, 'Your move, Peter,' and glared furtively at my rather drunken Australian friend.

Luckily they got along fine and I bought a fresh round of drinks. By this time I had learnt that Peter was down to his last five shillings on the African continent. 'Tex', our new friend, announced that he was hungry and broke and hadn't eaten for two days; this seemed rather unlikely as he was pretty drunk, and I assumed he must have had money to buy the drink.

Peter grandly ordered a meal, and Tex had to go off into another room to eat it. I thought this rather astute as it had unloaded Tex, who looked as if he could eat us both if he took it into his mind to do so.

'Always give a fellow a helping hand, if he's down on his luck,' Peter confided, although I knew I would have to pay. 'You never know when you may need some help yourself.'

I have followed his advice for several years now, and more often than not I have been duped.

It soon became clear that Peter was feeling ill; he became morbid about what the drink was doing to his insides. I hoped he wouldn't collapse on me, and I called a taxi which I directed should take us to the nearest local hospital.

'He'll be all right, just take him home,' said the doctor on duty. Peter was putting on a very good display of complete unconsciousness. I negotiated with the taxi-driver and he agreed to drive us to the block of flats which I hoped was Peter's address; this would cost me all my remaining money.

It was one o'clock in the morning when I left the Australian stretched out on his bed, propping a little note, with my name and ship's berth, on the dressing-table. It was going to be quite a walk back to my bunk that night.

As I neared the docks, my feet rang on the empty streets. I began to worry about the warnings I had heard, never to walk alone through dockland in the dark. I remembered the size of those Zulus who pulled the rickshaws, and just hoped they didn't change out of their feathers into bandit gear at night fall.

'Gimme a light!' demanded a voice from between two empty railway trucks. I was right in the middle of the docks. My mind flashed back to Saturday mornings at home, as a child, when I used to crouch over the small radio in my parent's bedroom, and listen to the omnibus edition of Dick Barton, Special Agent. During the week I wasn't allowed to listen to the serial as I had to do my prep. It was an old trick of Dick Barton to ask for a light, and as soon as his enemy struck the match Dick would knock him cold with a straight right to the nicely illuminated jaw.

Now, I stopped in my tracks, and my mind raced. Should I run for it and chance that I wouldn't be ambushed by a gang, who might step out from the shadows all the way down the line of trucks? I imagined the cold blade snickering through the skin and arteries in my neck, the captain writing to my parents: 'Dear Mr. Ridgway . . .'

Suddenly my enemy stepped out into the light. Big Bad Tex, drunker than ever, clearly didn't recognise the old buddy who had bought him a meal. I ran. He chased, but not half as fast as I ran.

Next day we passed through the whale-blood-stained water at the entrance to Durban harbour. I looked down at the sharks and thought of Peter and Tex.

From Capetown to Avonmouth took us twenty-eight days; it was a long slow trip. By the time we crossed the equator I had learnt only nine 'Rules of the Road' to recite to the captain at our Sunday morning study periods. He wasn't pleased, and Tugwell was smug because he knew them all. I was sick and tired of pacing up and down the twenty-five yards of open deck between our cabin and the deck cargo. I missed the open playing fields of school, the smack of the leather ball into my hands and the roar

of the crowd as I knocked down the fly-half. I didn't smoke
or drink and there was little else to do. I must have more
exercise.

As I left the gloom of the captain's cabin, and walked into the
bright sunlight, I looked across the sea towards the Canary
Islands. There, rising 12,000 feet into the blue of the sky, was the
superb volcanic cone of Pico de Teide. I had had the Merchant
Navy, there must be more excitement in life.

The weather was kind all the way home until we started to
cross the western end of the English Channel. Here we ran into a
true Atlantic gale. I was to remember it when planning other sea
voyages in smaller craft, in the years to come.

We were steaming north for Land's End. The huge rollers
strode in before the westerly gale straight on to our port side. Up
on the bridge I began to feel long-awaited tremors of excitement
up and down my back; here at last was the high adventure I had
expected from the sea. Steadily the storm increased, and as night
came the whole seething surface of the water became clouded
white with flying spume, until it was as if we were crashing over
some giant dipper in a mist.

By midnight conditions were grim and the engines cut to halt
speed to save the hull from damage. Occasionally we failed to
recover from a roll, before the next huge hillside of water
advanced and broke green and white over the whole length of the
ship. It was decided to rest Tugwell and me from duty on the
bridge, in case we were needed in an emergency.

In the cosy warmth of our cabin on the starboard side, we shed
our dripping oilskins, and screwed the porthole cover tighter than
before, but still it leaked. Our table and chairs were anchored to
the deck, but all our belongings, from toothbrushes to books,
moved from side to side of the cabin in time with the wallowing
ship. We decided to have a two-man party, and uncovered our
own trove of broached cargo, half a case of Guinness and a carton
of battered tins of peaches. This was the result of several months
of wandering round the holds as they were emptied; if caught
with the stuff it could be held as tantamount to pilfering and our
jobs might be forfeit. We were tucking in with some gusto, when
there was a loud knocking on the door.

'The alcohol has broken loose! One of you out on deck to help
me lash it down,' the mate shouted.

Fear glistened in Tugwell's eyes, all those years as a cadet and now if we were caught – dismissal. The surprise caused us to lose our grip on the box of bottles and tins, it turned over, and the deck was suddenly a mass of rolling, rattling contraband.

'What's going on? Get up!' the mate plainly wanted to come in. We panicked, throwing tins all over the place, but principally up on to my bunk. I covered them with an eiderdown.

'Just coming,' shouted Tugwell, while the door rattled with the mate's impatience.

We decided that I should go. I hastily donned oilskins, then clutching my sou'wester I half opened the door and hustled past the mate calling, 'O.K. I'm ready, let's go.' Luckily he did not enter the cabin, but followed me along the passage towards the open deck. He contented himself by muttering, 'What took you so long?' I didn't answer.

Out on deck the wind was shrieking across the ship, making white tongues of spray fly horizontally through the air in the pitch dark. Any speech had to be carried out by shouting straight into an ear through cupped hands.

About twenty black forty-gallon drums of industrial alcohol had broken their lashings. They were rolling to and fro in the open space between the hatch covers and the rails on the windward port side. Some had already disappeared into the sea, but in general the wind and water were keeping them pinned against the hatch cover towards the middle of the ship. Clearly we should have to try to round them all up in one corner and chain them firmly in place.

After securing a length of chain at one end, and selecting a mooring point for the other, we set about trying to corner the heavy drums. At first it seemed quite easy, we just rolled them into the corner and turned them up on end; the motion didn't seem too bad after all, we were quite pleased with the progress.

'That one next,' roared the mate, pointing at a drum jammed on its side between the rails and bollards, right on the edge of the ship. We had just levered it on to its end and freed it from the bollards when I glanced up.

'Hang on,' I shouted. The mother and father of all waves reared wickedly above us. The mate had one hand on the rail as he half turned towards the danger. Next second a pale green wall engulfed us; I must have looked like a shirt on a washing-line in a high wind, as I hung on to the rail with both hands. The strain on my arms was terrific but my grip held, then the heaving side of the ship cleared the water once again. I looked round but the mate had gone, and so had the drum.

There was a groan from between the winches and hatch cover amidships. I staggered over and helped the mate to his feet. Blood streamed from a gash on his forehead, but he was still aboard.

'Lash the remaining drums in the corner and go below, it's too dangerous,' he screamed into my ear. I nodded enthusiastically.

In the cabin once more, we patched up the cut on his forehead and he looked around suspiciously. Tugwell and I looked at each other and grinned. We had made it, no one would ever know.

Next day the wind and sea had subsided, as they always do if you can hang on. We found the pipes which carried steam to the holds, in case of fire below, had been torn from their steel fastenings all along the deck on the windward side. When we reached Avonmouth a few days later, this damage was photographed for the local paper.

While the big drums of tobacco were being unloaded I walked off the ship. It was May 1956 and I was pleased to be home in the early summer. Posters proclaimed, 'Tom Graveney, Pride of the West'. I caught a bus for the countryside, and as soon as we were out of the built-up area I got out and walked. I climbed a hill through a wood bright with fresh green leaves and gay with primroses and came to a long drive which led to a large Georgian mansion. It was plain to see that the old house was empty, and seemed to have been so for some time.

I was alone in the sun, at home after my first time abroad. I felt so happy that tears came to my eyes. The Hall had been a convalescent home for wounded officers in the First World War; all about there were memorials and plaques to valiant men who had died there. It seemed a kind place to die, after horror in the mud of France. I imagined pretty Sisters nursing men back to health in the green and pleasant seclusion.

Nearly eighteen years of age, I decided to go and look for life.

When the ship arrived at Glasgow, for a much-needed refit, I was informed that I was to be transferred to the *Clan Maclean*; one of the best ships of the line, on the Australian meat run. I was given fourteen days' leave, and I made sure that I packed all my gear for the train journey home to Datchet. I had finished with the sea!

My father did not seem surprised at my decision to leave the Clan Line; he had been rather surprised that I ever entered the Merchant Navy. I never told him that it was because I knew I wouldn't pass the entrance exam for the Royal Navy.

'Well, you have had your go, now I'll choose a career for you,' he said, as we paced the lawn in the late evening. 'You will go into Lloyd's.'

Mentally I could see myself rushing from desk to desk with bundles of policies done up in rubber bands. It was not my style.

4

National Service

MY father developed acute appendicitis in the early summer of 1956, just a few days after my return from South Africa. I saw a chance to escape from the career he was planning for me with Lloyds Insurance in London. While he was in hospital at Windsor I visited the Labour Exchange and arranged to be called up for two years' National Service with the army. Despite the fact that I was under age at that time, I was allowed to sign the forms to initiate proceedings. Within a month I was summoned to High Wycombe for medical examination and intelligence tests.

My reasons for choosing the army were simple. I had always admired the raincoats worn by army officers in war films, and at Pangbourne it was well known that it was easier to become an army officer than either an air force or naval officer. Besides I thought I had had enough of the sea.

At High Wycombe, my confidence failing as always at the critical moment, I gained support from an unexpected source. I was quailing inwardly as the intelligence tests were handed round to the dozen or so of us seated at our desks in a drab and uninspiring barrack-room, when encouragement came from a tough-looking fellow seated on my right. He nudged my elbow and asked if I would help him because he couldn't read or write. I had a

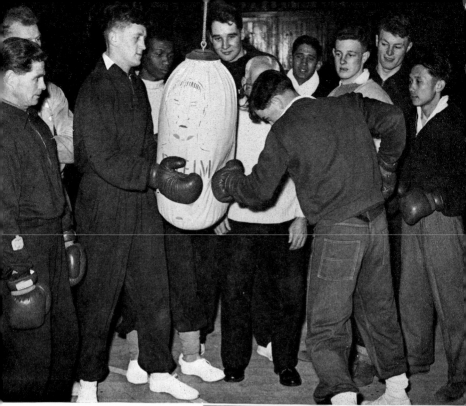

(*Above*) R.M.A. Sandhurst Boxing team, 1958; (*right*) intake 22 Marne Company after two years' intensive training; (*below*) right marker for Sgt. Ennis's drill squad in the first of six terms.

Arctic training in Canada with the Parachute Regiment, 1963; (*above*) with wind-chill the temperature fell to 83° of frost Fahrenheit. We lived in snow-holes 12 feet down; (*left*) waiting to jump—mukluks, mittens, snowshoes and all; (*right*) Fort Churchill, Hudson Bay in deep winter.

quick mental picture of Pangbourne, when I had persuaded my friend Terry O'Neil to read both our Morse signal lamp tests during the G.C.E. Signals Practical Examination. Although there seemed no way for me to help my illiterate friend in the timed intelligence tests we were about to tackle, he had at least given me some hope of success. I gave him a warm smile and suggested he told the examining officer of his problem. Glancing round the room I wondered how many others were illiterate. I passed that series of tests convincingly.

Then we went on to choice of regiment.

'What arm of the service would you prefer, son?' asked the stiff-backed but kindly looking Staff Sergeant, resplendent in No. 1 Dress uniform.

'The results of these tests qualify you for all arms,' he said.

'I'd like to be a commando,' I replied boldly.

'You can't do that, they're Royal Marines,' he said.

'Well, can I be a Royal Marine?'

'No, you are in the army.'

'What is the nearest thing to a commando, in the army?' I stammered.

'The Parachute Regiment, but you would have to sign on for three years, if you want to join them.'

'No thank you.' My recent experience in the Merchant Navy had taught me not to commit myself for longer than necessary to something I knew nothing about.

'What else is there, then?' I asked.

'Well, I am a Grenadier myself, but I doubt if you would pass the medical for that,' said the Staff Sergeant.

'Put me down for that please.' I fell for the bait, I'd show him.

When I got home that night, my father asked me how it had gone, and I was able to tell him that I was destined for the Brigade of Guards.

On the 20th August, 1956, I stepped off a train at Malvern station in Worcestershire, and climbed on to one of a line of army three-ton trucks which were waiting in the rain for the new draft. As we bumped along, I wondered what had gone wrong with my choice, for we were heading for No. 1 Training Regiment, Royal Engineers. Perhaps it was because my father was a civil engineer; certainly it was through no engineering aspirations of my own.

Over the first weekend I developed a heavy head cold, which did nothing to help my morale. I scrubbed my green web belt and

D

gaiters until they were white. That first belt became one of my most treasured possessions. I gained a lot of pride and pleasure from its supple and immaculate looks, after countless hours of scrubbing, hammering, emery papering, cardboarding, Brassoing and blancoing.

The camp at Malvern was built of the usual black timber huts. These were joined by corridors making small units known as 'spiders'. From our drying-room window, I could see in the distance, beyond the wire, the long ridge of the Malvern Hills. I remember thinking that if only I were free to get up there, I would soon shake off my cold. As it so happened, twelve years were to pass before I walked on those hills and looked down on the camp, the location of which was part of a map reading problem while I was on a Special Air Service selection course. I thought then of how, in return for my freedom and frustration, I had been taught many things. The years had not been empty.

After two weeks of basic training and selection, I was posted to 'Stalag IX' as No. 9 Training Regiment was known to National Service Sappers. Perhaps a move was a good thing, for one of our draft at Malvern had hung himself from a beam. I personally thought our treatment very fair while we were there; I felt sure that the poor fellow must have been rather unbalanced before he arrived. The special troop train to Ash Vale near Aldershot seemed rather dramatic to many of us eighteen-year-olds, but any film star feelings we may have felt on that journey, were cut short when the trucks rolled through the gate at Southwood Camp, Cove.

918 Party B Squadron was fifty-eight strong, and we were training at Cove from September 1956 – throughout the Suez Crisis – until January 1957. My life was dominated by one Corporal Harwood; days, nights and weekends, passed in a procession of room inspections; drill and P.T. Time and again my green steel locker, containing all my kit neatly laid out, was hurled face forward on to the polished floor.

Each week we were paid twenty-seven and sixpence; this covered cleaning materials and N.A.A.F.I. breaks. The small custard tarts with nutmeg sprinkled on top were my favourite buy.

Corporal Harwood stamped and snarled. His high-pitched voice urged us on, to build a bailey bridge, or cross a lake in an assault boat, that much faster than the squads competing with us.

We burnished jack-knives, polished curtain rails, we marched up and down, across and diagonally over the drill square. After twelve weeks I qualified as a grade 3B Sapper, and this entitled me to be paid an extra sixpence per week after six months' service.

A little before the end of my training at Cove, while squaring up the 38 pattern web equipment on the top of my steel locker, my helmet fell from the top of the pile and its sharp edge bit into the back of my head. Two days later I developed severe headaches and then my sight deteriorated. In the ambulance to the Cambridge Military Hospital in Aldershot I longed, for the first time in my life, if not the last, for peace, warmth and darkness. Fortunately, it was neither the suspected polio nor meningitis, but simply concussion.

Perhaps the most important lesson I learnt during that basic training came from another recruit. Eric Stonehouse was a gentle giant from Newcastle, and a welder by trade. Sitting on my bed in the barrack-room one November evening, I was hammering new studs into my ammunition boots on a last, which rested on the floor. Eric was pressing a pair of battledress trousers with the squad steam iron, using brown paper as an additional shield against the heat. His bed was three up from mine, and on the other side of the hut. We were all working away at our kit, we all hated Harwood, we all hated the army – it wasn't very difficult to hate each other.

With my back turned to Eric, I was concentrating hard, to arrange the studs in the correct pattern on the soles of my boots. I didn't realise the rising tempers, as the usual banter became more and more personal. Everyone teased Eric about his broad Geordie accent; without thinking I joined in.

'Look out, Ridge,' someone shouted.

I leapt to my feet, and as I turned, Eric grabbed the lapels of my battledress and heaved me towards him, smashing his forehead down on to my nose as he did so. Luckily he didn't follow this up with the customary knee in the groin.

Our room-mates dragged us apart as the blood streamed down my face. I protested in vain that we should go out into the dark and settle it; he could have killed me.

Eric had 'stuck the nut' on me. I have never forgotten the lesson. An aggressor, with the benefit of surprise, should cripple his opponent with the first series of blows. I have found a useful counter to this particular and widely used opening gambit; this is to drop the chin on the chest and slightly anticipate the butt. This results in the aggressor butting his face on to the hard dome of the victim's head with the combined weight of both bodies and the neck muscles of the aggressor. The victim, thus gaining the initiative, should follow up with the knee to the groin.

I applied for a Regular Commission, because I believed this to be more easily achieved than the National Service Commission for which most of my friends applied.

Towards the end of Basic training I was called forward for Unit Selection Board. I paraded, in best kit, on the verandah outside the Commanding Officer's office. The ten potential officers stood stiffly at ease, side by side, in a long line, each with our private thoughts as to how we might impress the Colonel that we were clearly officer material. I'd show Harwood.

At 1400 hours sharp by the Guardroom clock, after we had stood for quarter of an hour, the Colonel walked round the corner of the low wooden building and up the steps towards the door of his office.

'Call us up to attention, you bloody fool,' I shouted to myself.

It was the duty of the right-hand man to bring us to attention, but he forgot. Here was my chance to shine. Of course I just stood there and missed the opportunity. When asked during the course of my interview why I had not acted I replied weakly that it was the responsibility of the right-hand man. Surprisingly I passed.

In December 1956 I went down to the little country town of Westbury in Wiltshire for four days, to appear before the Regular Commissions Board. I decided to base my attack upon enthusiasm and physical fitness. I was keen to get into the Parachute Regiment, although by then I realised that officers only served for a three-year tour of duty in the Parachute Brigade after which they were posted back to their parent units. On arriving at Westbury, I was disturbed by the tough-looking Parachute Regiment candidates, who appeared in camouflaged para smocks while the rest of us only had scruffy denim suits. Fortunately, my voyage to South Africa was a help, for it provided a useful subject for both my lecturette and my essay. I felt sorry for those who had only just left school, with no such experience to talk on.

Luckily for me, we had several sparky fellows in our squad of twelve, and we all agreed to support each other with our obstacle-crossing problems. My own task involved moving a heavy oil drum across a ditch with the aid of some ropes, planks and a tree which grew in the middle of the ditch. Experience as a pack leader on the rugby field helped me to urge my four helpers to solve the problem by 'brute force and ignorance'.

After the selection test I returned to the Holding Troop at Cove, and rather pessimistically awaited the results of the Board.

The short January days were spent dashing from one warm drying-room to another, in an attempt to avoid being noticed by Authority. So I passed the working hours, stretched out on a pile of mattresses, idling away the time with other 'holdees'.

After ten days a letter arrived informing me that I had passed and should report to R.M.A. Sandhurst intake 22, on 27th January 1957. I was stunned, and for the first time I was quite hopeful for the future. I had at least shown Corporal Harwood, but I'm sure he never noticed.

Before going to Sandhurst I had to attend a Medical Board at Steeles Road in Aldershot. This didn't worry me; I didn't give it a second thought. I had worked on building up my physical fitness for years, to the detriment of my studies.

The Medical Board comprised three grey-haired doctors of the R.A.M.C. They met each week, in a musty Victorian barrack-room. These three told me to strip, eyeing me thoughtfully, then they weighed me, prodded me, tapped me to test reflexes and told me to make a sample of urine. I was confident.

'His feet look flat,' one said. My heart sank as they all looked at what I considered to be my weakest point. Surely I wasn't going to fail having come this far? The doctors weren't happy, but they told me to dress and mumbled to each other in a rather indecisive way.

This was a Permanent Medical Board. I was one of thousands they had examined; they seemed bored and disinterested in this average lump of flesh before them. Although I was trying desperately to impress them with my animal grace, clearly I was not succeeding.

After I had dressed, all three sat behind a table and signalled to a chair on the other side. As I sat down, I watched the eyes of the senior doctor, eager to anticipate any order he might give. They continued muttering to each other, while I sat tensed in my chair. 'They can't fail me, they just can't,' I said to myself.

'Putchered onthtable,' murmured the senior man in the middle, without looking up from a form on the table before him. I didn't move, I hadn't understood what he meant.

'Putchered onthTABLE,' he repeated sharply.

Surely he couldn't mean it.

Slowly I leaned forward in my chair, until my left ear rested on the table before them.

The doctors' eyes bulged in their pale grey faces.

'I said PUT YOUR HAT ON THE TABLE, NOT YOUR HEAD,' he shouted.

I jerked upright, my back straight as a ramrod. Trembling in my chair, I felt my face burn with embarrassment. My right hand reached sheepishly for my black beret and laid it on the desk before me.

'That's it,' I thought, 'I'm not officer material.'

This most irregular performance must have made them forget the feet. I passed.

After two weeks more in the Holding and Drafting Troop at Cove, I was put on the train at North Camp Station. Clutching two school suitcases and a sea kitbag, I alighted fifteen minutes down the line at Blackwater station, as an officer cadet.

5

Sandhurst

As we boarded the inevitable three-ton truck which was waiting at Blackwater Station, I immediately noticed that the sergeant instructor called me 'Mr. Ridgway, Sir.' The whole arrangement seemed better than Corporal Harwood and 'Stalag IX'. I was also relieved to see that the majority of the cadets were clearly straight out of the school and this gave me a much-needed feeling of confidence.

There were about 180 new officer cadets in Intake 22, of these perhaps twenty-five per cent were foreign students from the Middle East, India and various parts of Africa. Only twenty-five were 'Army Entrants', as we were called, who had come through the ranks, and thus avoided the Civil Service Commission Examination. We were to spend the first term on a separate academic syllabus, missing the intensive course of drill and weapon training, which the remainder of the intake underwent. If we passed the exam at Easter, we would then rejoin the intake and, hopefully, be commissioned five terms later as second lieutenants into the various regiments and corps of the British army in December 1958.

In spite of my unceasing dread of examinations, I have happy memories of my time at the Royal Military Academy, as indeed I thought I would.

In restrospect, the 1950s were, in many ways, a glittering Indian summer for the Establishment way of life in Britain, and Sandhurst was the very essence of this.

Twice yearly, in July and December, a whole intake is commissioned at a spectacular Passing-out Parade. At the end of this the Adjutant, astride his white charger, leads the new officers off the Square, up the steps and between the great pillars, and so on through the entrance of the massive white-walled building that is Old College. The faint puffs of white blanco are borne slowly away on the breeze, across the lines of blue figures standing rigidly to attention at the 'Present Arms'.

I have a memory of gracious college buildings, wide gravelled squares, impeccable green playing fields and hundreds of clear-eyed young men, all immaculately clad in uniform with knife-edge creases and shining boots. The motto gleaming on every cap badge reads 'Serve To Lead'. Honour is all.

Sandhurst, with its lofty ideals, its mental and physical fitness, sets a standard for the world – a standard which, I was sad to find, the world could never live up to.

Staff Sergeant Innis, of the Irish Guards, was keen on drill. Luckily for me I had done much more drill, while with the Royal Engineers, than the other sixteen members of the Junior Platoon of Marne Company, New College. He chose me as Right Marker, and so I dodged most of the trouble during inspections.

In the first few days we were issued with a whole wardrobe of fine quality uniforms, sports clothing and even a blazer. I loved it; it all seemed so like the West Point article I had read in a *National Geographic Magazine*. For me the glossy photographs were becoming reality, I was being transformed like some ugly duckling into a swan.

We were introduced to our Platoon Officer, one Captain P. D. Pauncefort-Duncombe of the Grenadier Guards. All I remember of him is the phrase he taught us – Some Men Enjoy Antique Cars – the first letters of which reminded us of that pillar of the British military art, the headings for the Orders Card; Situation, Mission, Execution, Administration and logistics, Command and signals.

I even gained the symbol for which I had joined the army in the first place, an officer's raincoat. Mine never fitted very well, and so it was hardly ever worn.

We were issued with cheque-books for our accounts at the

Academy's own bank. This was run by the R.A.P.C., and so we had to sign our cheques in the correct manner or suffer a vicious tongue-lashing from the Paymaster, a retired Marine Commando. It was this Bank which fascinated the Ceylonese cadet in our platoon, not the cold British climate. His plaintive cry, 'You are trying to KEEL me,' was often heard from the back of our night patrols, as we crept through the bushes and mud out on the Academy's own training area, on the fringe of the Broadmoor Mental Asylum.

One day there was a great fuss and my Ceylonese friend was put in close arrest; it seems he had stolen a number of Academy cheque-books and had been busy forging signatures like a real professional. Sadly he was not sharp enough for the Marine Commando, and he was locked up in the hospital under constant guard; while there he tried in vain to slash his wrists. After a time he was quietly dismissed, and returned home in disgrace. Later we heard a rumour that he had left the Ceylonese army and taken a post as a bank clerk; he was a friendly fellow with a broad grin, when he was warm.

Somehow I struggled through the written exams at the end of that first term and joined the rest of the intake.

During the summer of 1957 I sought a way of easing my passage through the remaining five terms of academic and military training. At nineteen I reckoned myself physically fit, but lacking any natural athletic talent. I also suffered a painful inability to concentrate on academic subjects. An easy passage was going to be tricky. A cadet was rated by the staff on two separate counts, his character grading or 'Charlie George' as it was known, and his academic achievement. Clearly my only hope was to develop some 'Charlie George'. I looked around for some guidance and found Terry O'Neil.

Terry had left Pangbourne and gone straight to Sandhurst. A languid giant of a fellow, with the poetic timing which had enabled him to snatch impossible chances in the slips on the cricket field at school, Terry lived in the dream-world of the sports commentator, always the World Champion. He turned his catlike grace to good use, and became the Academy heavyweight boxing champion throughout his two years at Sandhurst, losing only one fight in twenty-four, and that through laziness. Then he went on to box for the Army.

'Boxing is the secret, Ridge,' he smiled, when I arrived at

Sandhurst, one term after him. 'I don't have to do a stroke, I just win, and it's the only sport which the whole Academy and staff has to watch.'

At Pangbourne I had had two fights, and was easily beaten in both, but O'Neil was right – there was great prestige in boxing at Sandhurst. Surely I could learn. I could become fitter than any opponent because I would train so much harder. In my junior-term boxing, I had been beaten by a more determined rugby player called Douglas. I would simply have to get fitter.

Although I never missed a match in two years with the first XV at school, my feet and recurrent bronchitis had ensured that I had never run farther than half a mile without slowing to a walk. At Sandhurst I worked out my own cross-country course, round the lake and through the woods. Clad in track suit, ammunition boots and several pullovers, I settled down to run alone, two and a half miles every day, including weekends. Because of rather thin arms, I had started press-ups while at Pangbourne each night before bed. I was now doing 100 every evening.

O'Neil never seemed to bother about training; my fitness would have to make up for a lack of ability.

My first fight for Sandhurst was on the 14th February, 1958, St. Valentine's Day. The spectators paid to watch Oxford University win the first eight fights in the City Hall. I was on fight number 9, middleweight. My opponent, Neale of St. Edmund's Hall, was experienced. At twenty-four he had already done National Service in the Royal Artillery. In the previous term in a contest at Sandhurst he had knocked out a tough Rhodesian friend of mine in the first round, and the Rhodesians always did well at Sandhurst because they seemed so much more mature.

I was frightened. As the evening had worn on, I had begun to feel that cold sense of inevitability that I was to go out of my way to meet so many times in the years to come. Somehow it is a feeling of calm, like, perhaps, a very pure drug. The mythical chips are down and for a while, there is a mainstream life to be lived. Excitement, the rallying of all the senses for a vital effort. I have often wished for rousing music on these occasions, but always the cold spotlight isolates and emphasises the loneliness.

Alone in my corner of the ring under the hot bright lights, my feet shuffled nervously in the resin box. I smiled weakly at our silver-haired trainer outside the ropes. A round little figure in a white polo-neck pullover, he was the legendary 'Dusty' Miller, who had beaten the World Champion in a non-title fight after the First World War. 'Dusty' had been on the Sandhurst P.T. staff with Jimmy Wilde, 'The Ghost with a hammer in his hand'.

The referee called Neale and me to the centre of the ring for a briefing before the first round. As we shook hands and listened to the familiar, 'Now I want a good clean fight, break when I say break . . .' our eyes met. Neale's smile looked about as forced as I imagined my own must look.

Suddenly the lights failed in the Hall, and we three stood there in the middle of the ring. 'Now for a bit of psychological advantage,' I thought. I raised my open right glove, and placed it firmly palm down on the top of Neale's head.

'Last one up's a cissy!' I said, quoting Max Baer's quip to Primo Carnera, when they fell together flat on the canvas during their title fight at Madison Square Garden in New York, many years before.

The lights came up and we returned to our corners. The bell rang and I leapt to the attack. Neale fell back and I sensed he was unsure of himself; throughout that round I chased after him and by the end, I had built up a good points lead.

Coming out for the second of three rounds I was confident, and again forced the pace. Neale's seconds had evidently had serious words with him; this was a critical fight – if he failed he would not be picked for the next match, against Cambridge. His 'blue' hung in the balance. Neale did not fall back this time.

As I closed on him flickering my left hand into his face, he swivelled from the hips and countered with a smooth right cross.

'. . . 3–4–5.' I was all right. '6–7–8.' I rose shakily. The fight had swung right away from me, in just a few brief seconds.

Throughout the remainder of that round, I kept tasting the bitter jarring smell of leather and blood on my face. Now I could see how he had knocked out Thomson, and how he might catch me yet.

During the interval 'Dusty' and 'Spider' Webb extolled me to go after him in the last round.

'He's tiring,' they said.

'How the hell d'you think I feel,' I replied.

Luckily Neale wasn't as fit as me, and so I didn't undergo the same barrage that I had taken in the previous round. But sadly I lacked the experience to turn this to my advantage, and he took the verdict on points.

As I left the ring Terry O'Neil came in for the last fight of the evening. The score read Oxford University 9 R.M.A.S. o. He looked unworried.

Boxing languidly, with hands held high, in the 'Peeka boo' style he had copied from Floyd Patterson, he beat the inter-varsity champion at a canter.

In order to keep my weight down to within middleweight limits I didn't eat tea or have potatoes with any of my meals. After my run each day I always quenched my thirst with a glass of very strong Andrews Liver Salts, although I was never quite sure what good this would do me.

At about this time I became involved in my first serious love affair; it was extremely one sided. At weekends, and sometimes on Wednesdays, I would drive over to the Hind's Head Restaurant at Bray near Maidenhead, with a few friends who also liked good food. These fellows were all Old Etonians, and their leisure activities were often beyond my meagre means, but they made life seem very amusing. I admired their arrogant nonchalance, and the brains and determination which often lay hidden behind the façade.

On one particular Wednesday evening just before Christmas, we had all driven over in a Ford Consul, which my father had lent me. I had hit a taxi in London a few days earlier, after watching Terry Downes box at Harringay. The repairs had been effected at great speed and at my expense to ensure that my father should not find out.

As we drove home from Bray, I suggested that we should start carol singing, to pay for the expensive meal we had just had. Ascot, in the heart of the stockbroker belt, seemed a good target.

We did quite well, people paid quickly to be rid of us. We had all had a few drinks – even I had allowed myself two or three glasses of wine, quite sufficient to loosen my tongue. John Lockwood, a tall good-looking fellow whom girls loved to mother, suggested that we should try one more house, on the very edge of the race-course. Then we would have to head back for Sandhurst in time for 'Rounds' at ten o'clock, when each cadet had to be present at the door of his room.

As the car squealed to a halt in a shower of gravel before a large and elegant house, we all piled out and began to bellow our somewhat limited range of carols.

Two faces appeared at a bedroom window over the front door. They were girls in night-clothes. We sang louder.

'Go away,' said the girls after they had managed to open the window. There was a brief conversation and I was very much attracted by one of the voices. Half a crown clattered down on to the drive and we were away. I noted the name of the house.

On the drive back, there was the usual laughter and we were in a hurry. I failed to notice the change of road conditions as the frost set in. We bowled into the Academy grounds and I turned sharp right at the Chinese Bridge over the Wish Stream. Too sharp. The first model of Ford Consul was notorious for its poor roadholding on corners. We went into a gentle broadside up the road, then the back wheels mounted the grass verge, and the rear end finally collided with a young tree which, bending sideways, brought the car to a halt. Unfortunately, the car wouldn't move in forward gear. I was not allowed to bring a car into the grounds at that time.

We left it there wrapped round the tree, and ran across the playing fields to the lights of New College; breathless we made it up the stairs and along the corridors to our rooms just as the roll was called. Ten minutes later Lockwood and I crept down the back stairs and out into the cold night. We backed the car all the way out of the grounds and left it at a local garage in the town.

'I'm afraid I've had an accident,' I said to my father over the phone.

'Yes, I wondered when you'd own up,' he replied, 'we have just got the bill from the taxi-driver.' He meant the previous accident. . . . I felt even more nervous.

'No, another one, I mean. The car won't go forward, I'll have to get it repaired here in Camberley and come home by train tomorrow.' It was the last day of term.

'I'll see you when you get home.' Click – he rang off. I didn't laugh at Lockwood's jokes as we plodded back through the grounds. 'It's not going to be a good Christmas,' I thought.

As soon as I got back to my room I started to write to the voice I had heard from the window at Ascot. I described my predicament after the carol singing and suggested we meet somewhere, anywhere.

Young love.

By the time of my fight at Oxford the affair had almost run its totally negative course. While I could write the most dashing of letters, I found that, whenever I took her out, in my 1938 two-seater M.G. – which I had bought for forty-five pounds to replace the now confiscated Consul – I was quite unable to hold even the most simple of conversations. All I could do was glare across the table of which ever expensive restaurant we happened to be in.

Clearly my letters entertained her, for she managed to maintain this gay romance for several months before she finally announced her engagement to a subaltern in the Household Cavalry. I was heart-broken.

It seemed to me that the majority of the money the army paid its officer cadets at Sandhurst was spent on costly dinners in London for girls who were in fact earning considerably more than their meal-ticket friends.

The next boxing event was the inter-company annual championships. Following my display at Oxford, I was favourite to win the middleweight title. I was wary of a very strong chap called Christie. We were at opposite ends of the draw and would probably meet in the final.

In the first round of the competition I met Barber of Waterloo Company. A powerful red-haired boy, he stormed in, 'after the style of Marciano', as he told me later. I was able to keep him away until early in the third round when he accidentally butted me, in a clinch.

I reeled back and realised my nose was broken. I'd never had a broken bone before – it hurt!

I coasted through the rest of the round and won on points.

The semi-finals were not for another five days and there was a weekend in between so I went home to Datchet. My parents didn't really approve of boxing. My father had been a good centre threequarter in his time, and had played rugby until at thirty-five a cartilage operation put a stop to it. We often went to Twickenham together and I was always impressed by the way we never cheered – such a lack of self-control was never justified.

'Talk's cheap,' my father would say. A successful civil engineer, he worked twenty-four hours a day, seven days a week. Playing golf with him was like playing with a shadow; he would be far away planning a new bridge or harbour in some distant land.

'Now you must let him win,' my mother would say. He was never so far away that he didn't mind losing. My younger brother

Michael became a good player and he also liked to win; sometimes this resulted in rather poor weekends.

Our father was the rock upon which the family was built. A brilliant young engineer, he specialised in tunnelling for fifteen years until he became the country's leading expert in this field. At the early age of twenty-one, he was given a chance by an eminent engineer to control a substantial section of the tunnel work between Finsbury Park and Cockfosters on the London Underground. He didn't waste that chance.

In 1947, when faced with the cost of educating Michael and me, he was offered a directorship in his firm. He left that firm. For six months he was out of work; he wanted to start his own firm. A quietly determined engineer all his life, he needed an entrepreneur, and in Ernest Marples he found one.

Since 1945 Marples, an accountant and a successful property developer, had been M.P. for Wallasey. Marples Ridgway got its first contract in 1948 to build a wharf at the Poplar power station. Until 1951 when Marples severed his connections with the company on becoming Parliamentary Secretary of the Ministry of Housing under Macmillan, the business blossomed. Only two opposite personalities could have made such a successful team.

When Marples left the firm, my father pushed on alone, looking for tough propositions as a matter of policy. The difficult jobs paid better and cut some of the irresponsible opposition. The first contract to put the firm in the public eye was the Hammersmith flyover. Thousands of motorists passed the hoardings daily, on their way to and from work.

From his rather dark, pine-panelled office in Victoria, behind Buckingham Palace, he gradually expanded the firm abroad. He took another chance in 1956, by bidding a first tender in the Sudan, on the day Nasser seized control of the Suez Canal. I was aboard the *Clan Kennedy* at that time, off the East coast of Africa, and there was much speculation about the future of the Middle East.

As his business succeeded, so his prestige grew at home. Michael and I looked very dull; we didn't show any engineering aptitude. It became a firm principle of mine not to ask for financial help from my parents.

I won my semi-final against Hayes of Burma Company. He hit my nose three times in the first round and this caused the most exquisite pain; the nausea tasted like very strong onion in my throat. I was much fitter, and outpointed him easily in the second and third round and also avoided being hit again on my nose.

Christie, my rival, won with a second knockout. A natural athlete, good tennis player and cross-country runner, he was well built with a mop of fair hair over a strong face. Boxing in a square two-fisted American style, he moved like a panther; all his wins were knockouts. Swift reflexes ensured he was seldom caught; he knew all about my nose. I passed the medical examination on the day of the final in the early morning. The medical officer was still sleepy, and in the half light only looked at the boxers' hands.

Mentally I prepared myself for a great effort, one of the few really big efforts a man can make in his lifetime. I prayed for strength, in the darkness of the empty chapel, on my way down to the Hall.

The night of the Company boxing finals is one of the events of the Sandhurst calendar. The entire Academy is present, surrounding three sides of the ring. The officers sit facing the fourth side, dressed in the glittering uniforms of all the proud regiments of the British army. The band plays during intervals and the air becomes heavy with cigar smoke. Cheering is only allowed between rounds, and when the lights go down there is a complete silence, two thousand pairs of clear eyes watch and wait. Honour is all.

Christie looked as strong as a young bull as we came out for the first round. He knew about my nose and attacked it immediately. With a good strong boxer every blow carries a jarring detonation; it was like that with Christie.

The blood began to flow freely down my face and there was the sickening taste of it in my throat. Both of us began to get covered with patches of crimson of varying shades, and as the gloves hit home the canvas soaked up the flecks of flying gore.

I had one chance half-way through the first round, when I crossed his snaking left with my right. My arm straightened like a piston a fraction of a second ahead of his, jamming like a bar in the crook of his left elbow. We were both moving forward and my blow caught him, with our combined weight behind it, just too high on the left hand side of his jaw. His eyes glazed momentarily, but I was off balance and too inexperienced to follow up in time. He was off the hook.

Throughout the second round the merciless beating continued.

In the third round I was no longer experiencing any pain at all.

(*Above*) Beaconsfield Parish Church, March 1964, my parents and Lt. Colin Thomson on the left, Marie Christine's mother and brother on the right; (*below*) planning the rowing with Marie Christine at home in Farnham.

Rowing across the Atlantic, 1966;
(*above*) a rare moment of calm a couple
of weeks from the start; (*below*) my
hands after a month at sea;
(*right*) climbing aboard Shell tanker
Haustellum after seventy-one days,
some 750 miles off Land's End.

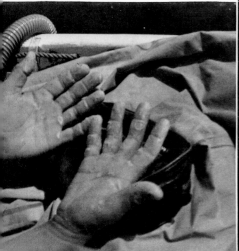

Occasionally I would find myself on all fours on the canvas, staring at the white-clad legs of the referee, and on under the ropes into the sea of pale faces in the darkness beyond.

I had never been stopped in my life, it was the last round and as I was feeling nothing I would make it all right. This was the time for the fight to be stopped; it was dangerous.

'Stop,' The referee held my face between his two hands, looked closely at the damaged nose and waved Christie to his corner. A wave of cheering broke out.

'No, no,' I shouted imploringly as I was led forcibly to my corner.

Tears streamed down my face on the way to the dressing-room, as the tension broke. On the bench my shoulders shook hysterically. The fight had been stopped. I had been stopped. Nobody knew what it meant to me. Throughout the light-heavy and heavyweight finals I wept, but by the time of the prize-giving I was calm and relaxed once more. Inside I had been hurt.

The cool O'Neil had won the heavyweight title with his usual first-round knockout; he added just one more award to his growing collection. I was awarded the bronze statuette for the Best Loser of the competition. It altered the course of my life.

In the officers' mess, a tartan-clad Highland officer said, 'You will have the pleasure of knowing that no one who saw you fight tonight will ever forget it.'

Next morning when I woke up, for a short while I was unable to open my eyes, so swollen was the whole of the front of my face and nose. At the hospital, they said the X-ray was clouded by the conglomeration of blood in the area of the damage.

It was at this time that I had to make a firm decision about my choice of regiment. Until my entry into the army, I had never had any military connections and, once in, I had only wanted to join the Parachute Regiment. As this was impossible I had taken a pin, shut my eyes, and jabbed firmly down at the other infantry regiments listed in 'Staff Duties in the Field'. The Royal Ulster Regiment was affixed to the table-top – that was for me.

Then just as we were to make our firm choices, the Parachute Regiment started to build a permanent cadre of officers. My priorities became Parachute Regiment, Royal Ulster Regiment, Royal Engineers.

Every one of the army entrants in my intake tried for the Parachute Regiment. I stood little chance. The 'Best Loser'

E

swung things my way. I was one of only two cadets chosen for interview by the Colonel Commandant, General Sir Richard Gale.

Again in Aldershot the 'Best Loser' pulled me through for I had nothing else to recommend me. I was accepted, and subject to passing out of Sandhurst satisfactorily, I would become the first officer commissioned direct to 3rd Battalion, The Parachute Regiment.

For a while things went well for me. I was able to arrange the operation on my nose for the very morning of the Military Law exam, a subject in which I stood no chance. Most fortunately I was actually under the anaesthetic while the others of my intake sat this exam. I never had to do it and was granted average marks.

Then at the end of the Easter term I was appointed Captain of Boxing for my last term which would be Christmas 1958. I settled down to enjoy the remainder of my time at Sandhurst; it looked as if it might be a memorable summer.

My Etonian friends knew how to enjoy life, and I was keen to learn. Between the five of them they had quite a collection of invitations to debutante dances for the 'season'. Just one invitation card was sufficient; we would ink-in 'and friends' after the name at the top left-hand corner of the card, and all stroll nonchalantly in. Sometimes we would go to two or three dances during one week. This meant sneaking out of Sandhurst in track suits at around eleven o'clock at night, driving to Henly's garage near London Airport, changing into evening dress in the lavatory and driving to the dance. We would troop in, give some fictitious name to the Master of Ceremonies, and gravely shake hands with the line of family at the door. Sometimes an old and wise greataunt would follow us down the line with beady eyes, looking to see which relative had issued the invitation. In such a situation I would choose a shy-looking girl in the line and overwhelm her with affection; nobody ever found us out.

I took to collecting breakfast menu cards at these magnificent functions; it was great fun and as a non-drinker it wasn't very expensive either for me or my unknowing hosts. We also met some rather bizarre girls, although neither they nor we had very much to say.

Eventually we were caught. Every term the Company had a dinner and on this occasion it was held at a restaurant near the main road bridge over the Thames at Windsor. During the meal spirits rose, and by the end it rather looked as if something would have to be done.

'Let's go for a row,' We were only a few hundred yards from the main Eton boathouse.

Four of us were in the first boat away from the pontoons moored alongside the bank. It was around nine-thirty on a mid-summer evening. As we drifted down towards the grey-stone bridge, many faces gazed down at us. Some were cheering us on for the bridge was to be the start-line for a race upstream. Just out of sight, round the bend downstream, we could hear the low rumble of the weir.

'Hey, look!' One of the revellers on the bridge pointed across towards the boathouse. The police were ordering our competitors from their boat. Sheepishly we pulled our boat back to the bank.

'You lot, come to the station,' said a burly officer of the law. We were under arrest, our names were taken and we were told we'd be hearing from them.

If charges were laid against us we would probably be R.T.U.d (Returned to Unit) from Sandhurst.

On the way back to the Academy, we decided to go out to a dance that night. When we crept up the back stairs, at dawn, we found notes pinned to each of our room doors, 'Report to the J.U.O.' (Junior Under Officer). The game was up. It was a pity we hadn't carried out our original plan of kidnapping an unpopular senior cadet, nailing him naked in a coffin and leaving the ominous black box at the foot of Nelson's column in Trafalgar Square.

The result of this was seven days' Restriction of Privileges, and fourteen days' stoppage of leave. This was an intolerable burden at that time of the summer. 'Strickers' meant we had to remain in uniform and wear white buff equipment to show others that we were undergoing punishment. Much worse, we had to report ourselves to the authorities at frequent intervals on each day.

During this period we managed to swim and dine at Eton some fifteen miles away (one of us had a sports car capable of 130 m.p.h.), go to Royal Ascot and actually dance, within touching distance of the hated Assistant Adjutant, at the Hurlingham Club in London.

One evening when Restrictions were over, I became involved in an argument about training for the assault course race, which our platoon had to compete in during that summer term. It was already eight o'clock in the evening and we had had dinner. During the afternoon, I had boxed one round with each of the eighteen cadets of the junior platoon consecutively, in preparation for their competition, and batted for half an hour in an inter-company cricket match. I was tired.

Next thing I knew, I was in a hand built Alvis-Healey, dressed in full battle order, as we sped towards London's Hyde Park Corner. Foolishly, I had accepted a 'gentleman's bet' that I couldn't march back to Sandhurst in time for breakfast roll call at seven-thirty next morning. Bill Leigh was a good amateur jockey; he specialised in driving the Healey hard, changing gears without the clutch. It was only a few months later that he had to be cut out of a wrecked van with the aid of a fireman's axe, after he missed a corner near the Hind's Head at Bray.

We arrived at Hyde Park Corner at nine-fifteen and it was beginning to rain. At nine-twenty I set out to cover the thirty miles back to the Academy.

Initially things went well. I swung along through the evening crowds feeling very fit and the rain held off. I was offered and refused lifts on two occasions. I made good time and certainly should be back for the parade. I felt tireless.

As the night wore on, and I drew away from London, darkness closed in and I felt tired. Gradually the lights went out in the houses lining the road. Near London Airport I bought three Mars Bars at a garage kiosk and strode on tearing great holes in the night. By the time I reached Staines my feet felt numb from the endless hammering of the studded boots on the pavement, and I was no longer enjoying myself. The five-mile intervals between Staines, Sunningdale, Bagshot and Camberley seemed an eternity. My left foot began to hurt more than my right and I started to limp. The red tail-lights of the big lorries seemed to remain in sight for such a long time on the straight stretches. Came the dawn, and I found myself dozing off as I walked; somehow I must keep awake and stop weaving about in the road.

By the time I reached a broken-down sports car outside Camberley, it was light and the dawn chorus in full swing. Bent over the cranking handle was the lanky figure of Rudge Penley. He was returning from a party and I gave him a push start. Rudge was the first officer commissioned direct to 1st Battalion, The Parachute Regiment. Tragically he was killed after landing in telephone wires at the end of a free-fall parachute descent, when he bounced off and broke his neck thirty feet below.

As I ran across the playing fields, the clock on the green-domed tower of New College read six-twenty. I leapt up the flights of stone stairs, three at a time, and burst into the room of my challenger.

I had an hour to spare so I had a shower and lay down on my bed for a rest. When I came to dress I couldn't get my boots back on. Stupidly they had been laced too tight on the march, and as my feet were prevented from swelling normally, the lower leg had puffed out over the top of the boot instead.

There was a very dull nuclear T.E.W.T. (Tactical Exercise Without Troops) on that day so I went sick instead. The M.O. put me to bed in the hospital, and I slept all day. Next morning I was sent back to work and charged with self-inflicted injuries. Fortunately I was only admonished.

Soon I was back to my old tricks again. The Consul, nearly rebuilt with a reconditioned engine, was ready for use. I drove carefully down to Pangbourne for Founders' Day. The new engine had to be run in at not more than 30 m.p.h. I was returning to the college at the end of a year's ban resulting from a raid we had made one night, and waking them all up with military pyrotechnics and thunderflashes.

After the usual speeches I agreed to meet several friends down at the Elephant Hotel in the village. Like Toad of Toad Hall, I turned the nicely resprayed pale green car down the narrow lanes; the leafy hedges restricted the already poor vision. Too late I saw the smart black Daimler coming round the bend uphill towards me. Wildly I twisted the steering wheel, and drove the inside wheels up on to the steep bank in a vain effort to miss the oncoming vehicle. There was a screech of tearing metal, then we were past. Sadly the Consul was too high on the bank and it began to topple on to its side. In the driving seat I saw the tarmac coming up to meet my door, so I pushed my right arm out of the open window in a Herculean effort to stop us from going over. For my pains I got a deep gash in the second finger of that hand from the door handle. The car came to a halt on its side – and the radio played on.

My mind raced. As a non-drinker my first thought was to remove the bottle opener from my key ring so the police would not see it. Secondly, I switched off the radio, and sniffed the petrol fumes as a full tank emptied on to the road. As I hauled myself out of the window on the passenger side, I thought at least I was spared the awful death I had often dreamt of. Near our home at Datchet one night, an exiled prince had left the road while driving home to London in a Jaguar XK120. His car had ended upside down in a ditch. The prince was drowned in a foot of mud. The radio played on and the wheels spun, emptily.

My father was in Cuba, negotiating a contract to build a sardine factory at the time of my accident. On his return he said I must buy the car and insure it myself – I never had any more accidents in that car.

During the Sovereign's Parade at the end of term, the commissioning ceremony for O'Neil's intake, I very nearly dropped my rifle. Sandhurst unquestionably produces the finest drill in the army. Dressed in 'Blues', and wearing white buff equipment, we marched round the Old Building Square, in slow and quick time, carrying the highly polished No. 4 rifles at the 'slope' on our shoulders, we looked indeed 'Every man an emperor'.

My left hand began to tighten with cramp on the brass-plated butt of the weapon. Thousands of proud parents watched as the 'cream of British Youth', as we were known in some quarters, (the National Stud in others), passed by. I felt the weight of the rifle begin to push its way out of my white gloved hand. Sweat started to trickle down my neck with the effort of holding my arm at right angles to my body. I just couldn't think what was causing the cramp.

Eventually, almost crying out with the pain, we wheeled, halted, faced up and stood at ease. Surreptitiously I was able to feel my left wrist with my gloved right hand. The button at the cuff was too tight and had restricted the circulation; I crooked my finger under the shirt and wrenched the button off. Immediately there was an improvement.

We came to attention, sloped arms, advanced fifteen paces in review order, and then crashed into the present arms, amid clouds of white blanco. All was well.

At the end of the annual summer camp at Brecon in Wales, after I had led the whole of New College, mounted in three-ton trucks and Land-Rovers, up a narrow windy lane through the hills to a very embarrassing cul-de-sac, I was appointed a junior under officer for my last term. The 'Best Loser' had saved the day again.

Part of the summer leave was spent at R.A.F. Abingdon, the

Parachute Training Centre, with the Edward Bear Club. Volunteer cadets were trained in all aspects of static line Parachuting, except the night descent.

Synthetic training presented no difficulties; the swings, fan exit trainer and high tower seemed quite enjoyable.

The first real introduction to jumping is from a cage slung beneath a barrage balloon. The cage bar is slammed into place after the five nervous trainees and the joking instructor have hooked up.

'Up 800. Five men jumping,' shouts the instructor.

The brake on the cable drum at the back of the truck is slowly released and the balloon climbs into the sky with the cage swinging beneath it. Everybody jokes, everybody feels sick with nerves – except the instructor. The balloon climbs to 800 feet, and the would-be parachutists, looking all the way down the steel cable to the truck, have a rather nasty sensation of height. I have never been able to appreciate the view from the top. The first jump was all right because the experience was unknown. The second jump, anticipating that sickening plunge of 120 feet before the chute developed, was, for me, quite dreadful.

From an aeroplane parachuting always seems a much more reasonable proposition than the cold-blooded balloon cage. Somehow the noise, sickness and fetid air in a troop carrying aircraft, conspire to make the jump a tolerable alternative to any continuation of the flight.

Sitting in two parallel lines, each of thirty men, with heavy steel helmets tight on their heads, main and reserve chutes and heavy weapon containers strapped to them, it is not long before one of the sixty begins to feel sick. On one such occasion, during a particularly bumpy flight, a man about half-way up the aircraft on the port side, suddenly reached up for one of the issue brown paper bags. Many pairs of eyes set in pale sweating faces watched the poor fellow bend forward and bury his face in the bag. With knotted stomach muscles and clenched teeth, we saw him remove the bag and hold it in his right hand; he made a few flat circling movements with it before he raised it to his lips, throwing his head back, and seemingly swallowed the contents. Suddenly the air was full of hands reaching for paper bags.

I glanced back at the man who had started this chain reaction; with a broad grin on his face he was now refolding his bag and placing it back in the rack. It was a pretty grim joke.

At the end of the two-week course we had completed our two balloon jumps, and sufficient aircraft descents to qualify for a parachute emblem to be worn on the left sleeve.

My last term at the Academy was spent desperately trying to learn enough to pass the final examinations. Also I was captain of boxing. Boxing had steered me through Sandhurst and it was only fair that it should inflict some more pain on me, now that I was set up to meet the best of the opposing teams as captain. I continued to lose more than I won, but I value the experience, for it accustomed me to decision-making and helped me to relax when under pressure.

There was always mental pressure before an important boxing match. I used to lie in silence on my bed, waiting for the rumbling of feet and voices which meant that dinner was over and the spectators were starting to make their way down to the gymnasium.

Luckily I scraped through my examinations and was commissioned into the Parachute Regiment. I was very proud.

The 19th December, 1958, the day after we had 'Passed Out' under the stern gaze of the Chief of the Imperial General Staff, dawned cold and bright. Pale sun, blue sky and frosted grass etched a memory in my mind. As I walked, alone with myself, out of the grounds for the last time, my heels first crunching the frozen gravel on the Square, then ringing on the tarmac road to the Staff College Gate, I knew that at last, after twenty years of training, I was going to make my mark on the world.

6

Young Officers

EARLY in January 1959 I presented myself to the Adjutant at Maida Barracks in Aldershot, the depot of the Parachute Regiment and Airborne Forces. After a brief introductory talk, he told me to go on up to the mess.

Nervous in my new Service Dress, I walked up the short gravel drive bordered with its neat flower-beds. Once inside the red-brick Victorian building, I found myself looking straight into the mouth of a tiger, which hung head-down on the far wall of the hall. On either side of him red-tiled corridors led away into the gloom, their regulation cream walls hung with charcoal sketches of airborne battles.

The officers' rooms opened on to these corridors, some neat, some in violent disorder, each with its wash basin and coal fire, travel posters on the walls, gramophones, uniforms, sports and civilian clothing, squash racquets and golf clubs. Adjoining the hall, on the left, was the high-ceilinged dining-room, with regimental silver on the tables and portraits of airborne generals along the walls. Off the hall on the right was the ante-room, identical in shape, but with airborne battle in oil, by David Sheppard. The whole building had an air of grim pride and austerity; there was no acknowledgement of a civilian world.

The officers of the depot were entertaining the sergeants' mess to drinks on that first morning in the ante-room. Second Lieutenant Pat Wood and I tried to hide in a corner; we had left Sandhurst together, he for the 2nd Battalion and I for the 3rd. Every so often, we were summoned by the Adjutant to meet various Regimental personalities. We smiled politely and tried to say as little as possible. We drank nothing from the pints of beer we carried throughout.

After a couple of hours' hard drinking, the party began to warm up, voices were raised and glasses occasionally fell and broke. The redoubtable Provost Sergeant, an ex-booth fighter and Arnhem veteran, quietly subsided down the wall and on to the floor into a sitting position by one of the doors, with a happy smile spread across his beaten face.

The party had gone as far as I expected it to go, The Regimental Sergeant-Major would surely now rally his men and leave, thanking all concerned. Pat and I would be free to go unscathed.

Two hours later, at four o'clock in the afternoon, the R.S.M. called for silence. I was feeling pretty frought by this time as some of the sergeants were looking rather belligerently at Pat and me. Surely this was the end, it must be.

The R.S.M. challenged the Brigadier to a fight. To my way of thinking this was rather like Jesus challenging God; it was the antithesis of three years of army learning. The most senior N.C.O. in the regiment glowered at the Commander of the Parachute Brigade. Locked together they both fell to the floor. At this point the sergeants turned on the officers and I was knocked to the ground. Fortunately Pat and I were sober, so I had no great difficulty in defending myself, but I was certainly not going to attack anyone. I managed to extract myself and retired into a corner, hoping, once more, to pass unnoticed.

Despite our diffidence during the party, one or two officers had clearly decided that we needed a good shake-up on joining the regiment. It was the same 'new-boy' feeling that everybody has when first joining school. Now, one of these officers, seeing me out of the fracas and presuming my cowardice, decided it was time for my come-uppance. He charged across the room and hurled me to the ground, seeking to force my submission with a wrestling hold. I soon realised he was not playing, but he had had several drinks, and he was attacking my only strong point,

physical fitness. Gradually he tired, and long evenings of wrestling in the gym at Pangbourne came to my help. The mêlée
continued in full swing all around us; I decided I could and would
force this officer to submit to me, and damn the possible consequences. He was drunk, I was sober, he had expended his energy
in his furious onslaught, I had attacked no one.

Now I had him face down on the floor, my right arm locked
round his throat and my body on his back and out of reach of his
arms and legs.

My grip tightened, the noise around us continued. I lowered
my head to look him in the eye – there was just him and me.

'It's unfair,' I thought, but then he would have had me.

Sweat glistened on his face, his eyes began to bulge.

'What if he goes unconscious?' I wondered.

He grunted submission, I let go and we both got up. He said
nothing but turned away and went off to another part of the room.
He never mentioned it again, and he never held it against me as
far as I could tell.

Soon, honour satisfied, the fight came to an end. All but the
hardened drinkers began to drift away from the party. Pat and I
left. I was amazed and asked him if this always happened. He
replied grandly, 'Oh, quite often.' I thought his recruit training
with the Parachute Regiment must have been very different to
Stalag IX.

Two days later I left Aldershot for six months, to undergo
various training courses prior to joining the 3rd Batallion, or
3 Para as it is known to the army. The last of these was the P
course, or pre-parachute selection course, and it provided an
unforgettable fortnight ending with my twenty-first birthday.
Eighty-two soldiers and seven officers assembled for selection at
Maida Barracks at the beginning of July, it was to be the hottest
time of that year. We were divided into six squads with an officer
in each. I was the seventh officer and because I was already in
the regiment, I was placed in a squad with an athletic Royal
Engineer subaltern some three years older than myself.

The first cross-country run took a heavy toll of the candidates.
This was followed by a period of confidence tests in the swimming
pool. For some reason I was unable to master the trapeze which
hung above the baths. Each time I stepped off the platform I
swung down along the pool, but as soon as the upswing began
towards the other platform, my grip failed and I belly-flopped

into the water. Another test which proved difficult, particularly to the non-swimmers, was a back somersault off the top diving board. I vividly remember my feeling of relief when the whistle blew to signal the end of the period – I was third in line waiting for the top board at that time.

As luck would have it I was in a good squad, and we carried off most of the competitions; this enabled me to save my energy for individual efforts such as the 'milling'. For this each man was roughly matched against an opponent of the same weight. They were then gloved-up and put into the ring for three rounds of fighting. It was far removed from boxing, and many of the fights were stopped through cuts inflicted by heads rather than fists.

My own opponent was half a stone heavier than me. An ex-boy soldier from Chepstow, he grinned malignantly and said he had never thought he would be given the chance to 'stick-it-on an officer'. I saw the milling as an opportunity to shine, so I went hard and won convincingly. Although tired I was quite pleased with myself as I stepped down from the ring.

Sitting back on the bench at the ringside, I wasn't really watching the next contestants, but congratulating myself on passing the course.

'Mr. Ridgway, sir,' the P.T. sergeant called, 'We've one lad extra, would you like another fight?'

I swallowed hard; why hadn't I thought of this? A lot of people were looking at me.

'O.K.,' I said, trying hard to sound keen.

Five minutes later I was in the ring against the biggest fellow on the course. I had put too much into the first fight and could not stem the bull-like rushes of my new opponent; the strength just wasn't in my arms and my feet were like lead. Time and again I wrestled him off, my head ringing with blows from the inside of his gloves. When the final bell rang the flag was raised in his favour. I was disgusted with myself.

The climax of the course was the infamous log race, which took place on a burning hot morning near the end of the second week. Each squad, by this time reduced to seven or eight men, had to run carrying a telegraph pole. The race was over a switchback course among the scrubland of the training area, two miles out of camp.

Clad in P.T. vests, denim trousers, boots and steel helmets, we joked nervously at the start line as we bent to fasten our short toggle ropes around the pole. Four of us on either side, shortest at the front, tallest at the back. The hemp loop cut into the back of my wrist. We were expected to break the record of fourteen minutes and thirty-two seconds, and were matched against a particularly fit squad. A poor showing in this and I'd fail the course; I must give it 100 per cent. I was twenty-one today, and on the left-hand side at the heavy end of the log.

From the start we went smoothly, and kept well in step, everyone pulling his weight. At the half-way mark we came to the foot of Trig Point Hill just ahead of our opponents, and slowly ground our way up its crumbling, nearly vertical face. At the top the P.T. instructor urged us on with good news; we were level with the record. On the way down, the leading man on my side stumbled and fell, releasing his rope; we didn't see him again.

Reduced to seven men, we ran on through the drumming heat. Eventually the finishing line came into view, some three hundred yards ahead through the bushes, along a deep sandy track. At the back, we were choking on the dust kicked up by those at the front of the log.

To this day I think of that last stretch whenever I am faced by anything particularly difficult. I just did not believe I could make it. As we crossed the line, all seven of us pitched forward into the dust with the log.

We had cut four seconds off the record. When I came to untie my rope I found it had cut deep into my hand, and yet I had never felt it.

Forty-five soldiers and three officers passed the course.

Next day I joined 3 Para.

As the commander of 9 platoon, C company, I was a part of the one regular parachute brigade left in the army. The Brigade was composed of three battalions of infantry, with minor units of artillery, engineers, ordnance and all the other supporting arms necessary to maintain the brigade as an independent force at war. Each of the three battalions comprised three rifle companies, a support and a headquarters company. Each rifle company had three platoons and a company headquarters.

No. 9 platoon, like all the others, was made up of three sections each of about six men, and a small headquarters which had two men on the 3·5-inch rocket launcher, a batman/runner, a wireless operator, a platoon sergeant and me. The grand total of twenty-four was well under strength, for there should have been thirty-six.

Sergeant Hilden, my platoon sergeant, a veteran nearing the end of twenty-two years' service, had been an Olympic trialist at water polo and had played for the army in a variety of games. A big athletic man, with a broad kindly face and striking blue eyes, he was known affectionately in the battalion as 'White Hunter', for his habit of running outside the camp perimeter before reveille whenever the battalion was abroad in the Middle East.

In the early days Sergeant Hilden stood as a barrier between the platoon and me; he allowed nothing to upset me. Standing with feet apart and his huge fists clenched, at the top of the wooden steps which led down into the platoon barrack-room, he would bellow at the soldiers to stand up whenever they spoke to me. I was grateful for his paternal influence, and I remember the sorrow in his eyes, when, after six months with me, he told me the result of his interview with the resettlement Board. After more than twenty years of pride in the regiment, they said all they could offer him was a demolition course, because labouring was the only job he could expect outside the army. Two or three times over the past ten years I have seen his powerful figure among gangs of workmen employed in demolishing those same proud red-brick barrack blocks which had housed British soldiers for nearly a hundred years. I wondered what he, typical of the old disciplinarians, thought of the new barracks, all space and light; and the new soldiers, born since the last war, with their own ideas of discipline and dress.

Of the three corporals who commanded the sections, Bickell and Graves were quite manageable and helped me gain confidence. The third was Corporal Taylor, an army lightweight boxer. He worked on the principle that only the strong should survive. Soldiers in Aldershot had a considerable respect for this young Cockney. Not much over five feet tall and weighing around eight stone, he spent every minute of every day looking for a fight. He feared no one. Hollow-cheeked and Roman-nosed, he would strut around the room demanding attention; the platoon adored him.

There was also a rebellious young Lance-Corporal who was always trying to fix a posting to the Special Air Service, his name was Chay Blyth. Stockily built and baby-faced, at eighteen he always sided with the soldiers against authority. I tried in vain to have him reduced to the rank of Private.

In September the brigade went to Norway for a month of

exercises near the Artic Circle. Initially 3 Para was accommodated under canvas near an airfield about half-way down the west coast. I was one of five officers and the company sergeant-major to share a large conical tent. We slept round the outside with our feet pointing in towards a wood-burning stove in the centre. Everytime the cry 'Logs' went up, I had to get reinforcements for that heater; it was like fetching the newspapers for the officers aboard the *Clan Kennedy*.

We flew 450 miles north for the main exercise and parachuted on to a piece of bogland between two snow-capped mountains. As soon as I hit the ground I looked up, fearing I might be hit by others still in the air, but all was well. The next wave of aircraft came in, and I saw the remainder of the Battalion streaming from the planes. High above me a black dot gradually grew larger as it fell, but I couldn't judge its size against the height. I wondered what piece of equipment it might be, for weapon containers weighing over a hundred pounds sometimes break free from a parachutist's legs and soon reach a terminal velocity of around 120 m.p.h. Strangely the falling object above me was simply a red beret which slowly spun down and landed just a few feet from where I knelt. Picking it up I made my way to the platoon rendezvous, and soon I was engrossed in arranging fire positions and reporting casualty figures over the radio to Company Headquarters.

Corporal Taylor had had a bad exit from his plane, and had failed to clear the aircraft effectively. He was number ten in a stick of fifteen from the port side of a Hastings, and when he came to make his exit there were already nine long parachute strops trailing along the fuselage. He stumbled on the sill of the open door, and failed to drive himself into space with sufficient power. As his feet were carried up by the slipstream, so his upper body fell back; luckily his neck was not broken by the flailing strop which caught at his throat. At the rendezvous he reported his section in, and told me he had lost his beret. As I handed him the one I'd found, I saw the burn stretching from under his left ear, two inches wide, across to his Adam's apple. Already it was weeping badly. We were due for seven days with freezing nights, but he refused treatment and never complained of the severe pain he suffered.

This was an example of the quality of the people around me; time and again I was to feel that if some of the soldiers had had the opportunities and education that I had been lucky enough to have, they would have proved greatly superior to me. During my years with 3 Para there were many occasions when we seemed beaten by the elements, opponents or simply officialdom; I would be ready to give up, only to see success rise out of sheer spirit and disciplined teamwork. Sometimes my eyes would cloud with sheer happiness and pride, just to be with them. Slowly I came to believe that most things are possible.

On that main exercise in Norway, 9 Platoon had to defend a small bridge until orders arrived for its demolition. The cold in that high latitude in September was intense, and at night we were unable to sleep in our trenches. The Aurora Borealis played like searchlights in the cold night sky, and we watched these for hour after hour, stamping our frozen feet.

Our Norwegian opponents were often bicycle troops towed behind armoured cars. If they wished to move across country, they simply carried the bikes on their backs over the mountains to the next road.

They attacked us one night and I heard Corporal Taylor's harsh voice in the dark, 'Fix Bayonets . . .Charge!' The Norwegians fled but they were no more frightened than I. Did they really fix bayonets, I wondered? Luckily it was bluff.

When we returned to England, the rest of the year was spent mostly in barracks and I was involved in the endless task of trying to keep soldiers busy with very little to interest them. It is difficult to select men of high calibre, train them to work as a team, and then expect them to maintain enthusiasm and fitness for year after year. A challenge is needed to combat the frustration of inactivity, and challenges are not easy to find when the number of training areas, both at home and abroad, is decreased each year.

About this time Second Lieutenant Colin Thomson, fresh from Mons Officer Cadet School on a three-year Short Service Commission, joined C Company to command 7 Platoon. As we shared the wrath of the Company commander, Major Malcolm Carr, we soon became firm friends. Tall and charming, Colin always regards himself as a wiry reincarnation of James Mason.

Early in 1960, I looked outside the army for a challenge. The annual canoe race from Devizes, in Wiltshire, to the Westminster Bridge over the Thames in London has been likened to 'A poor man's Everest'. Starting at timed intervals, on each Good Friday morning, about 300 men in 150 double kayaks of all shapes and sizes paddle their way along fifty-two miles of the Kennet and Avon canal, carrying their canoes round fifty-four locks, on the way to Reading. There they join the Thames for a further seventy miles downriver to London. The last eighteen miles is on the tideway, and it is most important to catch the tide at Teddington lock if a good time is to be achieved.

In late February 1960 four young officers of 3 Para, Ted Horton, Edward Gardner, Colin Thomson and I, decided to enter the race. We would train in our own time and at our own expense. Ted already had a kayak and Colin and I bought a Tyne folding canoe for sixty pounds.

For our first training session we decided to canoe the seventy miles of river from Reading to Westminster, over a Saturday night. First of all we drove the cars to London and left Ted's Morris Traveller near Westminster; both canoes were secured on my roof-rack and we drove to Reading. At half past three in the afternoon we set off downriver. By midnight we were passing Datchet and our strength had disappeared, our backsides were painful in the wooden seats, the glucose in our service water bottles tasted foul. The long deep stroke seemed the most efficient. Colin and I reached Teddington at four o'clock on Sunday morning for a favourable tide; we were ahead of Ted and Ed by a few minutes. The eighteen miles down the tideway in the dark was quite memorably miserable, the banks often seemed to undulate before our eyes and then we would steer for the middle of the river and drift off into sleep, nodding into wakefulness whenever the canoe started to roll over. The miles passed and Ted and Ed disappeared behind us. At first light we opened our eyes suddenly, to find ourselves under the stern of a dirty coal ship, moored alongside a power station wharf. The dripping of the crew's latrine outflow reminded me of the *Clan Kennedy* off Beira. From that point the new day sustained us, and we arrived at Westminster at half past seven to find Ted and Ed waiting with the car. They had given up at Kew Bridge.

With the race only a few weeks ahead we continued training in the canoes whenever time allowed us to get on to the course; we also had some afternoons on the nearby Basingstoke canal. Since the age of sixteen I had done press-ups before going to bed each night. I was still doing 100 each night and I used the effort for its psychological as much as its physical benefit; the self discipline required to perform 100 press-ups at four in the morning, after

F

a party, was useful in later years. We were also lucky enough to be advised in our circuit training by an R.A.F. sergeant who, with a Parachute Regiment colleague, was establishing a series of long-distance walking records, which culminated in an epic march across North America from San Francisco to New York.

The circuit which we did each morning before breakfast in Maida gymnasium, consisted of a series of ten exercises with very light weights repeated against the clock. At the first session, we established the maximum number of repetitions we could do in each exercise in one minute; then each morning we performed half of that maximum number, in each of the exercises in a cycle, three times through without a halt. Over a period of four weeks, I was able to reduce my time from fifteen minutes to ten minutes twenty-one seconds.

On the course we managed to find bed and breakfast at the White Hart in Devizes for eight and sixpence. The most serious accident on our training occurred in the dark at five o'clock on the morning of Saturday, 26th March. Both canoes were side by side on the canal as we approached the mouth of a long tunnel, some two hours before first light. We had been going for almost an hour, and were chatting away to each other; the plan was to reach Reading and continue a few miles downriver. About a hundred yards short of the bridge we disturbed four swans which started to flail the water with their wings in an effort to rise into the air ahead of us. When they reached the tunnel, they panicked, unable to see the light at the other end. They turned and came back towards us, necks outstretched, wings spanning six feet. They chose Ted and Ed's side of the canal. The leading swan was just clear of the water and rising when it cracked head-first into Ted's chest. Over they went in the weedy ice-fringed canal water. Ted was rather bruised and that was the end of that day's training.

The race itself went quite well, but Colin and I were both convinced that the other was not pulling his weight. The first canal lock is twelve miles from the start. I could only achieve eleven and a half miles before I told him we must steer for the bank so I could spend a penny. Colin would not allow this and fighting broke out. As the front man my feet controlled the rudder; by the time we reached the bank he was beating the back of my head with his paddle.

We reached Reading at the end of the day, one and a half hours ahead of schedule, and turned downriver into the night. The lights in the riverside houses began to go out and we paddled on into the dark. At Hurley we almost went over the weir by accident being so sleepy; we decided to wait on the bank for Ted and Ed, who had started just after us. When they arrived we said we might spend the night on the bank and continue in the morning; although this meant missing the tide at Teddington they agreed. We had given up any chance of winning. Next day we pushed on and finished well down the list; we had trained too hard over too short a time. I was not finished with canoeing.

The summer was busy, but I thought everyone too complacent, and longed for real adventure. On one of the many exercises we flew north to parachute on the west coast of Scotland by Loch Awe, but because the wind was too strong for jumping we flew across Scotland to Kinross near Inverness. From my seat in the plane, I saw the desolate beauty of mountain and loch for the first time. I decided that one day I would live there. We rode back into the exercise by coach, and I was so impressed with the open country that I persuaded Colin that instead of going to France, we should spend our leave on the West Coast. This meant a twenty-seven-hour rail trip back to Aldershot and a twenty-four-hour drive back to Loch Awe, but the fishing on Fionn Loch was worth it.

The quest for excitement led to horse-racing, and that led to an organisation called 'Moonraker' which sent me tips through the post. All I had to do was place one bet on each race on each day; if I won I stopped betting for that day, if I lost I doubled my stake on the next race. 'Nip' Eustace, the main bookmaker in Aldershot, was more than pleased to let me lay my bets by phone, from the Company office. I was soon making four or five pounds each week. Then one day it happened, the horses I backed just did not win. My stakes doubled: five shillings, ten shillings, one pound, two pounds, four pounds, eight pounds, sixteen pounds, thirty-two pounds – I stopped, I had lost nearly a month's pay in two days. 'Nip' put a new window in his shop, and I always felt I had at least helped towards the cost. Had I continued I should have had £1,024 on the horse which eventually won, five races later, and there would have been very little profit.

I gave up backing horses and flew to Germany next day for the autumn exercises. The Parachute Brigade was billeted in a tented camp on the island of Sylt of the west coast of Denmark.

We were known as the soldiers with cherry berets and white bottoms because we used to go for runs on the nudist beaches of the islands.

After the main exercise, C Company was attached to the Royal Scots Greys in Detmold and I had a glimpse of the palatial style of a cavalry mess, which counted the Duke of Kent among its members. A last cantonment of the British Raj, it seemed a museum of old silver. Every officer had fruit juice for breakfast and owned an aristocratic dog and an Aston Martin or similarly expensive sports car. Their playing fields were the autobahns and polo grounds, and they could recommend places of class off Hamburg's Rieper Bahn. They believed in élan, and when we worked with them later, they proved most efficient with their tanks.

At a guest night we played roulette after dinner, and I was able to win enough to take Colin and me to Hamburg for twenty-four hours. My stakes were mainly the chips I found scattered on the carpets at their aristocratic feet. I was helped by one of their officers who had been deported from Norway after a spectacular incident involving a suspension bridge and his Facel Vega sports car.

The most impressive part of that short time in Germany was a visit one morning to the cemetery at the Belsen concentration camp. The vision of those long mounds which serve as mass graves for tens of thousands of German Jews, will never leave my mind.

We returned to Aldershot and another winter passed, broken by a short visit to ski in Italy. In 1962 I began to look increasingly outside the army for excitement. I was much aware of the prime of my youth and the urge to live a full life was strong in me. In January I started to organise an assault on the canoe race again, this time at Battalion level. We managed to raise five crews. One of the men was Corporal Chay Blyth. The training was marred by an accident one night when we were repeating the Reading to Westminster stretch. As Colin Thomson and I led the five canoes into the bank by the weir at Cookham, the second, third and fourth crews dovetailed in behind each other. The fifth failed to get in, and overshot the landing place. Too late they saw the iron girders loom up in the dark. We shouted a warning and they back-paddled frantically; it seemed, as they turned broadside, that they would claw themselves away, but suddenly they were gone. The fibreglass canoe shattered and both men disappeared into the lattice work of platform and posts. The white water foamed in the dark and I felt sick.

As I ran to the gate leading on to the catwalk over the weir, I tried to make a plan. Second Lieutenant David Charles would have to look after himself; my responsibility lay with Private Jason Hazard, his partner. Once over the barbed wire above the gate, which was locked, I raced to the spot where the bow of the canoe still jutted forlornly above the tumbling water. It was jammed against one of the posts of the weir. The beam from my pocket torch made out the head and shoulders of a man. Seemingly trapped by his legs, the varying pressure of water sometimes forced his head above the surface, and sometimes dragged him under.

'It's Jason, sir,' Chay shouted in my ear, 'Gibby and I will swim down from the bank above and cut him free.'

'You bloody well won't!' I bellowed at him. Visions of four deaths instead of two leapt into mind.

I simply didn't know what to do. The minutes were ticking by, at nine o'clock on a January night. The roar of the water filled my head. I must do something, Jason couldn't last long, Jason couldn't last long . . .

We got a canoe round the weir and two of us tried to paddle up into the 'lion's mouth' in which Jason was trapped, but it just wasn't possible. As we came ashore David appeared; he had shot straight through the weir, and after a long time under water he had been washed to the surface, just as he felt he could no longer hold his breath. With failing strength he found himself being sucked round the weir pool and into the maelstrom again. Once more through the white water, once more downstream. Realising he couldn't survive another circuit he struck out desperately to reach the downstream current. He failed and was drawn round again; he felt he was going to die there in the dark. Suddenly his dangling feet scraped the bottom; in his effort to get downstream he had moved on to the outer edge of the eddy and reached the shallows. He crawled up on to a small gravel beach and lay there, wondering how Jason had fared. Soon he made his way to the weir and met us on the catwalk.

Jason couldn't last long . . . Jason can't last long . . .

We decided that Colin and Corporal Gibbins, in a canoe, should wait in the pool below. An inflated life-jacket would be lowered to Jason. At the same time two of us would climb down the front of the pier and try to shift the steel-wire cable which ran diagonally down through the water between the piers and seemed to be trapping Jason.

We noticed that his head was lolling now when it came clear of the water – he had been there nearly twenty minutes and in January the water is cold.

The canoe took station, we crawled down to the wire and saw the dangling life-jacket silhouetted against the night sky, close by Jason's head. He reached for it and we heaved on the wire. Suddenly he was gone.

Corporal Gibbins saw the jacket riding high on the water. It slipped past his bow and he grabbed as it came alongside – there was nothing with it. He felt a slight bump on the bottom of the canoe and thrust his hand deep into the water on the other side. His fingers closed on Jason's hair. They towed him to the bank. He was out cold.

The lock keeper was watching television and Colin lost his temper. Soon we had Jason laid out on the kitchen floor, and carried on with artificial respiration, but when the ambulance arrived half an hour later he was still unconscious. However, he recovered quickly in Maidenhead hospital.

Colonel Roley Gibbs, our Commanding Officer, never once remarked on what had been a horribly near escape, although there could well have been a regimental inquiry. Nothing was ever recovered of the canoe.

We held a trial on the course and only Colin and I finished the distance. We were very disappointed. On the race itself all five crews finished within twenty minutes of each other. The next year a team prize was offered.

The battalion was posted to Cyprus, and four of us formed a syndicate to buy a yacht. We planned to sail her out to Cyprus, and fit her out for a voyage round the world to the Caribbean, where we hoped to start a chartering business in the West Indies. We all agreed to pay twenty pounds each month into a joint account, to raise funds.

Over the Easter leave Colin Thomson, David Charles, Richard Sherjan and I chartered the small yacht *Chiriya*, and hired her skipper, Terry Fitzpatrick, to teach us to sail. That week in the Solent was made memorable by Colin's sea-sickness, Richard's bad losing at poker, David's early morning sickness from a shortage of cigarettes, and Terry's girl friend Delia. I upset everyone with my impatience and a long list of other major faults. Sailing that small boat seemed to present no great difficulty, and the project continued.

After Easter I was sent on an Army Support Weapons course, for I was soon to leave 9 platoon to take over the anti-tank platoon in Support Company. Unfortunately my interest in the course rather waned when we heard that *English Rose II* was for sale at Poole. David and I looked her over, David liked her and we bought her for £2,000. Built in 1898 she was a sixty-foot ketch which had long been the property of the Courtauld family. During the war she was sold, and her lead keel was replaced with railway lines set in concrete.

Foolishly we failed to have her surveyed. The mortgage company supplied the major part of the finance and we relied on their brief survey. From that time I began to realise what it is to worry. It was good training.

On every available weekend we travelled down to Bursledon on the Hamble River where we kept the yacht for convenience. The *English Rose II* had previously been a girls' training vessel, and there was much work to be done to fit her out for the long voyage to Cyprus. We repainted the graceful black hull, with its raking bow and stern, and transformed it to gleaming white. We cleaned the interior, and serviced the twin Coventry Victor diesel engines. The drab brown paint was scraped from the elegant teak decks, and we set about recaulking them with pitch and oakum. Several firms offered equipment and stores for the voyage; several famous sailors answered our letters in which we sought advice. The crew was to be David, Richard and myself, with a further seven soldiers all from 3 Para. Colin was posted out of the battalion to the depot, but retained his share.

We had been working on the yacht for nearly three months when, in July 1961, the trouble flared up in Kuwait. 2 Para flew there from Cyprus, and 3 Para was ordered to stand by for a posting to Bahrein in the Persian Gulf. Colonel Gibbs quietly told me that *English Rose II* would have to be left in the United Kingdom or sold. The search began for a buyer with only two months before the battalion was to fly to the Middle East.

We decided that we should cruise out to Cherbourg and the Channel Islands during our August leave, but because we were soon to go abroad most of the crew wished to visit their families. Lieutenant Rod Liddon, Lieutenant Alec Larkman, Sergeant

Gibbins, Colin and I were all who had turned up at Bursledon by half past seven on the morning of 5th August. We slipped our moorings and motored cautiously down the winding Hamble River. Colin's broken ankle and fatalistic disposition to sea-sickness did not make him an ideal sailor.

Once in the Solent we hoisted the sails on the short masts, which had been drastically reduced to balance the replacement lightweight keel. The engines were switched off, and we headed for the open sea at the eastern end of the Isle of Wight. The wind was rising from the west; we decided it was too rough by the time we reached the Nab Tower. Turning back we slowly made our way westward along the Solent, hoping to return to the Channel by the Needles Rocks at the western end of the Island. There was a fair amount of tacking and during the squalls we blew out several of our old canvas sails, lost the log and line, and finally lost our burgee over the side. We spent half an hour trying to find this little flag as it drifted away on the tide in the choppy water.

By four in the afternoon we had only reached Cowes, and so decided to call in to buy a new log and line. It was the last day of 'Cowes week', and the Fastnet race to the south-western corner of Ireland was already under way as we groped past the Royal Yacht *Britannia* and her grey naval escort frigate. Several times we nearly collided with some of the hundreds of glossy yachts moored in the river at Cowes, but we managed to secure our-selves to one of the wooden piles in midstream without any real mishap. Colin and Sergeant Gibbins stayed aboard to prepare supper while the rest of us went ashore to buy stores.

We sailed on the tide at eight o'clock in the evening, and passed the Needles Light at one o'clock in the morning. It was quite rough crossing the Channel and the whole crew of five felt rather grim. At three o'clock Colin rushed up from below and was sick all over the gleaming teak deck; it was immediately clear that he and Sergeant Gibbins were guilty of deceiving the crew. At supper we had all complained of army stew and asked where the spaghetti was. Colin denied all knowledge of any spaghetti aboard. It was now clear for all to see.

Later, I rushed up on a similar errand, very lightly clad, and tossed a brand-new pair of gym shoes on to the deck ahead of me. They bounced straight into the sea and disappeared astern in the darkness. It had not been a happy voyage, when we tied up at Cherbourg late next afternoon.

Colin and Rod Liddon both had to fly back to England next morning and this left Alec, 'Gibby' and me. We knew that the *English Rose* had a crew of fourteen as a girls' training vessel, but we felt we three could take her round the Channel Islands. The weather forecast was bad, storm Force 10 from the west within twelve hours. The Frenchman at the weather station assured us we could make the short voyage of some thirty miles west, down Channel to Alderney, if we left before six that evening on the favourable tide.

We sailed at half past five and found strong easterly winds just outside the harbour, so we fairly sped down Channel under full sail, goose-winged with main and mizzen sails boomed out on opposite sides.

The weather worsened, still from the east. Night came on, and we were unhappy about the tricky entry into Braye harbour on Alderney Island. Running free before a near gale from the east, we had to align two lights as we passed along the north coast of the island, then we should turn sharp left through the harbour entrance. If we failed we should either be swept on out into the Atlantic towards America or, worse, be wrecked on the wicked remains of the German breakwater, now partially submerged.

Alec was standing between the masts when the main boom gybed. It came over with crushing force, but he was just on the other side of the steel wire shroud which stopped the boom a few inches from his head. Had he been knocked over the side, Gibby and I would have been unable to pick up his unconscious body in the dark.

We decided to start the engines to help us make the sharp left turn when the time came to enter the harbour – the wind would be very confused in the entrance. We had long been in the Swinge, a notorious tide race which sometimes reached five knots.

It was completely dark when the two lights came into view and the moon and stars were obscured by racing clouds. Gibby's burly figure bellowed sea shanties to the wind, in his strong cockney accent. He lived for excitement and was thoroughly enjoying himself.

We were rather worried when the starboard engine caught fire, but clearly it was imperative to reach the shelter of the break-water, so we carried on hoping the fire would not spread. Smoke from the engine obscured the lights for the helmsman, so Alec called directions to me from the bows as we went in. Once inside the harbour we dropped the anchor some distance from the other yachts in case they should drag their anchors when the wind veered to west. The fire was mainly smoke, and the extinguisher quickly put it out. A hot cup of cocoa and we settled down for the night, one on anchor watch and two asleep.

At six in the morning, it was Alec's turn in the cockpit; his head was lolling drowsily on his shoulders. Twenty-four years old, he was a big man with short fair hair and a dry sense of humour. He had not been to sea before, and was pleased to find himself unaffected by sea-sickness. Now, he felt safe in harbour and it was beginning to get light. The waves booming on the breakwater outside seemed to lull him to sleep. He swayed, the way I had seen him nod off during lectures in Aldershot. Fitfully sleeping below, I was worried in case the anchor should drag and let us drift across the small bay to the rocks along the shore. The wind was still around severe gale force and it had veered to the west.

'Look out, one of them's broken loose,' shouted Alec.

Gibby and I scrambled from our bunks and reached the cockpit just as a yacht much bigger than *English Rose II* impaled itself broadside on our bowsprit, snapping it off like a spent match. The *Arminel* was jammed across our bows, and the pyjama-clad crew jumped about in great excitement as our broken bowsprit jutted through their saloon window. Fortunately our anchor held both us, and the ninety-ton *Arminel*. After some alarms the bigger yacht managed to free herself under engines and she anchored again some hundred yards clear of us and parallel with the wind.

We settled down to breakfast and waited for the wind to abate. With a crew of only three, the scrambled eggs were made with six eggs each. At two in the afternoon the master of the *Arminel* summoned us with a loud hailer and we went over in our dinghy to 'talk turkey'. It was a clear-cut case and as we were covered by insurance it worked out satisfactorily.

On the next day the three of us made an appearance at the islands' annual sports. While Alec, who played wing three-quarter for Berkshire and was the 3 Para sprint champion, won all the short distance events, Gibby devoted himself to raising a visitors' team to defeat the Islanders at tug-of-war for the first time in memory. 3 Para were army tug-of-war champions at this time, and the sight of red blood trickling down the side of Gibby's chest where the rope had been pinned by his arm made him an island folk-hero. I simply sat and ate the boxes of chocolates they won – athletics was never my strong point.

While in Braye harbour we met a Colonel Brewis who eventually bought *English Rose II* from us. Leaving her in the harbour, he kindly gave us a lift home to Portsmouth in his chartered boat. When he had *English Rose II* surveyed, she was found to be of rather different construction than we had thought. We were lucky to get £1,250 for her, despite the work we had done.

After only five months we had lost £750, and I had learnt a valuable lesson. The Regimental Colonel said, 'Time is a great healer, Ridgway.' I felt like healing him.

Sitting alone in my room, in the mess in Aldershot, I read a short book by a man named Chichester who had won the first single-handed trans-Atlantic sailing race. I thought that the last big race would come soon, a single-handed race round the world non-stop, and I tried to imagine how I would compete.

In October 3 Para flew out to the Middle East and set up camp on a flat sandy island in the Persian Gulf, called Bahrein. It was the base from where the operations in Kuwait, a few hundred miles distant at the northern end of the Gulf, had been mounted. We settled into a tented camp on the Muharraq airfield and awaited developments; 2 Para flew home.

The tents of the officers' and sergeants' messes were situated on one side of the runway and the company lines were on the other; down the runway flowed a fetid drain. The sand was always damp as we were only a few feet above the level of the surrounding sea.

It was hot and humid, the Arabs did not particularly like us, and there were dissidents who supported the Kuwaiti rebels. One night a Beverley freight aircraft touched down on the airstrip and its cargo of ammunition was rapidly unloaded. The plane was parked across the runway from our mess, which was next to a fuel dump of hundreds of thousands of gallons of petrol in polythene drogues and metal drums. Around midnight, just as I was turning in, the Beverley exploded. Across the runway we could see it wreathed in flame.

'If they hadn't unloaded that ammunition . . .' I thought of the petrol outside.

Apart from occasional incidents life was unbearably dull in Bahrein. Most of us trained desperately in an effort to tour Kenya with one of the battalion sports teams. Each day the sun came up, a huge fierce ball, first red, then yellowing as it rose in the coppery sky. It passed almost over head and sank again into the sand on the other side of the camp. Our training areas were much restricted, so we sat and sweated it out. The endless competition began to irritate everyone.

Bahrein was the classical scene for the girl friend's letter from home, which starts, 'Dear John'. So many soldiers had them that it shouldn't really have come as a surprise when it happened to me. But it did. The affairs of my heart had settled, over the past two years, upon a young and attractive girl from near Oxford, who was barely sixteen when I met her. The same selfish nature which had so upset my parents eventually turned her against me. Perhaps it served me right that the parting should come in misery in Bahrein. I was certainly miserable.

I had been in command of the anti-tank platoon since June 1961 and at Christmas I got a new platoon sergeant. Chay Blyth was only twenty-one, which is young for a sergeant in the Parachute Regiment. In my early days in 9 platoon, I had tried to have him stripped of his lance-corporal's stripe for he seemed a born rebel. Now, two years later, we worked well together. The platoon was never more than twenty strong, and most of them were experienced men of a higher calibre than the soldiers in the rifle companies. We had a good team, and they knew how to look after themselves, but in Bahrein very little happened. We did have one good spell on patrol in the lonely mountains of Oman at the other end of the Gulf, but this was an interlude.

My Christmas leave was spent in Kenya at the home of an officer of the 17/21 Lancers, a squadron of which shared our mess on the airfield. Kenya was so green and Bahrein so sandy that I decided to take up boxing again in order to join the battalion's Kenya tour in February 1962. When I left Sandhurst my nose was in poor shape and the hospital said I should not box again. My nose seemed a small price to pay to get off Bahrein, so I started training in earnest with the team every morning before reveille and every afternoon after duty.

As it turned out, I had to take responsibility for the team because the boxing officer had to return to England for a course. The tour went well and I had only one fight, in Nairobi, which I lost against our own light heavyweight. Once more I gained a 'Best Loser' trophy.

We returned to Aldershot in May 1962 and since then my craving for the sun has been completely cured. I remember saying I wouldn't mind if it rained every day in England just so long as I didn't have to return to that runway in Bahrein. I still feel the same.

The summer passed and I searched for some adventurous way of life outside the army, but could find nothing. Colin, who had been educated in Perth, visited Australia House and asked if we might join the Queensland sugar cane gangs; the immigration officer asked to see his hands.

'As I thought, never done a day's work in your life,' he said.

In Bahrein I had taken a correspondence course on diesel engines with a view to starting a big game fishery with a Kenya farmer in the Seychelles Islands in the Indian Ocean. Unfortunately, the airstrip did not look as if it would be built there after all, so there would not be enough American tourists to support us.

In July Rod Liddon, Keith Farnes and I did the Nijmegen Marches together. This meant thirty miles on four consecutive days along the flat roads of Holland and I was not as good a marcher as Rod and Keith. We went fast and in the towns I felt fine, but in the empty country roads I felt dreadful.

After six good weeks in Greece on exercise the battalion returned to Aldershot and I was given the task of entertaining an American airborne officer for a week.

On the final Saturday night of his visit I took him to a roulette party at a wealthy country home near Beaconsfield. Seated in my dinner jacket at midnight with a good pile of chips at my left hand the world seemed quite a reasonable place, and I quite a reasonable fellow. Concentrating hard and alone, I had followed the pattern of the red and black with some success; I looked up and down the table for a likely girl to share my winnings, preferably with some of her own. The prettiest girl sat at the left-hand end of the table, with a nice pile of chips, but she was not alone. 'She wouldn't be!' I thought. 'But I'll have a go.'

The heavy chips felt solid in my pocket, giving me confidence, as I moved round the table.

'I think it'll be red,' I said placing a one-pound plaque.

'We'll see,' she said and pushed out her own stake.

'Rien ne va plus,' called the croupier.

We watched the ball race against the spin of the wheel; slowly it dropped down the bowl and then clicked into place.

'Rouge, vingt cinq,' the croupier's mechanical voice announced.
'Well done,' the girl smiled.

We were friends.

'I'm Marie Christine D'Albiac; have you met my brother
James?' she asked. I was home.

Years in Aldershot had given me a good knowledge of London.
There must have been hundreds of 'big nights' when I drove up
for dances, parties or simply to take girls out. On balance, I
usually drove home rather poorer feeling a singular lack of
achievement, but I always returned. Those nights, and pounds
wasted resulted in a rather casual approach to girls and an attempt
always to hedge my bets in case I might be let down. It was not
surprising that Marie Christine began to think I was a spy, but it
would have surprised the army.

The autumn passed and we got to know each other. As the
New Year came in we were driving my old white M.G.A. through
a blizzard in the Kings Road in London. It seemed we could
compete a little better if we were together. It was the luckiest
decision I ever made.

On Arctic trials at Hudson's Bay in Canada I was in a snow
cave we had cut in a twelve-foot drift; the outside temperature,
accounting for windchill, was the equivalent of 83° F. of frost. I
said, 'I'll soldier no more [or words to that effect], I would rather
be an insurance clerk.' Chay Blyth smiled.

When we returned to Aldershot I planned the first Parachute
Brigade Canoe Race for March, a seventy-five mile overnight
race in two-seater canoes from Reading to Westminster, when
the Thames should be running fast and high. Chay and I were
the favourites; we started last in order to gain some measure of
how we were overhauling our opponents.

It was already dark at half past seven in the evening, as we
slipped away from the start under Caversham Bridge with the
whole field of thirty-five canoes ahead of us in the night. After a
half mile we carried our canoe round the first lock, with the
economy of time and effort which came from considerable practice and experience. It was those few seconds we hoped to gain at
each lock which would give us a marginal superiority over our
opponents; the race was on a time basis and therefore if we
completed the course in the shortest time we would win. We
should have the benefit of passing other crews all the way down
the course.

Three-quarters of an hour later we approached the short cut we used to get round Shiplake Lock. Here the weir lies on the right-hand side of the river as the canoeist approaches from upstream. We always aimed for the downstream end of the concrete weir apron, and carried the canoe across the slipper silk weed at a quiet part of the weir itself, just down from the main sluice gates or 'lion's mouths' as they are known. The idea was to make use of the swift weir stream rather than paddle through the safer lock-cut. The river was high, and the weed underfoot more than usually treacherous in the dark. We slipped the canoe down into the black water below the apron. Every second counted. The booming weir drowned our voices; there was a misunderstanding. Instead of the bow facing downstream it was facing up. The quickest way to rectify this was to turn the canoe across the current, once we were both in. Chay leaned over the apron sill and held the canoe firmly alongside as I gingerly lowered myself into the steering position at the bow. Once settled I held my paddle with my left hand and kept us against the bank so Chay could clamber down into his seat. The bow had moved out a little when I was settling myself, and now the fierce current pressed along the whole seventeen feet of the canoe, pushing the bow farther and farther out into the weir stream. My hand slipped on the weed and the gap widened. Chay decided to jump and save time, rather than let the canoe turn right round and face downstream.

Sadly my paddle was still firmly clamped in my left hand, along the gunwhale; if I had had it in both hands across the canoe, I might still have saved us. As it was we rocked heavily to the left and then back to the right, before slowly subsiding upside-down to the left.

We didn't feel the cold at first, as we went to either end of the upturned canoe and hung on to our precious paddles. The current led us into a big eddy which drew us swiftly towards the main lion's mouth. Chay pulled at the gas bottle on his airborne life-jacket and it inflated; I decided to wait and remain manoeuvrable.

We were suddenly in the roaring white water below the sluice, and I hung on as everything disappeared in a welter of foam, then, just as suddenly, we shot out on the other side. Chay was still there at the stern, clutching his paddle.

Twice we went round the pool and back through the white water. 'We're not getting much nearer the bank, I'll swim ashore next time round and hold out my paddle for you,' Chay shouted as we reached the spot where we had capsized.

He made it ashore, and I went on alone, hanging on to the bow. I was beginning to feel the cold and my legs were numb. I hoped Chay would reach me with his paddle on the next circuit.

It may have been that the current pushed the canoe farther out to the edge of the pool with only one man attached; anyway, we passed much closer and I grabbed the end of Chay's outstretched paddle without difficulty. He carefully drew us into the bank.

We had lost half an hour, and expended much nervous and physical energy. Soaked through on a raw March night, the wind seemed to cut into us as we stood shivering in the stark electric light on the catwalk above the weir.

The next ten hours were a turning point in my life.

'What do you reckon, Chay, call it a day?'

'No! We're going to win, ain't we?' he replied in his usual jokey Border accent. Only this time he wasn't joking. The short figure, inclined to run to fat in times of ease, and the round baby face with curly black hair belied the hard blue eyes. For the first time I really saw Chay; the youngest of a family of six children, he had had to fend for himself since leaving school at sixteen.

We had lost half an hour in a race which would surely be won in under twelve hours. We weren't that much better than our less experienced opponents, most of whom were as fit if not fitter than ourselves. It was logical to assume that statistically we would be unable to make up the lost time. I was prepared to accept this. I had unconsciously come to accept losing as a characteristic in my life. My mother often contrasted the brilliance of my father with my own inabilities. I had only ever won one race at school, the hundred yards for twelve to thirteen year olds; the favourite went sick with chicken pox on the day of the race and I beat 'Fatty' Good by inches in a field of four – it hardly made head-lines. From then on I had never been placed in athletics, and only reached the first team at games through training harder than anyone else, never through ability. At boxing I was a good loser. My academic career, which had been sacrificed as part of the strategy to gain the first team at cricket and rugby, was certainly not that of a winner. It would be fair to say that I lulled myself with the American saying that 'Good guys don't win ball games'.

Now I was with someone to whom winning meant progress, who wanted and, indeed, was used to, progress. I was twenty-four and he twenty-one. He knew we would win, I knew we wouldn't.

'Come on,' he said, 'let's go.'

When we started, I knew that, lurking at the back of my mind, there had always been this thought, to be prepared for a major effort when my chance came. Now, in this obscure race, of absolutely no importance, on this dark night, with a half-hour handicap, I knew that for me it was the time to make that effort.

We were so cold and wet that we decided to sprint for the remaining sixty-five miles of the race. Although near freezing at least it was not raining; our clothing would dry out on our backs as we went on through the night.

In my mind I came to believe that we might win.

Two locks and some ten miles farther on we came to the first of the 3 Para checkpoints, manned by our wireless operators who were helping with the safety aspect of the race. The half-hour gap between our time and that of the race-leaders had been worked out at this checkpoint. They had been worried about us and although clearly relieved at our arrival, their faces showed disappointment that we should have lost the race at such an early stage.

We sprinted on through the night, and the checkpoints began to tell us that we were slowly making up the lost time. At Maidenhead we were slightly delayed by a crew from another unit, which rushed to the bank ahead of us to impede our portage round the lock. Cursing I hauled the bow of the canoe up the bank and gulped down the hot soup handed to us. I was furious at the gamesmanship of the other crew and shouted this out in the best military style. As we pushed off from the bank I noticed a girl under a street lamp.

'That was my wife, Maureen,' said Chay.

'Well, she'll remember this race if only for the language,' I replied and struck out downriver.

The cold helped us to maintain the spirit. Chay comes from Hawick, a small Scottish border town with a keen swimming team; years of rigid training twice a day at the baths during his youth had developed strong shoulders and a barrel chest. The power he supplied at the back kept us churning on our way. There was nearly always someone not far ahead to be overhauled; the checkpoint gave us the information and spurred us on.

Land-Rovers and even private cars appeared at the bridges as we neared London to give us news of our progress on the race leaders. We hit the tide just right at Teddington, with eighteen miles to go and no more locks. We were stretched right out but were still in with a fighting chance; each bridge brought us more news. Everything slotted into place to help us maintain the spirit.

The last four miles were covered in daylight. Chay was all in and beginning to falter; he felt dizzy and the banks started rising and falling before his eyes. He felt sick and once stopped paddling, but feeling himself toppling out of the canoe he started again. The race seemed no longer a race, it meant something more to both of us. We were ready to die for it.

We shot under Westminster Bridge at 0647 in the morning, and weakly paddled across into the steps by County Hall. The police launch covered us in in case we should come to grief at the last moment. Lying like stranded fish in the rain on the wet stone steps on that Saturday morning after eleven hours of intense effort, we were told we had won by eleven minutes. We had made it!

We were in a state of collapse. Alec Larkman and Gibby helped us across to a café and fed us breakfast. What a night!

At seven-thirty, when nearly all the crews were in, a familiar figure came walking across the Westminster Bridge smartly turned out in a suède coat with a huge fur collar. Holding a small umbrella to keep off the rain, she looked rather incongruous among the dishevelled and haggard faces of the competitors. I decided to marry her.

'Hello, Johnny, I've brought you some aspirins. I thought you might have a headache after all that effort,' said Marie Christine.

I smiled through tears of happiness.

That night I wrote in my diary, 'The big difference between 1st and a place is the will to WIN *ONLY!*'

As the spring warmed to summer, it became clear that 3 Para would return to Bahrein during 1964 for a further year. The idea appalled me, but my application to join 21 Special Air Service Regiment had been turned down on the grounds that I needed administrative training. It was agreed that this could best be effected by a period as second-in-command of one of the 3 Para rifle companies. I did not want to leave 3 Para unless it was for the Special Air Service, and when I was later offered the Signals Platoon I settled down to prepare for an Army Signals Course.

Rod Liddon, who now commanded the Machine Gun Platoon also in Support Company, suggested we brighten the inevitable

Bahrein tour of duty by learning to fly, buying an inexpensive
Tiger Moth and flying out to the Middle East. I was much taken
by the idea but the training season kept us out of Aldershot so
much that we were never able to start the flying lessons, and in
any case we were short of money, as always.

One of my tasks during that summer was to organise a week's
training for Support Company at Ardnamurchan, a beautiful and
lonely peninsula on the west coast of Scotland. I was there for
several days before the Company arrived at Fort William on the
train, and during this time I visited the various estates to arrange
clearance for our cross-country movements.

As I watched the haunting islands of Rhum, Muck, Eigg and
Canna slowly turn to purple in the mid-summer sunset, memories
of Loch Awe came flooding back to fill my mind with the half-
forgotten dream of making a home in this inspiring place. However, the practical problems were quite apparent – there was no
work available and the housing situation was practically impossible.

Three nights later I met Rod Liddon on the Salen road, which
runs north and south and cuts across the peninsula at its
eastern end where it joins the mainland. This leaves a finger of
rock and heather some twenty miles in length and five miles in
width, jutting out towards America.

As we walked down the peninsula all through that night, in the
bewitching mid-summer half light, a discussion began which
was to last for five years before it was finally resolved.

Rod had joined 3 Para from Sandhurst, during 1961. Powerfully built with unruly black hair and a handsome ruddy face, he
was one of the kindest people I had ever met. Nicknamed 'Badger',
his main delights were field sports and rolling up his sleeves for
muddy work. He was intensely practical. A real gumboots man,
his whole outlook made him a most suitable person to attempt a
life on the west coast; it was simply a matter of finding a way of
life which would provide an acceptable standard of living. Rod
had just become engaged to Jeannie Dudgeon, a pretty-dark-
haired girl who had lived much of her life close to the Devonshire
moors. He felt sure she would love the west coast. Shortage of
money to start any kind of venture was the outstanding problem.

After a brief visit to canoe on the fast upper waters of the River
Loire in France during our summer leave, I returned to go on a
carefully planned fishing holiday with my father.

We had ten days at Altnaharra hotel in Sutherland, and although neither of us had any experience, we were lucky with both brown and sea-trout. Because no fishing is allowed on the Sabbath, we drove around the north-west coast together, and subsequently I resolved to write to all the landowners in search of a ruined croft house. I intended to buy a motor-cycle, keep it in Inverness and ride it the hundred miles from the railway station to my as yet only notional croft on the north-west coast.

My father remarked on the bleak landscape and the lack of trees; I felt he couldn't understand, so there was little point in trying to make him. And yet I believe he did understand what I wanted, but could see no practical way of carrying it out. In any case such a feeling is private to one person, and only that person can really work it out for himself.

Perhaps it was connected with winning the canoe race earlier in the year, perhaps it was simply a perfectly natural step in the process of growing up. Certainly many of my friends in the Parachute Regiment felt the same vague frustration with service in time of peace; an inability to fulfil the ambition and ideals learnt at school and Sandhurst. Great captains of the past like Malborough and Wellington had to be studied for examinations, but in contrast the austerity and pride of the grim old barracks were tumbling. In their place rose new and yet strangely soul-less constructions of plate glass and concrete, oriented mainly towards a public relations image rather than the honour, pride and discipline of the past. These were the lines along which many of us thought. The socially accepted measure of achievement seemed to lie in material possession and financial wealth; so we talked endlessly of plans to make money in civilian life.

From my father I came to believe that the accumulation of wealth would in fact take many years and that there was no honourable way of achieving this quickly. The professions did not attract me, and the future seemed insoluble. I longed to stand free and independent of others, in a place where I could think, my mind uncluttered by the petty cares of life. I wondered how many men over the years had felt the same – my mind focused on the North-West Highlands. When we returned home I started to write letters of inquiry.

Philip Carte, a fellow-lieutenant in 3 Para, was on a three-year tour with the Parachute Regiment from the Durham Light Infantry. Lightly built, with thinning fair hair and an infectious enthusiasm for life, he suffered from asthma. After a particularly bad attack in the autumn of 1963 he lay in the Millbank Military Hospital in London, his army career finished. Mimicry and a vivid imagination had made him many friends in the mess. When Marie Christine and I visited him in hospital he outlined a plan for himself and me to undertake a voyage round the world under sail just as soon as he was discharged from the army. He recalled the sad tale of *English Rose II*, and urged me to recoup this previous failure with him now; he would buy the boat, he said, and asked me to think it over and give him a reply within a week.

As soon as we were out of the hospital Marie Christine made her position quite clear: 'If you go, don't expect me to wait for you, it's him or me!'

I had heard this before and it didn't take very long to decide in favour of Marie Christine and Scotland. Shortly afterwards we became engaged and I resigned from the army. The wedding was arranged for the first day of spring 1964, at the Beaconsfield Parish Church in Buckinghamshire where Marie Christine lived. My army career was to end on the 31st April that year when we would move to Scotland. All that remained was to find employment and a home up in the North-West Highlands.

My old white M.G.A. was sold, and we bought a diamond engagement ring and a second-hand mini-van with the money.

On the first available weekend we took the night train for Inverness, hired a car and visited Lord Vestey's 300,000 acre estate around the little fishing village of Lochinver. Major Farran was the factor of one of the few estates which had cared to reply with any interest to my letter asking for a ruined house which I might improve with my own hands. Also I hoped to find work at sea on one of the small seine net boats working from Lochinver.

Old croft houses were being leased but not sold on the estate. This meant that the old shell of a farmhouse on Stoer Head, which had seemed just what we needed, would have to be almost rebuilt and then at the end of thirty years it would revert to the estate. We were looking for something better than that and it would clearly be difficult to find.

Work on a fishing boat would also be difficult, because we discovered that the fishing boats came from the east coast and the crews returned home each weekend by car, leaving their boats at Lochinver. This meant that whenever a new hand was needed to make up the crew of only five or six, they were able to take on an experienced man from their home town, possibly even from their own family. They were a tight-knit little community and did not welcome in-comers.

Over my Christmas leave, I spent ten days driving around the west, north and east coasts making inquiries and sleeping in the back of the green mini-van. The outlook was not encouraging. Most people smiled knowingly when I mentioned living on the west coast. Nearly everyone, it seemed, knew of people who had tried and failed; now this young Englishman with no home, no money and no qualifications was to be added to the list.

There were several more visits to the north-west coast in the New Year, but we achieved nothing positive. My parents kindly offered to give us a caravan from their farm in Sussex as a wedding present. This would at least give us some flexibility during the summer while we searched for a home. Once we were living and working up there we would qualify for the Assignation of a croft in the eyes of the crofters' commission. If only we could find somewhere so remote that a family would wish to be rid of it, and so assign it to us in return for a few hundred pounds for 'improvements' rather than let the building fall into ruin and gain nothing in return.

We were married on the 21st March, 1964, and Colin Thomson, who had been in Germany as an A.D.C. to a general, was best man. The previous night had been the regimental dinner at Claridges in London. We had won a little money playing roulette at a gambling club later, and then spent the rest of the night in the turkish baths in Jermyn Street. Repeated challenges over endurance in the hot room had left both of us very weak by the time of the wedding itself; but in spite of this all went well, owing to the efforts of Lady D'Albiac, my mother-in-law. There was a guard of honour from 3 Para, and during a rather long wait before we came out of the church they threatened to impale the photographer on their swords.

Our honeymoon was spent in the Scilly Isles, over Easter, and there seemed to be only honeymooners on the islands. I resolutely practised tying trout flies, in case I might have to earn a living by this means if all else failed in Scotland.

7

Planning to Row the Atlantic

AT seven o'clock one grey October morning, I was counting cars in the rain outside Hammersmith Underground Station as part of a Ministry of Transport survey of London traffic – it was better than the dole. Marie Christine was working as a temporary secretary with Kilburn Town Council. The future seemed none too bright, and I determined that no matter what might happen, we must do better than this.

I was lucky, in that Lieutenant-Colonel Farrar Hockley, still commanding 3 Para, supported my request to return to the Parachute Regiment. I hoped to rejoin 3 Para, which had been engaged in active service in the Yemen during my six months in Scotland and latterly London. However, at Aldershot the Regimental Colonel told me I was due to serve my two years in the depot. I was in no position to argue.

After a short spell with the Regimental Battle School at Brecon in Wales, Marie Christine and I decided to try to recover our bad luck of 1964 with a recklessly expensive ski-ing holiday in Austria, over Christmas. In the New Year Marie Christine took a job as secretary to an estate agent in Farnham, near Aldershot, with the intention of finding us a house in the district, while I settled down to an office job as second-in-command of Recruit

Company. The staff work involved, although tedious, proved of great value during planning phases in the future.

We reduced the housekeeping money to three pounds a week, and I made a determined effort to reach a peak of mental and physical fitness. All my spare time was devoted to the complicated correspondence course in preparation for the Staff College examination, still some three years ahead. Each day for lunch I took a brown-paper bag containing one hard-boiled egg and an orange which I would eat alone in the office after a three-mile run over the short steep hills where I had once run the log race. Circuit training and running served to reduce my weight to just over twelve stones, and this fitness training was sustained for eighteen months while at the depot; I often wondered for what purpose. I fell into the old routine in which there was a mental need to run every day.

The croft at Ardmore remained our sheet anchor for the future, and throughout the year I continued the struggle to determine legal tenure. Whenever possible I travelled the 700 miles each way for long weekends, using my free rail warrants and sleeping in the guard's van in my lightweight sleeping bag.

Marie Christine found a tiny red-brick eighteenth-century terrace house, overlooking the parish church across a narrow cobbled lane in the middle of Farnham. After some difficulty we managed to secure it with a mortgage. The month of August was spent on summer leave at Ardmore, with Rod and Jeannie Liddon, and during that time we continued the discussion which had begun at Ardnamurchan two years before. Eventually we would find a way to live and work there, three miles from the road where the North-West Highlands roll down into the Atlantic.

At twenty-six I was in good condition, and waited daily, balanced both physically and mentally, for an opportunity which I felt certain must occur. While at Ardmore we heard of David Johnstone's plan to row across the Atlantic, but another six months passed before my own idea began to take shape, and by then Rod and Jeannie had gone to Bahrein with 2 Para.

On the 27th February, 1966, *The People* newspaper headlined the news that David Johnstone and John Hoare were to row across the Atlantic from Boston, Massachusetts, to Land's End in England, in their specially built boat, the PUFFIN. The attempt was planned to start around the 1st June.

The idea of my rowing had rather faded during the winter;

but on reading their plans I spent that Sunday afternoon on a detailed military appreciation of the problem, with Colin Thomson. We concluded that it would be possible to win a race, but that we had only ninety-two days to find a boat, a partner, and the necessary provisions and equipment. In that time we would have to move everything to Boston and get started. I was £120 overdrawn in the bank at this point, but we reasoned that if *The People* were backing the *Puffin*, then another national paper would back us. Two thousand pounds would cover the cost of the venture and Colin agreed to row with me.

I telephoned Hugh Belayse-Smith, an old friend from my days at the Nautical College Pangbourne and now a master mariner, and he agreed to help me brush up on navigational matters.

I was a complete novice in business affairs, and had no belief in my ability to make money. In the days before the long single-handed sailing ventures there was no indication that rowing across the Atlantic might be a means of financial advancement; indeed it was difficult to imagine 3,000 miles in an open boat in that light. A friend on the *Daily Express* spoke optimistically of that newspaper buying the rights to our story, and thus covering our estimated costs of £2,000. This seemed a huge sum of money and I rather doubted that anyone would pay that much.

I soon realised that Colin, a chronic sufferer from sea-sickness, had clearly only agreed to row with me out of friendship and had no wish to undertake the voyage for his own sake. James Emson, another wiry Parachute captain, was keen to accompany me if his doctors would release him from the rehabilitation course he was undergoing at Headly Court to mend a pair of shattered heels. In the event a specialist vigorously advised him against the voyage.

In early March I wrote in my diary of the need for a mighty thrust to throw us clear of the human race for one short summer. This reads rather ridiculously now, but it reflects a basic need to attempt something worthwhile in life, after all the years of physical training and frustration with the realities of existence.

The *Daily Express* continued to show interest through the early part of March, and Colin Mudie, the designer of the *Puffin*, calculated that a similar boat could still be built in time for about £1,000. These large round sums of money went to my head and I became anxious about the whole scheme. James D'Albiac, my brother-in-law, himself a London stockbroker, offered to try to raise the £2,000 through a syndicate in the City, but he estimated that thirty per cent interest would be required on such a loan.

Lieutenant-Colonel Tugwell, my C.O. at the depot, agreed to support the venture; without this the voyage could not have been made. Following his agreement the Ministry of Defence granted a period of unpaid leave for the duration of the voyage. It had to be unpaid leave, because in the event of our demise, questions might be asked in the House of Commons about public funds being expended in training soldiers only to send them to their death at sea.

At this point the *Daily Express* announced our intentions in its gossip column, and as a result several other newspapers started to show interest in the venture. With eighty-four days left to the 1st June there was no boat, no crew, no stores and no money. Colin became ill with worry about letting me down, and on the following day I heard that the *Daily Express*, having had its story, now 'regretted that they could not support a funeral'! Again in the event of our death, they did not wish to be hounded by the other papers for seeking publicity at the expense of our lives. A man from *The People* suggested we meet for 'a jug of beer in a neutral corner'; but when we did meet, Colin and I were so clearly undecided that he returned to London satisfied that we posed no threat to the *Puffin*.

Now the first of the 'agents' appeared, suggesting several newspapers who would buy the story and so cover the £2,000 costs. Colin and I agreed on a seven day contract with them, but on the next day we panicked and sent them a telegram cancelling the whole project.

James D'Albiac telephoned and said that a City syndicate would require fifty and not thirty per cent interest on a loan of this kind. I told him we couldn't take that risk. That evening the 'Roundabout' radio programme announced the quote of the week to its audience of commuters returning home from work by car. A certain Captain Ridgway, when asked by a newspaper why he wished to row across the Atlantic, had replied, 'Because afterwards, when I come into a room, people will say there is the man who rowed the Atlantic.' I smiled at myself, and thought, 'How foolish, and yet how true!'

On that Sunday *The People* published, 'Paras pull out'; we were not going after all. But I still saw the venture as the opportunity I had waited for; it was a golden chance after the disappointments and dole of 1964. If I failed to grasp this chance, then I did not deserve another one, and must resign myself to a life of dull compromise and mediocrity.

Colin Thomson, James Emson, Alec Larkman, Mike Edwards and R.Q.M.S. Genever – my companion on the lunchtime runs – all declined my invitation. I wondered whether they would have felt the same had they known the bitterness of the dole.

With seventy-five days left, I visited Mr. Lee at the Admiralty in Bath. He was enthusiastic about the venture and offered to supply me with plans for a boat, and a long list of manufacturers who would probably supply raw materials. He gave me a separate list of Service experts who would advise on rations, medical equipment, clothing and survival at sea. I decided to go ahead with preparations and hope a partner would come along in due course. There followed endless telephone calls and visits to manufacturers. Now, experience gained over the past year spent in the office helped me considerably with this planning.

I still had no backing and decided to finance the operation myself; this would at least end the waste of time and the humiliation of seeking money from outside. However, the voyage would have to cost considerably less than the original £2,000 I had estimated. The building society declined to extend my mortgage in order to make available a greater part of my months' pay of £110 to help towards the cost, but they tactfully suggested the bank might give me an overdraft. Fortunately this was the case; against the mortgage pass book and life insurance policies, the manager agreed to £300 over and above the £120 I was already overdrawn.

There were sixty-seven days left when Hughie Ross wrote from Ardmore about the improvements to our croft home up in Scotland; he also enclosed a brochure detailing folding lobster pots in which Rod and I had shown interest during the previous summer. On the last page of this leaflet there was a photograph of a Yorkshire Dory. 'If anything can do the crossing, I think this design will,' he wrote. On that day I rang the builders in Yorkshire and bought the very twenty-foot dory they had shown at the Boat Show at Earl's Court in London that year for £185. They only had the one, because she had aroused little interest; still, she would do better at the next Boat Show! While keen to sell, they were a little perturbed when they heard what I had in mind.

Now I had a boat. As soon as it arrived in Aldershot, modifications to make it more buoyant, by decking in four feet from either end with compartments of solid expanded polystyrene, were expertly carried out by Sergeant Sermon, the pioneer sergeant in the depot cinema. Rations and stores began to arrive, but still there was no one to row with me and time was slipping by.

Since relinquishing command of 3 Para, Lieutenant-Colonel Roley Gibbs had served on the military staff in Washington, and he had now returned to command the Parachute Brigade with the rank of Brigadier. He summoned me to his office and said he would write to people in America, to smooth our arrival on that side of the Atlantic for the start. Only much later did I see a copy of the letter to his successor in Washington, asking him to allow me $500 from his personal funds if the need should arise and urging him to keep the matter quiet. I was much impressed by this remarkable gesture of goodwill. It was comforting to know that this man had faith in the idea.

On my return from Ardmore after Easter, the race against time continued. I had abandoned the idea of free equipment from manufacturers, and taken to paying cash without mentioning the rowing at all. I had found that trying to obtain goods free often became nerve-racking, because even the release of small items usually required decisions at board meetings which take place infrequently.

The second 'agent' appeared as a result of inquiries by another brother-in-law within his firm, Ind Coope. The new man was running an independent public relations agency in London, and it turned out that he was almost as unfamiliar with the marketing of rights and the handling of syndication within Fleet Street and abroad, as we were ourselves. He believed the story would be valuable but he failed to convince me.

In the middle of April the only fresh candidates for a place in the boat with me were a number of recruits who had failed their training at the depot. I was only interested in people within the Parachute Regiment, because at least our minds would work along the same lines, and I could rely on a high level of steadfastness. I was constantly plagued by doubts about the voyage and dreaded that it might go off at half cock; above all I feared an embarrassment which might bring the name of the regiment into disrepute.

At two-thirty on the afternoon of Friday, 15th April, there was a knock on the door of my office, just as I was arranging for the famous oarmaker from Oxford, Fred Collar, to attend the preliminary boat trials on Hawley Lake on the coming Sunday morning. Sergeant Chay Blyth came into the office with a grin on his face.

'I heard you were looking for someone to go on this rowing trip, sir,' he said.

'You're damn right,' I replied, 'but I don't want any married fellow along, though.'

'Oh well, I've talked it over with Maureen and she thinks it's a good idea, but it's up to you.'

I smiled across the desk. It seemed as if the sun had come out after a long cloudy spell.

'O.K., you're on the short list,' I said. 'Can you make the trials at Hawley Lake on Sunday morning?'

'I'll be there,' he said. 'Can I bring Maureen?'

'Fine, we'll load the boat here at eight on Sunday morning.'

The short list comprised Captain Colin Thomson, Sergeant Chay Blyth and Lieutenant Charles Shea Simonds, whose wife was clearly against the idea. The selection would not take long.

As we slipped the boat from the army truck into the calm waters of the small tree-lined pool that is Hawley Lake, the morning sun glinted on the Tudor rose and her name *English Rose III* painted in red on the white gloss of her bow. *English Rose III* was really the only possible name – after all, she could only do better than *English Rose II*.

All morning we rowed about the lake trying various combinations of load and crew. With half a ton of fresh water in polythene containers, beneath the false bottom Sergeant Sermon had built in, we were pleased at the speed with which she still moved on her flat bottom. It was clear that she could carry a much greater load without difficulty.

Although Chay had never rowed before, we soon fell into the team rhythm of our canoeing days. I had found the right man at last. There were forty-three days left before our starting date from America.

Colonel Tugwell recorded the whole sequence on colour film in case anyone should ever be interested. As Fred Collar went away with the rough sketches and measurements for the special oars he was to make, he was heard muttering that he wouldn't chance crossing the Thames in that, let alone the Atlantic!

Chay and I settled down to plan the crossing together. We both felt that as long as the boat would stay afloat, then we would stay alive. We had worked together for nearly six years on and off, and knew each other pretty well. Survival training in Europe, the Middle East and the Canadian Arctic had knocked off a lot of corners. We were both aware of the paramount importance of not falling out with each other in mid-ocean.

When I met 'Blondie' Hasler at his home a few days later he was optimistic about our chances and the weather conditions in the North Atlantic during June, July and early August. I valued his opinion as someone who had sailed across alone on several occasions.

As we were tied to no backer we were able to avoid newspaper reporters. *The People* had published that we would not make the attempt and the other papers considered the story dead. I dreaded the inevitable day when the story must leak out once more; once we said we were going to try there would be no pulling back. *The Sunday Times* sent a reporter and photographer down to the little house in Farnham two days before the sea trials which Chay and I had decided would finalise our plans to proceed with the crossing. As I posed grimly for their photographer, leaning on a tombstone in the graveyard across the lane, I hoped that it would not be an ill-omen. In their story they described me as 'a taciturn, straight-backed Sandhurst man', which I thought a far cry from the shambling figure in the dole queue of 1964.

The sea trials took place on a breezy Sunday at the end of April, in the Solent at the entrance to Portsmouth harbour. We rowed up and down, accompanied by a large Service launch I had hired for the day for fourteen pounds. Marie Christine and Maureen must have had many thoughts as they watched *Rosie* riding the choppy sea. They didn't feel ill, but poor Colin was sick on several occasions. Everyone was satisfied with the trials and our 'agent' took a photograph of us with the liner *United States* in the background; this, he thought (wrongly), the newspapers would like captioned 'Fastest and Slowest'.

Unbeknown to us the *Puffin*, with Johnstone and Hoare, was aboard that liner headed for New York. I had not seen David Johnstone since the brief meeting we had had one evening the previous October, and I never met John Hoare. We were so in-

volved with our own problems that we scarcely even thought of
them during the preparations and simply hoped we would meet
in Boston and set off together. I had booked *English Rose III* on
the same cargo ship as the *Puffin*, which was due to sail from
Glasgow for Boston on 10th May. It came as a surprise to learn
they had advanced their passage by two weeks, and this indicated
that they wanted to start before us. On the way across in the
United States, it seems the navigating officer urged them to start
from Norfolk, Virginia, some 600 miles south of Boston. He
reasoned that the Gulf Stream passed much closer, only some
thirty miles from the coast at that point, on its way north and
east across the North Atlantic. From Boston we would have to
row some 150 miles across the cold and foggy southward-flowing
Labrador current, before we would reach the warm but stormy
Gulf Stream. We did not expect the Gulf Stream to help us much
as we would only settle some twelve to fifteen inches in the water,
and the wind would play a much greater part in our progress, or
lack of progress should there be easterly winds. In any case I
could not afford to change our starting point.

The newspapers showed little interest in us, even after our
agent informed them of the successful sea trials and our intention
to proceed with the attempt. We were really quite relieved.

A hairline crack, the result of a slight collision with the launch
as it took us in tow at the end of the sea trials, had been discovered
on one side of the boat near where the oars rested on the gunwale. Mr. Lee said he must withdraw his support for the venture
unless we had the boat sheathed with Cascover, a heavy nylon
cloth affixed to the marine plywood hull with epoxy resin. We,
too, were keen on the idea, but *Rosie* had to be in Glasgow within
the week and we could not afford the cost of the treatment.
Fortunately, the Cascover people kindly agreed to work over the
weekend and charge us nothing – this probably saved our lives.
The boat now seemed as if it were enshrouded in a thick nylon
stocking and we felt she would stay afloat. Now it was up to us to
stay alive.

As I drove in the truck with *Rosie*, overnight to Glasgow, I
hoped my stocks of 'three o'clock in the morning courage' would
be sufficient to meet the fast approaching test.

Our agent decided to withdraw from the venture just eleven
days before we were due to leave for America; he had achieved
little, but had tried hard and we parted friends. At least we were

still not tied to anyone. At this point the venture had cost me a
little under £500 and I was still just within the £300 overdraft.
Lieutenant-Colonel Tugwell had been an enormous help, while
most people treated the whole thing as a joke.

On 9th May, Chay and I drove down to Plymouth in my green
mini-van to visit the R.A.F. headquarters there at their suggestion. They gave us special Search and Rescue Beacon Equipment
(S.A.R.B.E.), fixed to the training frequency of R.A.F. Shackleton aircraft. They told us that if we extended the aerial and let it
send its automatic signal from 1300 to 1400 G.M.T., on every
Tuesday and Thursday after we reached half-way across the
Atlantic, then they would surely visit us as the aircraft were out
on training in that area, on those two days of each week. Once a
ship had reported our position to Lloyds, then they would know
where to look, as we would only be moving about thirty miles to
the east each day. They also issued us with another S.A.R.B.E.
on the normal international distress frequency, which we should
use if the worst came to the worst. From another branch of the
R.A.F. we drew two one-man jet fighter liferafts which Chay
believed would give us a psychological boost although its doubtful
if we would have survived for longer than just a few days in them.

Five days before we left the country, James D'Albiac's wife
Carole put us in touch with two new agents who were experienced
men from Fleet Street. No paper bought our story, but one or
two took options on the right to read it first after we landed and
then decide whether or not they wished to pay the price our
agents asked for it. As I remember it, there options amounted to
something under £200 when we left the country, only a tenth of
the sum I had originally forecast as the cost of the venture, for
which I had hoped just one newspaper would pay. Glamorous
tales of huge sums are often greatly exaggerated in these matters.

On Friday, 13th May, Marie Christine and I attended a dance
at the depot mess. I don't usually dance much, but on this occasion the steel band from 3 Para, which had recently returned
from duty in British Guiana, played a number of Calypsos. The
wild beat of the West Indian music seemed to summarise my
release from all the frustrations of the preceding years. At last I
was on the threshold of a real life; perhaps it would be the end of
me but at least I should go out through the front door in
style.

I danced until Marie Christine was exhausted, and then on

and on through the night feeling the old rhythmic power that had sometimes come to my legs when ahead in the final stretch of the lunchtime runs, or going through the towns on the Nijmegen marches, or when the going was good in the mountains on exercises with 3 Para, or during long training sessions with the boxing team at Sandhurst. 'At last, at last,' my body seemed to say. 'After all the years of training now there is reality, a chance to be fulfilled and make one joyous leap clear of time and the pettiness of life.'

On the previous day I had split my left foot on the lunchtime run, but I had thought little of it as I intended to run no more. Now the hours of dancing caused this foot to become infected. Perhaps I was run down from all the worry of the preparations, the constant delays and letdowns. I had never suffered any kind of blood poisoning before, but over those last few days in England, my left foot began to swell ominously.

Colonel Tugwell took me into the camera shop in Farnham on the day before we left and I bought an old Kodak 16-millimetre movie camera for eleven pounds. Back in his office, at Maida Barracks, he set the speed at twenty-four frames per minute, with a broken piece of matchstick and Sellotape. It would have surprised us both if we'd known then that the film used after the voyage, but taken by that battered old camera, was to sell at five pounds per second.

At twelve-thirty on Tuesday, 17th May, Chay and I flew out of London Airport bound for Gander, only six hours away in Newfoundland. Maureen and Marie Christine smiled bravely and went home to wait. It was a sad parting.

As we cleared the west coast of Ireland, I could see the long sweep of the rocky coast far below in the bright sun of the early summer's day. There were just a few flecks of white on the deep blue of the ocean.

Half-way across, my left foot hurt so much that the stewardess offered to bathe it for me. I wondered if the First Sea Lord, for whom this Comet 4C flight had been arranged, knew we were on the plane in the spare seats at the back, but the stewardess said she was sure he didn't.

At Gander the pain was rather worse, and I almost missed the take-off for Ottawa because the sick bay sister took so long with another dressing. When we landed at Ottawa it was still winter, and soon we were on our own, with little money, four heavy

H

suitcases and a long journey ahead of us, via Montreal by Grey-
hound bus down to Boston.

Next morning the bus filled up as we approached the end of
our ride and we had to stand to allow lady passengers to sit. My
foot throbbed painfully and I began to feel definitely under the
weather.

Brigadier Gibbs had indeed arranged for our arrival in Boston.
The British Consul introduced us to Lord Frank Margeson, who
had kindly come from Washington to ease our passage into the
1st Naval District in the city. My condition worsened considerably during the afternoon and I was admitted to the Chelsea
Naval Hospital with severe blood poisoning. After a thorough
medical check and three blood tests, I was treated with a daily
dose of two bottles of intravenous sugar and penicillin, and four-
hourly penicillin injections. My backside began to get rather sore
for rowing.

Chay, whose only experience of the sea was a channel crossing
in a steamer from Calais to Dover, was assigned to an office with
a set of telephones and a sign which read 'Supreme Commander
North Atlantic Dory Command', but it didn't bother him.

On the 20th May the papers carried the news that Johnstone
and Hoare had set out from near Norfolk in Virginia. Lying in
that small white hospital room on my own, my feelings were
probably not unlike those experienced in a death cell before the
scaffold. However, it would be at least another two weeks before
we were ready to walk on to our scaffold.

After five days in that excellent hospital, I picked up Chay
from 1st Naval District and together we drove out to Cape Cod
with *Rosie* on the back of a huge flat-bed truck which a road
haulier had kindly offered to drive for us at his own expense.

Cape Cod, just south of Boston, is a narrow peninsula shaped
rather like a man's arm bent at the elbow, as it projects into the
Atlantic. While the inside of the forearm shields Plymouth on
the mainland, some ten miles away across the Cape Cod Bay,
the sandy sweep of the outside forearm faces the broad ocean. We
decided to base our operations at the little township of Chatham
on the outside elbow, and to set out on the voyage from Orleans,
another little township some five miles north along the outside
edge of the forearm.

At Chatham we found a ramshackle boatyard of the old style.
This jumble of gaunt clapboard sheds, mysteriously named the

Chatham Marine Railway, was presided over by a cantankerous but kind-hearted, and successfully retired, liquor runner of the bad old Prohibition days. He was known simply as Kenny. Here foregathered the old guard of crusty fisherman, left over from a bygone age of schooners and line fishing, after cod and halibut, far out on the Grand Banks. These ancient dorymen had, some of them, survived hurricanes in their little dory boats, only to find themselves alone on the ocean, lost by the mother schooner in fog or blizzard. Then there would be nothing for it but to row home or die. Now these men looked kindly on our little dory and proffered advice. They relived their own long-departed past. They approved the age-old design, but snorted at the new-fangled construction. After hours of discussion, hunched in rickety chairs around the great cast iron stove in Kenny's office, they drew up a plan of campaign to refit *Rosie* and give us 'A fighting chance'.

Captain Johnny Stello and Captain Fred Powell left their nets to carry out the plan. The dory took on a new appearance, stronger yet, with sides raised nine inches and capped with oak. A carefully designed rudder fitted to her stern with steering lines led forward to the new, wider, thwarts which served the double purpose of strengthening the dory shell, and at the same time providing seats for us to row on. We had planned a small keel but this idea was scrapped by the old men, who reasoned that the seaworthiness of the dory relied on its flat bottom. When the Atlantic rollers neared the vertical, the dory would slip off the wave before it could break and swamp the little craft. Fred Collar's beautifully made oars were discarded, and twelve one-piece ash oars of varying length were lashed along the inside. Four more were laid ready to slide through the newly fitted oar locks. Everything was simple and easily replaced or repaired.

On Thursday, 2nd June, Kenny announced, 'Well, I can't vouch for you two young fellows, but the dory's ready, she won't let you down. Now, if you take my advice you'll set off on Saturday; nobody goes anywhere on a Friday, it's unlucky.'

At five-thirty on the afternoon of Saturday, 4th June, 1966, *English Rose III* shot through the rapids of Nauset Inlet, Orleans, accompanied by a fleet of small craft. Clutching the twenty-five dollars the N.B.C. T.V. crew had paid us to wear the same grey T-shirts we had worn while practising, we set off in the gathering dark. I hoped for darkness so that I might be sea-sick with fright with no inquisitive cameras to disturb me.

As the stormy westerly wind helped us pull away from the last land we were to see for three months, I felt there was no task for which I was better fitted.

Now we were to live a real life. Every day was to be an achievement.

8

Ninety-two Days in a Rowing Boat

WE divided the 3,000 miles of rowing into three separate phases, each of a different length. The first was 300 miles or so, through the fog and across the cold waters of the Labrador Current (48° F.), out on to the edge of the warm, but stormy, Gulf Stream (70° F.); this we hoped would help to carry us across the North Atlantic towards Europe.

During this first phase, which should take about two weeks, we would row together for twelve hours using four oars. Then we would both sleep for eight hours while *Rosie* lay to her sea anchor.

On reaching the Gulf Stream the second phase would begin. We would drink the bottle of white wine given us by Mrs. Norgeot, mother of 'Skip' Norgeot, the young Orleans harbour-master who had been so helpful at Cape Cod. Once in the Gulf Stream we expected to row for twenty-four hours each day, having reached a plateau of fitness during the first two weeks of the voyage. Each twenty-four hours would be split into twelve hours of rowing together with four oars, and then twelve hours at night with one man rowing and one sleeping. At night each would alternate with two-hour periods of rowing, then two hours of sleeping, and so on. Thus *Rosie* would be always moving forward through the water twenty-four hours each day.

The third and final phase would begin in the middle of the Atlantic, at about longitude thirty degrees west of Greenwich. Here we hoped to make contact with the Shackleton aircraft of R.A.F. Coastal Command, when on Tuesdays and Thursdays of each week they expected to be on exercise. The S.A.R.B.E. Mk. III radio which they gave us, specially tuned to their training frequency, should make it possible for them to fly over us at least once every fortnight during the second half of the voyage. This would mean three and perhaps four visits while we pulled our way across the imaginary 'fences' of longitude thirty degrees West, and twenty degrees West to the west coast of Ireland at fourteen degrees West. The Parachute Regiment places a great deal of faith in the R.A.F. from both the parachuting and air supply aspects of their work. Neither Chay nor I had any doubt that if only we could reach half-way across the ocean, then if it were humanly possible the 'great iron birds' would find us. This, as much as anything else, spurred us on.

During the first week of the voyage we were in considerable pain, for the boat was so full of food, water and equipment that our movement was greatly restricted. Sometimes it was so foggy that we could hardly see the ends of our oars; then we could only keep on rowing, steering by the compass. This was fitted in the middle of the forward edge of Chay's plank seat, and so it was just in front of my knees when we were both rowing together. I would keep an eye on the compass, and adjust the steering lines, which led from the rudder on the back of the boat to either side of my plank seat, in such a way that we could each row with an even pressure on both oars.

After twenty-four hours the sea-sickness left me and I was able to concentrate whole-heartedly on the rowing. Chay never felt sick in the early stages. Despite sore hands and backsides we made reasonable progress. Unfortunately, the prevailing westerly wind which was expected to be our main ally on the voyage, much more so than the Gulf Stream from which we expected little help, failed us badly. Fairly strong winds from the east kept us pinned too close to the American seaboard for our liking.

After a week of fog and adverse winds we encountered a day or two of sun and calm. I decided to fix our position using the sextant, and this meant getting an accurate time check before-hand. We had a good portable transistor radio, which we had bought at a most advantageous price from a gun-toting policeman in the Boston docks. With this set we were able to receive the Washington W.W.V. time signal, and so synchronise a pair of Smith's wrist watches we had with us. At noon I calculated our latitude by sextant meridian altitude, and at three in the afternoon I worked out our longitude by the chronometer method. Our position changed little in the intervening three hours between obtaining the latitude and longitude, and thus we determined our position with some accuracy every two or three days during the voyage.

Accuracy, however, came a little later. My first sight placed us some 700 miles inland in Vermont. Chay seemed unimpressed by my claim to navigation at O level in G.C.E. The U.S. coastguards had publicly declared that we stood a ninety-five per cent chance of suicide, and now, finding that we didn't know our position, I became rather worried. The fear of having to call for help on the emergency radio, and so endangering other lives on our behalf, was our greatest single worry on the voyage. A failure at this stage would mean a serious embarrassment to the Parachute Regiment, and to ourselves.

'The situation is seldom either as good or as bad as it is first reported,' says Field-Marshal Lord Slim in his book *Defeat into Victory*. Working on this theory, I decided that we should sleep for an hour or two that afternoon, hoping that our situation would look better when we awoke. This was the case, for when we started once more I remembered to check the sextant and found that a screw had worked loose. I tightened it and the new sight re-sulted in a more realistic longitude.

We were nearing the end of the two weeks' supply of fresh food and were about to start the first of the polystyrene boxes, which each contained one week's rations, when we heard of Hurricane Alma in a news bulletin on our transistor radio. 'The first hurri-cane to be spawned in the spring for sixty years is making its way up the Eastern Seaboard, and will be in the area off Cape Cod at 0600 hours tomorrow morning,' declared the announcer, his confident voice issuing from the warm safety of a skyscraper somewhere on the mainland.

Chay and I had a good sleep that night. At dawn we awoke with a start when a huge wave broke over *Rosie*, and filled her almost to the gunwales. We both bailed hard for a quarter of an hour before she was dry. It is difficult to describe the experience of a hurricane in a small boat. The sea becomes a giant switchback with moving hills and valleys, all covered with foam which looks rather like icing on a cake. The water comes in over the side of the boat, and it has to be removed with buckets and pumps faster than it comes in for longer than the storm lasts, or else the crew will drown. If the water ever succeeds in filling the boat right to the gunwales, then in those seas every bucketful removed will spill in again immediately, the water level inside and outside the boat being the same.

Fortunately, I believe Alma was nearly spent when she reached us, and we were able to survive, one bailing and one resting until a big wave would swamp us. Then we would both bail frantically for a while, usually ten minutes or so, before returning to the usual routine of one bailing, one resting. The worst weather held for about six hours and then passed on. We were left in the gathering darkness to cook our evening meal over the Bleuet gaz stove. We were soaking wet; nevertheless we felt triumphant. A dozen seagulls, which had sheltered on the sea close under our lee-side as we drifted broadside before the storm, took off and disappeared into the night. We were sad to see them leave us.

Next day I calculated that we had made only 150 miles, after twelve days of almost continuously adverse winds and soaking fog. It was nothing like good enough. Also, our ankles were beginning to swell alarmingly; this was because our feet were always lower than the rest of the body, thus preventing the plasma from draining back as it normally does during the night, in a proper bed. We did not know this at the time, and feared all sorts of ailments from blood poisoning to dropped arches. Chay's determination and logical appraisal of the situation constantly boosted my own flagging spirits.

We often saw schools of small whales, but the larger ones seemed to travel alone or in pairs. The explosive hissing noise they made, when they came up to blow, sounded eerie in the fog. One Thursday afternoon we were thinking of our evening meal, when it seemed as if a big whale far off in the fog was getting nearer to us; every half minute the hissing seemed louder as the monster came up to blow. We felt secure enough; our little world ended where the blades of the oars faded into the grey curtain of fog. Surely the whale would never come that close.

Quite suddenly, we entered a small clearing in the racing mist, and about thirty yards out on the port side the waters parted. Something like a black nissen hut surfaced. It was heading straight for us.

Psssshhh! went its spout and we smelt the stale oily air drifting over us. The smooth back of the whale looked as broad as *Rosie* was long, and water drained off it rather as it pours off a rock in the surf after a big wave. I could see one eye looking at me.

'Fit the belts,' cried Chay, and we both reached for our safety harnesses. It seemed now as if the whale could not miss us, but with a long sigh it gently subsided once more, and was well below the surface by the time it passed under *Rosie*.

Some thirty seconds later we heard it blow again, away in the fog. We were safe to plod steadily eastward into the lonely night.

On the 19th June, at eight o'clock on a sunny but still misty morning, we rowed up close alongside an American oceanographic vessel, the *Albatross IV*. She rolled heavily on an oily swell in an otherwise calm sea. The crew, who were fishing for lobsters deep down on the edge of the continental shelf, were delighted to see us. Based at Woods Hole, not far from Orleans on Cape Cod, it seemed they had read of us in the papers. Suddenly everyone wanted to take photographs, but we had to keep on going towards the Gulf Stream.

The officer of the watch said we were over a subterranean canyon and in an eddy of the Stream; the main current was seventy miles E.S.E. Given favourable winds we thought we could reach it in three days.

Hurricane Alma had caused sea-water to seep into the poly-styrene ration boxes, through the lids broken by our feet in our efforts to sleep comfortably in the early days of the voyage. We had to unpack every item, down to the last packet of Spangles, and then repack it all in new bags of heavy-gauge polythene we had bought for such an eventuality. Rice and biscuits were particularly badly contaminated by the sea-water, and in all twenty-five per cent of our rations had to be thrown over the side. It was a grim task to be throwing food away when only a few hundred miles out from America.

The reorganising of the stores was done on a hot calm day, with no shade but our floppy white 'Jonesey' hats and sunglasses. It felt rather as if we were on the runway in Bahrein once more. The stowage took two hours in the hottest part of the afternoon –

I did the bows and Chay the stern. I finished first as the space in the bows was taken up more by the radio and other equipment than by rations. 'Away in for a swim,' said Chay, busily working in the stern.

I felt like Lawrence of Arabia crossing the Nefud Desert. The sun seemed to vibrate overhead. As always we had sat unshaded since dawn, and would continue to do so until dark. All I had to do for relief was to slip over the side. The water temperature was 68° F. in the Gulf Stream eddy; it looked cool and inviting.

'Go on, away in for a swim,' repeated Chay.

'No, I'll start rowing again,' I replied, glumly easing my nine-foot oars through the cast-iron rowlocks into the water. The leather rubbing strips had worn out long since, and the hard white ash of the oars was highly polished and slightly indented where it pressed on the 'u' of the rowlock.

As I pulled gently away, hardly rippling the glassy calm, I was trying to calculate how long we could last on our reduced rations. After nearly three weeks at sea we had only covered some 300 miles, or ten per cent of the total distance, in the right direction. At this rate of progress . . .

'Look at that!' screamed Chay, leaping to his feet and pointing over the stern as if unable to believe his eyes.

The shark which had been lying sleepily under our stationary boat, unknown to us while we repacked the rations, had suddenly found his sunshade removed. Now he surfaced slowly in the sunlight just astern of *Rosie*. Neither Chay nor I had ever seen anything like it before. The dorsal fin, the one in the middle of the shark's back, was six inches thick and tapered to a point about eighteen inches above the water. Grey-black in colour, he was criss-crossed with white scars, and flopped awkwardly to one side because so much of him was above the surface. The tip of the shark's tail was fully fifteen feet behind the battered dorsal fin, and it just cleared the water.

I kept rowing steadily forward, watching the shark and wondering what he would have done if I had gone in for a swim. After a moment's hesitation, he decided to follow us, and so enjoy the shade afforded by the bottom of the boat. He didn't have to be very fit to keep up with us at about one and a half miles an hour. Rather like an ostrich hiding its head in the sand, he edged forward and the menacing fin crept slowly nearer the rudder until it was almost touching.

The shark kept station with us for ten minutes or so, and during this time it was possible to look over one side and see him, and then look over the other side and see the same dark brown mass. We nicknamed him 'the Dark Feller', and felt rather sad when, eventually, he flicked his tail and disappeared in a splash of foam.

When he had gone, we decided that he was a basking shark, and would not have eaten us, anyway. However, there have been many occasions when these monsters have smashed small boats when annoyed, and this one was nearly twice the length of *Rosie*.

It was growing cooler now as the sun began to dip towards the horizon in the late afternoon. We calculated that at the present rate of progress we should arrive in Ireland on the 27th January, 1967, but that we should have starved to death during October 1966. Something had to be done.

We decided that we were close to, if not actually in, the Gulf Stream; on some days our floating thermometer registered 70° F. and on others barely 50° F. Now was the time to start rowing twenty-four hours a day until we reached the other side. Twelve hours together with four oars; and then two hour alternately alone, during the twelve hours of night. It was now mid-summer and there were few hours of real darkness.

The situation was really quite simple: we had to row or die. We didn't want to die, so we rowed.

If only the wind would change to its supposed prevailing westerly direction, then we really would make some progress, with the Gulf Stream bearing us along as well as the wind.

Chay prepared the usual curry dinner in the pressure cooker while I continued to row. After he had eaten his share with the wooden spoon, we changed places, and he rowed on the forward seat while I scraped the cooker clean and then washed it in the sea.

He took the first two-hour 'stag', rowing from the forward seat where he could see the compass. I made myself comfortable in the four-by-five-foot space between Chay's empty seat and the buoyancy compartment in the stern. My head rested on one of the life-rafts beside the aluminium tube of the stove, and my body lay in a Z shape across the boat. 'Five minutes, Number One,' I heard Chay say. The two hours were already over. For four minutes I wrestled with myself, trying to shake off the awful feeling of drowsiness.

'Come on, Number One.' I had fallen asleep again. Chay made a spurt at the oars and I took over while the boat continued to make way through the water.

'Damn, I've dropped one of the oars, Chay – it slipped into the sea. The safety line must have come undone,' I said. Chay and I looked hopefully over the side but the oar was gone in the dark and it took several minutes to unlash another matching pair from the inside of the boat. If anything fell over the side during the night, it was gone for ever. Chay and I looked at each other. 'Whenever one man is asleep, the other must wear his safety harness,' Chay said. This became a cardinal rule; we thought about it in much the same way as parachute drill in an aircraft.

'When it's time to call me, only give me one minute's notice, will you? I saw how you suffered for five minutes; it's no good,' came a muffled voice from the figure huddled in the stern under the crinkly space blanket.

The night passed and soon it was breakfast time on a balmy Sunday morning. In bright sun of the mid-afternoon Chay, using a lifeboat heliograph, attracted the second ship to see us during the voyage. The reflection from his tiny tin mirror was picked up on the bridge of the German ship *Rigoletto* as she steamed along on our horizon. She was carrying a cargo of American cars to Europe. With true Prussian efficiency, the officer of the watch turned his ship towards that little flash in the empty sea, hundreds of miles from land.

If they were surprised to see us, they did not show it, but simply asked what we required. 'Our position', I bellowed through cupped hands. Then there was a pause for about three minutes. 'Your position is 44° 55′ N, 63° 14′ W,' boomed the loud hailer from the port wing of the bridge, which towered high above us.

'Is there anything else?' it called again.

'No thank you,' I replied.

'Well, goodbye, and good luck,' said the German.

Soon the ship was gone and the slight east wind fell calm. We came to a patch of sea where the surface was disturbed by water welling up from below, rather as the waters of a river in flood will well up just downstream of the piles of a bridge. The difference was that the disturbance covered hundreds of yards and the temperature of the pale blue water was 68° F. Surely this was the edge of the Gulf Stream.

We always shaved and washed all over on Sunday afternoons, weather permitting, in just half a pint of fresh water each. After the expense of the alterations on Cape Cod, I had had only enough money left for two packets of razor blades; so Chay shaved first and I 'doubled up' on the same blade. We had an old brush which had once belonged to Chay's uncle. After the ablutions, we changed into clean underwear, and washed our dirty socks and underpants in sea-water and soap and then gave them a final rinse in fresh water.

While I was absorbed with the luxury of shaving, Chay rowed. An old schooner, converted to motor with cut-off masts, hove into sight. Seeing us it came up quite close alongside. She was the sword-fishing boat the *Robertson II* out of St. John, New Brunswick, and was on her way to fish with mackerel-baited lines farther out in the warm waters of the Gulf Stream. Her crew were amused to find two 'limeys', one shaving and one rowing in an open boat. We were deliberately matter of fact about the situation. I continued to shave nonchalantly. They offered us fresh mackerel but we declined politely. They looked rather puzzled as they left us, alone on the ocean.

A few days later we found westerly winds and felt really on our way at last. About this time I developed a boil on my neck, on which Chay planned to operate using a method which he had learnt as a boy in the Border country between England and Scotland. The idea was to heat an empty orange squash bottle, which we still had aboard, and then press the hot opening of the bottle against the boil; as the air inside the bottle cooled so it would contract and thus draw the boil. I said we should wait until Chay got a boil and try the method on him first.

I had only had one boil in my life before this, and I felt sure that it must be a recurrence of the blood poisoning I had experienced in Boston before the start of the voyage. Chay, using his knowledge as a first aid instructor in another style, applied a paraffin gauze dressing and I started a course of tetracycline tablets supplemented with vitamin B.

Soon Chay complained of a pain in his side and recalled a period in the Bahrein hospital with a grumbling appendix. It was not a happy outlook. Although we were clearly in the main shipping lane across the North Atlantic for Europe, and could therefore easily attract a ship with our emergency radio, it would mean the end of the voyage if we did so. We decided to give it one more day; if the pain increased or even continued, we would radio for help and Chay would take a crash course of tetracycline to minimise infection. We rowed on.

The following day brought strong south-westerly winds and Chay felt better. We attributed the pains to cramped rowing and sleeping conditions. A big westerly gale set in and we crashed on – as long as *Rosie* was held pointing in the right direction she would surf on the waves. She would continue, somewhat slower, even if left on her own; adopting a position broadside to the sea she would skitter along the surface before the wind and breaking sea.

Within twenty-four hours the wind subsided and the sea fell smooth again but for a gentle swell. We were still seeing seabirds every day, usually the tiny storm petrels and the occasional tern. The calm was not longlived for in the early hours of the next morning we found ourselves in the middle of a tropical thunderstorm.

I could see the great black clouds on the horizon in the half light of early dawn, the lightning flickering in blue-white veins. Gradually, as it came up on us, the rain began to fall. Chay, sleeping under the blue plastic sheet of his space blanket, by now literally patched with black masking tape, was quite unaware of the approaching storm. When the rain began, he was protected by the faded green tarpaulin which stretched between the two sides of the boat over the sleeping area.

'What's up?' he called, when a crack of thunder awoke him with a start.

'A thunderstorm,' I replied, rowing steadily onward. 'You keep under the tarpaulin, I can handle it. You've still got half an hour before your two hours is up.'

I began to remember stories of men sheltering under trees on golf courses, and of how the trees were sometimes struck by lightning, with fatal results for the golfers. Surely on a flat calm sea the lightning would be likely to strike *Rosie*. I felt a sort of naked fear, just a speck in the path of a colossal power. I wished Chay would wake up.

Now it was raining so fiercely that when I turned the plastic buckets upright on the bottom of the boat, they rapidly began to fill. The water inside the boat soon rose above the floorboards, and I had to stop rowing and pump, to prevent Chay from getting wet.

'It's all right,' he said, 'I'll pump, you row. I can't sleep in this. I feel more frightened now than at any time on the trip. Pumping will give me something to do.'

'O.K.,' I said, trying to sound confident. The sheer power of the lightning, thunder and rain prevented me from saying anything more. There was nothing we could do but keep on going.

Quite soon the storm passed and the sun came out. Chay took over the oars and I cooked our breakfast of rice pudding and jam, with the inevitable packet of hard-tack biscuits to follow. We drank neither tea nor coffee because the chlorine injected into the water-bags before we set off tasted so foul that only cocoa with plenty of milk powder and sugar could hide the flavour. During the day we drank the water on its own. We had one airborne mug of cocoa between us after the evening meal, just as the first two-hour 'stag' began.

On 1st July, after we had been out very nearly four weeks, we met our fourth ship, the Monrovian tanker *Liquilady* bound for Montreal. We were now off the south-west corner of Newfoundland, and although we had made a poor start we were beginning to pick up the distance at last with favourable wind and current. Next day the water temperature rose to 74° F. and the wind continued from the south-west. After supper, I gazed up through the two holes in the sweat band of my floppy white 'Jonesey' sunhat, and drifted off to sleep feeling that all was well. It would take a long time but we could make it. Chay never doubted it.

Good weather never lasted long. Three days later, towards evening, the wind rose sharply into another gale, again from the west. We decided to have one man resting all the time, in case an emergency should arise where a major effort might be needed.

'John, get up, it's a white-out!' I heard Chay cry as the boat reeled before the breaking crest of a particularly big wave. I was flushed out from under the tarpaulin by something rather like a fire hydrant. I glanced at my watch. 'I'll have a go, my two hours is about up.'

Darkness was coming quickly with the gathering storm. When the huge phosphorescent crests broke around us, *Rosie* surfed, and everything went white in much the same way as a 'white-out' in the blizzards of the Canadian Arctic, where we had undergone cold weather trials in 1963.

I soon realised that this was the most severe test yet. The sea became confused and waves came at us from several different angles. Soaking wet, there was every reason for me to feel miserable and afraid, as I had done on so many previous occasions. Yet I felt strangely elated; at last I was face to face with death. There was a feeling of calm and relaxation as I struggled to keep *Rosie* on a straight course before the waves. I would do my best – beyond that it was not in my power. The tremendous growling roar, as a wave breaks along a front of perhaps 150 yards, defies description. If we were to die, then at least for a short while we had lived free from all the pettiness of everyday life, and we had given of our best. I was conscious of a definite conviction that this moment was to be lived and enjoyed.

The storm only lasted a few hours. During the night the wind veered to the north-west then fell away to nothing, and the sea quickly subsided to a flat calm. The sun burned down with an intensity that could almost be heard. We were both tired from the previous night and our usual nagging persistence fell rather low. We discussed our depression, as we discussed every angle of life, at great length. We decided to play the malaise like a fish on the end of a rod and line – when it was bad we should let it take line off the reel but would be ready to take up the slack again at the earliest opportunity. In our case we knew we would cheer up with a breeze from the west.

Instead of bemoaning our lot, we fell to discussing the water situation. After thirty-two days at sea we should have used sixty-four gallons of fresh water, but in fact we had used only twenty-five gallons. From this we deduced that we were carrying some thirty-five gallons, or the weight of two light men, uselessly across the Atlantic. While we both agreed that only a fool would throw drinking water out of a lifeboat in the middle of the ocean, nevertheless it would be silly to burden ourselves with extra weight on such a long voyage. Chay felt that we should keep the water anyway, but I reckoned that as long as we replaced the remaining fresh water with sea-water in the polythene bottles under the floorboards as we used it, then we should jettison the extra. Eight hundred pounds of water or eighty gallons under the false bottom would maintain our self-righting capability.

We discussed the problem for several hours and then dumped seven five-gallon jerrycans, containing fresh water, over the side. This immediately increased the sleeping space in the stern, but I felt rather apprehensive as the string of bright yellow polythene containers bobbed away in the distance.

On my twenty-eighth birthday, the 8th July, we introduced a new ration policy. As a result of hurricane Alma and the adverse winds of the first month we found that only four and a half of the big polystyrene boxes remained. This meant four and a half weeks, or thirty-one days, of the normal ration. However, we had various types of emergency rations with us; these had been acquired at odd times during our visits for items of equipment, to different branches of the Services, and Horlicks Ltd. Some of the boxes were several years old and we hoped they would not have deteriorated too much, but until they were opened there was no way of finding out. Our plan was to eat one Horlicks two-man motor rally ration, on one day of each week. These needed no cooking and had been bought primarily for storm conditions when the Bleuet Gaz burner might be blown out by the high winds. In addition we were to extend a normal seven-day ration box to eight days. By this means we would make the thirty-one days into forty days from 8th July, that is until 16th August. Beyond that there were four Verkade, three Debren, two low-water rations and three supplements; enough to last until the beginning of September at the most.

As a birthday treat the first motor rally ration was not a howling success, but the party was enlivened by a snatch of B.B.C. World Service on the radio. This was the first English, as opposed to American, we had heard since leaving London Airport. It had seemed a long time, but now we felt we were really coming home.

Next day fog closed in and everything was soon soaking wet. Our world shrank once more to the ends of the dipping oars. Into this little circle bobbed a wide-mouthed white polythene jar about a foot long, which had once held fruit salad. We took it aboard and decided that it would make an admirable container for the logs and films which we hoped to hand over to the next ship we might meet. We each wrote brief letters to our wives, and I wrote to Colin Thomson asking him to ensure that our 'Red Berets' were dropped to us by the first Shackleton.

Storms, sun and fog continued as we pulled on towards the middle of the ocean. Our rendezvous with the Shackleton aircraft provided the impetus to get us there. Twenty-five per cent of the month of July was taken up with east winds, although this was

I

four or five times their average incidence according to the navigational chart we never streamed the sea anchor and kept pressing on relentlessly. There was never enough time to carry out all the little tasks of maintenance which cropped up – if a man was not rowing then he must either be cooking or sleeping. No reading or fishing, or any action not directly related to keeping the boat moving through the water was allowed. At night, the hand-over of the oars was always carried out in such a way that *Rosie* never lost her momentum through the water. We became obsessed with keeping going steadily through the water.

The big westerly storms which occurred about every ten days served to break the monotony of the routine, and allowed us longer periods of rest. When the weather became too bad to row, we let *Rosie* run along before the storm, while both of us huddled under the strip of faded green tarpaulin stretched between the gunwales in the sleeping area. Chay would have his head on one side of the boat, and mine would be on the other, as we lay, with our knees bent, across the boat. Whoever was against the cooker would be left to sleep for twelve hours before changing with the man lying nearer the middle of the boat; the man in this position was responsible for bailing whenever a sea slopped over the side.

By leaning across Chay's seat, it was possible to reach either pump handle, one on either side of the boat, amidships between the two seats on which we sat when rowing. When the bucket lying on the floorboards between the seats started to slop around, it was time to bail. A hundred strokes with one arm, and then a hundred with the other, and so on until a sucking noise announced that *Rosie* was dry again. One night, when on duty, I counted 7,000 strokes between six-thirty in the evening and one-thirty next morning.

Birds were always apparent, even when the nearest land was Cape Farewell, far away on the southern tip of Greenland. Little fluffy storm petrels circled us, trailing their sparrow-like feet in the water in such a way that they seemed to walk even on the biggest waves. The dark brown bulk of the Great Skua, with a flash of white on each wing, would sometimes appear alone, gliding in from the horizon. After a cursory inspection he would swoop away.

Sometimes at the end of a day of calm, as the sun sank into the west, we had a mystical feeling that we were really a part of the natural life of the ocean, that we were the first humans to see it in this setting. We were now south of the main shipping lane and the sea was deserted. Unlike a speeding steamer or sailing boat, we would plod quietly up to a flock of a hundred birds as they settled down for the night on the glassy surface of the ocean, rising and falling to the eternal swell. In the fading light, diffused with soft hues of pink and gold, the drowsy birds would hardly move as the rhythmic dipping of the oars carried us through them. We were rather like any of the baulks of floating timber on which they loved to perch.

Around this time of day, large schools of porpoises, dolphins or small whales would cruise into sight, barely dimpling the surface as they came up for air. If they found us among a flock of floating seabirds they too would join in for a period of gentle play. Surfacing imperceptibly from just beneath a sleeping bird, they would cause it to rear back in alarm, unfolding its wings. When the porpoise subsided, so the bird would float off to sleep immediately. At other times the shiny black porpoises would rise languidly, to nudge at the floating down which was always in abundance around a flock after the evening preening session was finished.

I was rowing alone one night, looking back over the stern at the T section on the top of the rudder. It climbed up the starlit sky with each following swell that overtook us, only to fall and dip below the horizon as *Rosie* slipped down into the succeeding trough. Suddenly there was a heavy splash not far out in the dark to my left. Coming fast towards us was a writhing shape, two feet wide and perhaps forty feet long. On and on it came, and just as it seemed that it would smash against our side, it disappeared under the boat. I was still gazing to the left at the vivid fire of its phosphorescent path, when there was another heavy splash, this time out to the right, behind the shoulder of a wave. Of course it could have been the track of a porpoise, approaching through a lumpy sea, but it needed no great imagination to believe the splashes had been the head of a sea-serpent.

We had been at sea for many weeks, living only a few inches clear of the water; we were used to the ocean and felt a part of it. I was surprised at being surprised, and searched for some logical explanation. I regretted that Chay had been asleep. I could well understand how a superstitious mariner of old, similarly surprised, might attribute the experience to a sea-serpent.

We both preferred to see things together, for we could then

discuss the matter at length, and at the same time feel confident that there had been no halucination – an experience we always expected but which never actually occurred.

Only the day before a pale grey shark with notched tail and a vicious expression in its staring eyes had decided to rub itself against the boat. Although only some eight feet long, the vicious creature made *Rosie* shudder when it butted the hull; it then disappeared into the depths, with streaks of green Tropikop paint on its sandpaper skin. A few second later it returned and struck again; this performance went on for several minutes.

'Do you think he is trying to shake us out – like peas out of a pod?' said Chay.

'I hope it's just that he's got an itch,' I replied.

The shark then took to hitting the rudder, which rattled with each assault. We looked at each other, feeling slightly worried for the safety of this important piece of gear.

'I'll hit him with my oar,' Chay suggested, but to no effect; the shark just ignored the blows.

'Next time he comes past, I'll grab his fin.' Chay was getting bolder. The shark turned and swam lazily along the starboard side to hit the rudder again, its dorsal fin just cutting the surface. Chay reached over and grabbed; there was a tug and Chay let go suddenly. The shark hit the rudder and turned for another attack.

'I'll try a spinner,' said I, foolishly. We hastily lashed some eight feet of strong line to the handle of an oar, and attached a heavy cod 'ripper' to the other end. I dropped the spinner in front of the shark and began ripping it up and down enticingly. The shark ignored the line and hit the rudder again.

'What about the shark repellent?' grinned Chay, fumbling among the row of unused blue cartridges. 'We'll see how he likes this stuff,' he cried, tearing the lid off a bright yellow can about the size of a family tin of baked beans. Inside was a coil of string, which he pulled, then out came a small mop covered with black powder. The string was then tied to a rowlock and the mop hung over the side in the water, which soon clouded over as if a bottle of ink had been spilt from the boat. The shark continued to attack for another couple of circuits through the inky water and then disappeared, apparently repelled. I don't know if the shark would have eaten us, if either of us had been in the water during the intervening two or three minutes after the repellent mop was dipped into the sea.

We went in for a swim on only one occasion, on a calm hot day after a severe storm, when I feared that the pintles and gudgeons which secured the rudder to the hull might have been damaged by the heavy seas. The water was some two miles deep at that point and we had seen several sharks; with no swimming trunks the idea of a dip did not seem welcome, despite the awful heat of the sun.

Chay was an army swimmer and it seemed to me that he was just the man to inspect the rudder. He didn't agree, contending that with Seamanship at O level in G.C.E. mine was the expert eye which should examine the fittings. The discussion raged all day long. Chay was placed in close arrest, then had to be released in order to row.

Eventually at four in the afternoon I was defeated, so slipped hesitantly over the side. The rudder was completely as new; there were no gooseneck barnacles growing on the hull as yet, to slow us down. I splashed around in the cool, cool water, feeling free and clean.

'One last dive under the boat,' I thought, and as I glided under the surface I looked down through the colours; silver bubbles, pale green against the anti-fouling paint on the hull, then blue, purple, black.

'I'm two miles above the ground and there are sharks around.' I kicked for the surface, and hauled myself anxiously back over the side into *Rosie*.

'Go on, Chay, it's lovely,' I smiled. Over he went, but he didn't stay long. We never went in again.

We had not seen a ship for twenty-six days, and we were feeling guilty for the suffering we knew we must be causing Maureen and Marie Christine. We were nearing the middle of the ocean so we started to use the S.A.R.B.E. Mk. III on the special training frequency used by the Shackleton aircraft, from 1300 to 1400 hours on Tuesday, 26th July, but the 'great iron bird' never came. We consoled ourselves with the thought that we were still some distance from the border 'fence' of their territory, at longitude thirty degrees West. Then we saw four ships on one day, but none of them noticed us, although we wasted many of our precious little mini-flares in our efforts to attract their attention. At last, at five-thirty in the afternoon a ship seemed to be coming in our direction.

The black and yellow cargo ship, S.S. *Madaket* of New York, was returning to America from Europe and seemed to be travelling light. When it seemed possible that she might actually run us down, Chay fired a warning flare high into the air and her engines went full astern. She went on past us and then turned back in a big circle through the calm sea.

'What the hell are you doing,' drawled a Yankee voice over the loud hailer from the port wing of the yellow bridge.

'Oh, we're just rowing home to England. We've been out fifty-one days – can you give us a position?' I replied. We had had a shave two days before, and looked pretty chipper in our shorts and track-suit tops in the warm sun. We'd show these Yanks a thing or two.

'Sure, hang on a minute,' the voice replied. By this time most of the crew seemed to be on deck with cameras and were calling to us to wave in all directions.

'46° 56′ N, 37° 39′ W. The weather forecast is bad, you know – a hurricane six hundred miles south is coming north,' called the officer of the watch.

'Thank you. Would you please signal our position to Lloyds of London so our families will know we are safe,' I shouted, holding up the painted sign which gave our name and destination.

'O.K. Anything else – do you want some provisions?'

'No, thank you, we are all right. Thank you for stopping.'

'Well, we'll be on our way then. Good luck!' The bells rang in the engine room, a familiar sound from Clan Line days; then the great propeller churned the surface and the ship started to move forward. As she left us, the crew lined the decks, shouting and waving. Caught in the turmoil of her propeller, *Rosie* bobbed and curtsied.

Chay and I faced each other grimly. 'Another hurricane,' we both said.

'At ten knots, it would reach us in three days,' I thought aloud. 'Well, anyway, we are half-way, and the fix he just gave us is only a mile and a half different in latitude and it's just about smack on for longitude. How's that for a tribute to British education, after twenty-six days without a check?'

'Not bad,' said Chay. 'At least we know where we are, and we're in pretty good nick at half-way.'

There followed a wonderful night of flat calm, but I felt worried by the narrow margin of rations left us by Hurricane

Alma. We were both suffering from the effects of salt water on our bodies. I was in continual pain from a sort of nappy rash on my thighs and backside, and Chay had sores on his wrists and neck from chafe.

Rowing alone that night, under a glorious moon on a flat calm sea, I tried to imagine the effect of S.S. *Madaket*'s signal to Lloyds of London. The arrangement was that they should telephone Captain Colin Thomson, now Adjutant of the Depot, the Parachute Regiment, at Maida Barracks in Aldershot. Colin would first stick a red pin in our position on the chart of the North Atlantic which he had hung on his office wall. Then he would telephone Maureen Blyth in Newcastle and Marie Christine in Beaconsfield. At least they would all be pleased after no news for five weeks. The *Rigoletto* of Bremen had, in fact, been the last ship to inform Lloyds of our position.

At five in the morning I was again at the oars, in the last two-hour 'stag' before dawn. A gentle breeze had rippled the moonlit sea into a golden fleece. Conditions were so good that I tried the radio to help me keep awake. A cellist called Rostokovitch was playing Tchaikovsky on the B.B.C. World Service. Who would believe we were in the path of an approaching hurricane?

Gradually through the day the wind rose from the south-east and a long, ominous swell began to run. A little black-headed tern, with a bold white stripe along the top of his crown, played inquisitively around us, attacking any other bird that approached. The slamming jar of the sea on the ends of the oars at the start of each stroke had a cumulative effect. The east wind pressed us back hour by hour; it was dreadful to watch the floating seaweed drift past in the wrong direction as *Rosie* was forced backwards through the water. 'Good character training again,' I thought. At the end of a long day at the oars, we were farther from home than we had been at breakfast. A series of rainstorms ran through during the day and the seas were huge. We switched to one-man-rowing-one-man-resting in order to maintain energy for the crisis ahead.

The wind dropped a little at sunset and Chay heard us reported safe as the last item on the B.B.C. World News at two-fifteen in the morning. As I had been asleep, I tried the five a.m. news; just as the last item was about to be announced a rogue wave came over the side and silenced the radio. At least the R.A.F. Shackletons would know where we were, if they flew out next day, but we were still outside their limit of thirty degrees West.

That day was grim. The wind continued to blow at gale force from the east. When we changed over at the oars *Rosie* would swing away from the wind, and only a great effort could bring her back. We couldn't afford to waste our energy, so we slipped the sea anchor for the first time in five weeks.

Huddled together in the five-by-four-foot space in the stern we forced down curry and cocoa, but neither of us felt much like food. We knew the position and were simply afraid. Great grey seas rolled by endlessly.

Next day the wind was still from the east, rising to storm Force 10. We lay and bailed and waited. My rash, like pins and needles, extended from knees to hips. Chay was also in continual pain where his clothes had chafed him; his wrists and neck were ringed with angry red lumps. The tops of the waves were sliced off by the wind and the sea was covered by white foam, which also filled the air. Huge hills and valleys rushed by and there was little difference between daylight and darkness. The most dangerous waves could be heard breaking in the distance. It was rather like being on a road bridge over a railway when an express train is approaching. In the final roar, *Rosie* would always manage to rise up and avoid the worst. One of us was bailing as the other tried to rest up against the cooker. The sea was two miles deep and this allowed the waves to grow to enormous proportions.

Close together for warmth we talked of life in a new light. Stripped of all comfort and faced with imminent death, we talked of the night train to Scotland, Hawick, Ardmore and of our families. We talked of some of the mean things we had done, and of how much we wanted to go on living. Simple humility and a wish to live a better life filled our minds. Here was something which neither of us would ever forget.

I remember bargaining with God for another day of life.

Next day the wind dropped and backed to the north. We emerged from under the tarpaulin and started to row again, feeling much older. During the afternoon the wind strengthened and backed farther west, then south-west; the seas reared up again and soon we were recovering the distance we had so recently lost.

Just dabbing with the paddles was agony on our salt-pickled backsides; we were down to the last tin of soothing foot powder, and there had been no chance to wash or even to dry ourselves.

The following day we began to fear the onset of exposure. The wind varied in direction from south to north-west but continued above gale force. The seas defied logic, and we lay under the tarpaulin trying not to look at them. Our clothes were soaked through and felt as if lined with sandpaper. Time passed in a haze of bailing and checking the course as we drifted helplessly before the wind. Either we were to die, or we were not to die. We must just hang on and await the outcome.

The storm had now continued for five days and Chay kept saying, 'It's almost over, soon it will be a memory.'

There were three of us, *Rosie*, Chay and me; we were as one. There was no disagreement, just a continual effort to cheer the other two.

Chay had managed to cook two hot meals by using airborne initiative to its limit. Other than that, we lived on a diet of biscuits, cheese, raisins and chocolate, washed down with cold water. 'What the lions drink,' as my mother used to say when I was a child.

Next day the wind rose higher yet, and the string holding up my waterproof trousers broke to make life just the little bit more miserable. We used some of the precious calamine compound from our last tin to ease the salt irritation and hung on. Chay looked very tired, with dark sunken eyes in his unshaven face. I wondered if I looked any better. The seas seemed like great mountains covered in icing sugar as they marched towards 'Angleterre' – I was trying to teach Chay French.

During that night the frame which held the tarpaulin across our sleeping space at gunwale level broke at the connection on the port side. We lay in abject misery, shrouded by a soggy pile of canvas. It was uncertain whether it was worse to be on watch, or resting. On the seventh day the storm fell away and we were alive to continue on our way with the oars. It had been a searing week.

In the days that followed we made good progress, but quite clearly we were beginning to 'fade'. It was as if we were being rubbed down with sandpaper. The succession of storms and the reduced diet, combined with the extra duration of the voyage, caused by adverse winds, was wearing us down. We agreed that although we still had food for another month, until 4th September, we should take food from the next ship which stopped. We

reasoned that we should not allow ourselves to become so weak-
ened that we might have to use the radio to call for help from a
ship, thus endangering other lives unnecessarily.

Hunger became the dominant topic of our conversation; we
planned the meals we would have when we landed. We dreamed
of the army 'hard tack' biscuits which were, we knew, being
thrown away on Salisbury Plain Training Area at that very time.

We always had a snack during the five-minute break in each
hour while rowing. This was usually sweets, cheese, or raisins,
with Horlicks Enerzade glucose tablets with we took like medicine.
Now we tried eating Spangles, keeping the paper on to make them
last longer: when Cadbury's awarded us the 'C.D.M.' after the
voyage, they could never have known we held the world record
for making a piece of Dairy Milk chocolate last so long. If the
break meant a small knob of army 'Compo' cheese, we would
cut it into four tiny pieces and take one each quarter of an hour,
sucking them carefully to try and make them last until the whole
hour was up. I was sorely tempted to sell Ardmore to Chay for
his week's supply of one small tube of Smarties.

We were now within the limit of thirty degrees West, but the
'great iron bird' never came. 'Of course we might be anywhere
after the hurricane,' we thought. 'They'll come after the next
ship reports us.'

Alone at night, it became increasingly difficult to maintain
two hours at the oars. Somehow we both believed that we were
going to make it to the land. Surely some Almighty Presence,
which ordered these things, would have killed us off by this time
if he intended we should not succeed.

We prayed that the *Puffin* would arrive before us; they had
thought of the idea and we, for our part, wanted nothing but to
land. If we could finish second, but in a slightly faster time than
the *Puffin*, we would be more than pleased.

During the day we planned great walks across the mountains
at Ardmore, and Chay promised to call his home Foinavon, after
the mountain outside the front door of croft No. 80. Thoughts of
Ardmore, and of a simple life there, kept me going.

One evening, just as we were preparing the usual beef curry, a
container ship, heavily laden and bound for Europe, wallowed
through the heavy seas perhaps only half a mile from us. I fired
our last two mini-flares but the ship steamed on. A big sea broke
over the port side and Chay just managed to get the lid on the

pressure cooker in time. As soon as we had finished bailing out with the buckets, I returned to the oars and gazed after the cargo ship as it vanished into the grey curtain of rain. Suddenly I felt a steady grip on my bare head. It felt like the clutch of doom!

'What the hell is it?' I asked Chay.

'Och, it's one of those wedge-tailed skuas,' he replied. We had seen several pairs of these predatory seabirds usually flying north to south – perhaps this one was tired.

After a few moments it took off. We looked at the ugly sky and I felt it had been an ill omen.

Luckily, the curry wasn't spoilt. It was in fact only half a curry with a 'coalie' fish bar. 'Kedgeree à la *Rosie*', was the only dish on the starvation menu.

We had been nearly seventy days at sea and we felt as if, perhaps, we were just two little ants on a piece of matchstick trying to cross a puddle to a rock, on which were crowded many other ants. What was the purpose? What part could we play in all this, with our brief passage across the ocean beneath all those stars? Why had we been spared, surely there must be something more than just to return and continue the struggle to acquire material things in order to impress our fellow-ants? If we lived, how were we to carry on after the voyage? It certainly appeared now as if we were being protected at every turn. Surely we must show some improvement as a result of our trial? We must remember how we had felt in the hurricane. Perhaps suffering is the greatest gift a human can be granted. Somehow it opens the eyes afresh and banishes from sight the worthless trash of life.

These were the thoughts which played on my mind when rowing alone at night. I became certain that there must be some Almighty Presence ordering the sea and the storms, and at the same time preserving our lives.

We discussed the situation at great length over a period of many days. We concluded that if we lived then we would hope to be humbler, more tolerant and more appreciative of the brief gift of human life.

We imagined that the total length of the voyage was the equivalent of Dover–Ardmore–Dover–Ardmore–Dover, and that we were now on the last leg of the journey. One more month should see the end of the ordeal; surely we must have sufficient reserves of strength – although it was now rather like opening a tin in the larder, to find there are no sweets left inside.

For a few days we passed through an area where there floated several huge teak logs; these were encrusted with the same goose-neck barnacles which were starting to grow on *Rosie* beneath her waterline. Perhaps the massive logs had been washed from the deck of a cargo ship. If we should collide with one of those battering rams in a storm, then *Rosie* would be severely damaged. She might even be stove in and capsize.

On the 12th August, seventy days out, we decided to divide the remaining rations into sufficient portions to last us for another thirty days. We had a further 900 miles to row and I had three boils on my thighs. Painful glands in my groin indicated a serious build-up of poison, so I started another crash course of tetracycline tablets, supplemented with vitamin B. The paraffin gauze dressings proved effective. Chay prayed we might meet a ship; I did the same.

Early next morning, on a calm and sunny day, we had just finished a sparse breakfast when we looked round and saw a west-bound tanker, only a mile or so away, on our port bow. She was heading straight for us. We waited nervously to see if there would be any response to our signal – a red anorak waved from the top of our thin telescopic radio aerial. She put her engines into reverse and stopped; soon we were hauling ourselves up the rope ladder and on to her deck. The friendly bo'sun stayed aboard *Rosie*, and held her off from the steel sides of the ship, as she rose and fell in the gentle swell.

Captain Mitchell of the Shell tanker *Haustellum* received us on his bridge. We were clean-shaven and deeply tanned from two and a half months in the open air. Even our track suits looked quite clean and we were in high good spirits.

'What'll you have to eat,' smiled the captain as he led us down to his quarters.

'Scrambled egg,' we echoed, padding along behind him, barefoot on the steel deck. Our weekly meal of scrambled egg powder was the highlight of the breakfast menu; now we could have real eggs.

'I'm bound for Venezuela. I'm afraid we can't stop long, but I'll have them load your boat with provisions,' said Captain Mitchell.

'Thank you very much, sir. Who won the World Cup?' I asked.

'England, didn't you know?'

Chay and I smiled at each other. We had wondered if we would be the last to know the result.

I shall always remember those scrambled eggs, the black coffee, and the toast and marmalade on that sunny morning; also the calm efficiency of the British ship and the way our legs couldn't walk straight.

At 46° 22′ N, 23°15′ W, we were 850 miles south-west of Land's End. Captain Mitchell suggested we make for Falmouth, his home town, but we felt that the West Coast of Ireland would be easier to reach. I was keen to make land at the earliest possible time, to avoid the unsettled weather at the end of the British summer; besides we were getting rather tired of rowing.

We were aboard the tanker for one hour. After we left the bridge, clutching a tin of biscuits which the captain had saved for his wife, but given us, we met many of the crew by the ship's side, where the ladder hung down into *Rosie*.

'I read the *Puffin* was seven hundred and fifty miles out five days ago,' someone said, as we clambered over the rail. It was the only news we were to hear of the other boat; it seemed they were a hundred miles ahead. We hoped they would land soon.

'Good luck,' said the bo'sun, gripping my hand. His blue eyes stared into mine from a strong broad face. 'We've done two thousand miles,' I thought, 'eight hundred and fifty more will be no great problem. We're almost home. I wonder why he looks so concerned?' Meeting a ship always created a false rise in our morale.

Rosie was full of fresh fruit, bread, 'Longlife' milk, eggs, sardines, and all the good things we had longed for. The *Haustellum* pulled away from us as we started to eat and eat.

'Marie Christine and Maureen will hear in a few hours,' said Chay.

'Yes, and the Shackletons.'

'We should do the crossing in a shorter time than the *Puffin*, but I'm glad she is nearly home now,' Chay murmured. 'Let's get going.'

That night I was violently sick from over-eating.

We headed north-west aided by southerly winds. Four days later we held a shouted conversation with a French tuna-fishing boat; with her rakish lines the pale blue motor-boat looked positively unsafe.

'Boy, I'm glad I'm not on that,' said Chay.

We pointed at our unrolled chart. 'Quarante huit et dix neuf,' the wild looking Frenchmen yelled against the wind. 'Forty-eight and nineteen,' shouted Chay, airing his newly acquired knowledge of French, for he could now count to a hundred.

We plodded on; our oilskins were beginning to disintegrate and the painful rashes caused us both a lot of misery. Gradually the sea birds became more numerous and varied; gannets, terns and fulmars appeared. We were nearing land, but we were wearing out, despite the massive increase in diet. In addition to huge meals we each had a full tin of sweetened condensed milk daily, but still it seemed as if we were nearing the end of our tether.

We made endless plans of how and when we would land.

'Excuse me, I wonder if you could give us a cup of tea, we're both rather tired,' I imagined myself knocking on a lonely cottage door, and asking some little old lady.

'Perhaps if they have a telephone, I could make a reverse charge call to Marie Christine's Uncle Norman in Dublin. He'd lend us the money to fly home to London,' I said to Chay.

'D'you think he would?' he replied.

'Well, I hope so.' I wasn't quite sure. Why should he? I was broke, really broke.

The Shackleton planes never came.

Whenever we were really miserable Chay would strike up with the old Scottish songs of his childhood. 'The Road and the Miles to Dundee' never failed to rally my spirits; he was tremendous when things seemed really grim. I pointed out that our chances would be slim if our arrival off the cliffs of Eire coincided with another storm. I offered to use the emergency radio if he felt that the risk was not warranted.

'We'll go on,' he said without hesitation.

'O.K.' If he wanted to, then I would go on and on and on. I don't know why.

In the calm late afternoon of Saturday, 27th August, we met the Finnish cargo ship M.V. *Finnalpino* bound for Montreal from the English Channel. We were only 250 miles west of Fastnet Rock on the south-west corner of Eire.

'One week, Chay. Fair winds and we'll make it in one week.'

'Soon it will be a memory,' he replied.

The pain, the wet and the cold were bad in these northern waters in late summer. The wind blew a gale from the south-west; it looked as if we might land at Clifden, just north of the large bite of Galway Bay. The aviators Alcock and Brown, friends of my late father-in-law, had landed there; it would be fitting if we could do the same.

I had a dream, which was very unusual, on the night of the 31st August. A girl carrying a bundle of man's clothing walked past me on a country lane.

'Whose are those?' I asked. But she looked away and wouldn't reply. It didn't bode well for a landing on the cliffs.

Chay, *Rosie* and I were one small team working in perfect harmony; somehow we'd find a way in. At least there would be no fuss. The *Puffin* would have landed and if there had been any public interest it would be over. All we needed now was luck, and a calm day.

At ten a.m. I was just finishing my breakfast in the stern while Chay rowed alone. As we started to change around so that he could have his meal I noticed a faint grey line just above the horizon, well to our left.

'There it is, it's land!' I said as calmly as I could.

'Well, I won't look now because I probably won't be able to recognise it,' said Chay. He had never been to sea before and we had seen no land for the past ninety-two days; not since leaving Orleans, Cape Cod, at five-thirty on Saturday, 4th June.

As the land was to our left, or north, we decided to turn towards it in an attempt to reach it before nightfall. I believed I had sighted the Aran Isles on the west coast of Ireland, some ten miles west of Galway. We had nine or ten hours of daylight left and wind backed to south, blowing us towards that faint smudge of land far ahead. Steadily it increased and we realised that the landing would be dangerous.

There are several islands which go to make up the group known as the Aran Isles. We were concerned with only three, those directly ahead of us, with the mainland of Ireland some ten miles beyond them to the north. The three run from east to west. The main island of Innishmore is about fourteen miles long and one mile wide, and at its western end lie two small islands each about half a mile in diameter and each separated by perhaps a quarter of a mile of sea. We aimed to pass through the 400-yard gap between these two end-most islands to land on the sheltered side of the western island, as it had a lighthouse. It was here that I planned to make the reverse charge telephone call to my wife's uncle in Dublin, to ask him if he could lend me enough money for our fare to London.

As we approached the islands it began to blow a gale; soon we were being blown so fast that we turned the stern towards the gap and just balanced the boat with the oars. By two in the afternoon the wind was severe gale Force 9 from the south, and we could see the great rollers smashing themselves against the distant cliffs.

It was difficult to judge if we would make it through the narrow sound between the islands, because rain squalls frequently blotted them from our view. Neither did we know if there was a tidal stream dragging us across; we prayed there was not, because there were no beaches ahead, only those grim cliffs. Nearing the land after ninety-two days, the soft green of the grass, framed by racing black clouds and white-grey seas, seemed to be welcoming us home. But between that soft green and *Rosie* lay the black cliffs laced with foam where the raging sea clawed in vain to reach the emerald carpet high above it.

A heady sense of pleasure overtook me as I realised that this was one of the supreme excitements of our lives. We had taken every precaution we could; survival kits were already secured to our waists; now it was no longer in our hands as the wind drove us inexorably nearer the cliffs. Within a few minutes, we should know if we were to succeed or fail, live or die. There would be a final result after three months of patience.

Somehow we made it through the sound and into the lee of the little lighthouse island. In fact we shot through the gap backwards, feeling rather like a cork in a street gutter after a storm. We had to land on this island or be blown beyond on to the rocky coast of the mainland during the night, for it would be dark by the time we covered the intervening ten miles.

There were two men from the lighthouse down on the shore, in a little cove on the leeward side of the island. One of them ran to fetch the keeper, who appeared clutching his brass telescope. He was dressed in rough blue serge like the others. As we hauled at the oars to close the shore, we could see the men waving us away towards the main island across the wind. We could not hear their shouts above the deafening roar of the wind and sea, but it was clearly too rough to land anywhere on the lighthouse island.

It was now five o'clock in the afternoon and only three hours of daylight remained. We had to think rather quickly and come up with a new plan. The only place to land, it seemed, was in the

(*Above*) Landing at Galway to a civic welcome. Twice I nearly fainted with claustrophobia; (*below*) going through our written logs caused some anguish in the Great Southern Hotel, Galway.

(*Left*) Landing at London Airport with our wives;
(*right*) Princess Margaret came to see *Rosie* at the
Boat Show, 1967; (*below*) *Rosie* in Trafalgar Square.

shelter of the main island, protected by the cliffs 500 feet high on the Atlantic side. Between us and the main island lay the other small island.

At this point, another factor further complicated the situation. I had been wanting to go to the loo with increasing urgency all day. It was now quite clear that unless I used the plastic bucket we kept for this purpose, in the very near future, any landing we made would be extremely embarrassing. Chay decided that we should both row with all our might, using four oars, and crab across the wind into the shelter of the little island half-way across to the main island. Then, while he made a Herculean effort with two oars, I should take my chance with the bucket.

Picture the situation now, with *English Rose III* steadily crabbing across the wind through clattering rain squalls which obscured the land every few minutes. The lighthouse keeper, in blue serge suit, peering through his telescope from the top of the lighthouse. He was a worried man, responsible for safety precautions; he didn't recognise the boat and thought it must have been blown down from farther up the coast before the wind backed south. He could hardly think that that clumsy-looking twenty-foot open dory had come the other way – across 3,000 miles of the Atlantic from America. As the battered-looking little boat drew in to the shelter of the small island just within his sight he saw the oarsman in the bow stand up, pick up the bucket from the stern and bend down.

'They're in trouble, they're bailing out, radio for the lifeboat!' he shouted to his subordinates.

And so, unknown to us, at five-thirty on a stormy Saturday evening, the Kilronan lifeboat put out from the tiny fishing village of that name, some nine miles farther east along the sheltered side of the main island of Innishmore.

Meanwhile after I had finished with the bucket, we crossed the menacing rollers and the remaining distance to the shelter of the main island. The miserable weather continued, but we found ourselves in relatively calm waters which were nevertheless, still swept by the storm shrieking down from the tops of the cliffs on the windward side of the island. We had lost some distance in the manoeuvres from the lighthouse island, and now we had about half a mile to row into the wind, before reaching a sheltered pebble beach in flat water. We thought we could cover the distance in about an hour, rowing hard with four oars. We were

K

singing now, songs like Barbra Streisand's 'Second Hand Rose', and we were all set to make one last gigantic effort to land before dark.

At seven o'clock, the Kilronan lifeboat appeared through very poor visibility and horizontal rain. She commenced circling *English Rose III*. We were the only two boats on the sea and it was still quite light. We couldn't hear what they were shouting but clearly they hoped to take us in tow. Chay and I had lived in an open space twelve feet by five feet for a quarter of a year while rowing some 3,500 miles in a rather erratic course across the Atlantic. We were keen to finish the last quarter mile under our own steam.

'What shall we do now, Chay?'

'Just pretend we can't see them and keep rowing.'

The lifeboat crew were clearly puzzled by our tactics.

After about twenty minutes, we were so embarrassed by looking down at the bottom of the boat, and pretending we couldn't see the lifeboat circling only about thirty yards from us, that we decided we should let them take us in tow. After all, these kindly Irishmen had come out on this bleak night when they could have been enjoying a drink at home instead.

So it happened that at seven-thirty we boarded the lifeboat and watched *Rosie* yawing at the end of a short rope from the stern, while she was towed along to Kilronan. In the lifeboat cabin there was time to sit alone and wonder what might happen next.

The lifeboatmen conversed in Gaelic; they did not know if the *Puffin* had landed. They heard about us on the wireless, but did not connect the little dory with those reports until we told them who we were. They were surprised.

Chay said, 'I'm not getting back in that boat for no one.'

We chugged slowly down the coast in the gathering dark and I talked to one of the crew, a young lobster fisherman, about the new American-style creels they were trying with great success. My mind turned to the north-west coast of Sutherland and Ardmore – my 'haven under the hill' as Chay's song went. It was from here that my friend Hugh Ross had sent the catalogue for lobster pots, with the photograph of the twenty-foot dory on the back, suggesting that it might be suitable for the rowing trip.

We arrived in the little harbour at eight-thirty in slashing rain and high wind. It was pitch dark but a small crowd had gathered under the single naked electric light outside the warehouse. They didn't know what to expect.

We tied up alongside the stone harbour wall, between two fishing boats, and a man came aboard and shook hands with us.

'Welcome to Aran,' he said. 'I'm Father McMahon, a Jesuit priest visiting the island.'

I was shaken. The last person we saw as the last escort boat from Cape Cod turned for home, on the 4th June, had been another Father McMahon. He had blessed the boat for us at Chay's request. It was another coincidence, much the same as my wearing an Aran Isle jersey for the whole trip, and now we were landed on Aran.

It *was* all a memory now.

9

The Aftermath

WE dragged *Rosie* on to the sandy beach in the harbour and after some discussion we were driven through the night in a Dormobile, by Sean Conneeley, to the family guest-house at Kilmurvy, where we were invited to stay the night. They had seen us struggling towards their beach before the lifeboat took us in tow. Everyone wished we had landed at Kilmurvy.

At ten o'clock that evening, the phone rang while we were eating great plates of stew. It was *The People* newspaper for me, calling from London. They told me that during the voyage *The People* had signed a contract with our agent. We were not to talk to any other newspapermen. We agreed – after all there were no reporters on the stormbound island.

Unknown to us, half an hour before the phone call, the editor of *The People* had taken the tricky decision to change the front page of his newspaper to the headline 'THEY'VE MADE IT', without knowing for certain if we had made it or not. Later we felt rather sorry for the girl reporter who had been infiltrated into Red China to send exclusive reports on the purges by the Red Guards. Our story replaced hers.

We settled down again to more stew, anxiously awaiting the telephone call from our wives which *The People* had promised us would be coming through very soon. Both Maureen and Marie Christine had been out on a trawler, chartered by Associated Newspapers, from the Scilly Isles. They were now stormbound in St. Mary's.

While we sat in front of the fire in the warm kitchen at Kilmurvy, on Innishmore, Maureen and Marie Christine sat in a cinema on the Scilly Isles. They gazed with unseeing eyes at the screen and thought of the storm outside; the trawler had been forced back into port by the foul weather. They both wondered if *Rosie* could survive in such conditions.

Quite suddenly the two girls were called out in the middle of the film, much to the annoyance of the audience. When told we had landed safely in Ireland and were on the telephone, they both burst into tears of relief and happiness. It was wonderful to hear Marie Christine again and feel the dry land firmly under my feet.

Next day, when they tried to ring again, they found they were ninety-fifth on the list of calls waiting for us from all over the world. They flew in a hired plane from St. Just to Cardiff then on to Dublin. After this they were driven to Galway, to evade the waiting reporters at Shannon Airport. We were taken by sea to Galway for a civic reception, and later we were kept behind locked doors in a suite at the top of the Great Southern Hotel. When Maureen and Marie Christine arrived at the back of the hotel at one in the morning, dustbin lids slowly rose as waiting photographers focused for their shots. In the hotel lobby and lift, fighting broke out, and this was televised for the National news.

Telegrams came from all over the place, including one of 130 words from the Chief of the General Staff of the Army. Our Commanding Officer immediately put us back on full pay. Two days later we flew to London and were met by a guard of honour led by the Colonel Commandant of the Parachute Regiment. After a T.V. conference at the airport, a Rolls-Royce drove the four of us to a hotel in London. Although we don't smoke or drink, the bill for the next ten days apparently came to £1,300; this was fortunately met by the newspaper.

On our first evening we gave a small dinner party. During the meal I was called from the table to discuss a proposition. I was to call at No. 10 Downing Street and challenge the Prime Minister to a duel with my dress sword. While I politely declined the suggestion, I couldn't help smiling at the effect such a scheme would have had on my military career. Surely it was all a dream, and I

would soon wake up, wet and miserable, when Chay called me for
my next spell at the oars.

In our hotel suite, a relay of typists worked round the clock to
transcribe our pencil-written logs into type for the first part of
our story, to be serialised on the coming Sunday. Telephones
rang incessantly. We had our hair cut in the suite while we
carried on a series of interviews with reporters from foreign
magazines. Within a few days we were overcome by the new diet
of rich food. *Rosie* sat in state in Trafalgar Square, and *The People*
brought the lifeboat crew over from Galway to join in the celebrations. We made short visits to T.V. studios and the Ministry
of Defence. From time to time Chay and I looked at each other
and just smiled.

Six days after landing we were given a 'Tribute Luncheon' by
The People at another London hotel, and the Secretary of State
for Defence (Army), during his speech, gave us a fortnight's
leave. After a string of speakers, I got to my feet before a distinguished audience. Nervously I tried to compare the sumptuous
banquet of that Friday afternoon with the meagre fare of the
previous Friday, before the cliffs of Aran.

Chay, confronted with a barrage of T.V. cameras and micro-
phones, upstaged everyone by saying, 'You may have heard that I
did all the rowing – this is not true. Captain Ridgway did do
some rowing – when I was cooking!'

The excitement of our landing on Aran on the Saturday
prevented us from sleeping much. It seemed incredible that we
could keep going, but some kind of nervous energy sustained us.
One morning I awoke after only three hours' sleep.

'Look out, it's a storm!' I shouted to Marie Christine, asleep
beside me, but it was only a pneumatic drill in the street below.
They were working just outside the hotel, where I had counted
cars for the traffic survey only two years previously.

The days passed and life seemed strangely shrouded in a mist of
voices; I felt as if I were Walter Mitty. Now that the two ants on
the piece of matchstick had made it across the puddle to the rock,
all the ants on the rock were reacting in a most peculiar manner. In
the rare quiet moments, such as when relaxing in the luxury of a
hot bath, I thought of the dramatic change in our lives. I couldn't
help feeling that we were allowing ourselves to be carried away
on a tide of back-slapping, which was far removed from our
intention to become 'humbler, more appreciative people'.

Of the *Puffin* there was still no sign, and our thoughts were often of Johnstone and Hoare, and how the position could so easily have been reversed. In a warm bed, the misery of the open sea seemed far away, but all the same it didn't need much effort to remember.

As soon as we were allowed to go from the hotel, Marie Christine and I visited our little home in Farnham for a couple of days. We bought a saloon car to replace the mini-van, which before the voyage had cost four speeding endorsements on my driving licence. Then we set off for a quiet holiday together at Ardmore, 700 miles north. I was feeling absolutely drained of energy and worn out; several medical tests had been made and it seemed that we were still fit, although very tired. To the average person we met we appeared perfectly fit, but it was an illusion.

On the way up, we stopped for a night at Hawick. Next morning I looked round the old border town of which Chay had talked so much while we were out at sea.

There was a gale blowing when we arrived at Skerricha late next evening. Clearly it was no night for the boat trip across to Ardmore in the dark, so we stayed at the Garbet Hotel seven miles along the coast at the little fishing village of Kinlochbervie. Next morning the sky had cleared and the wind abated. Hughie met us with the boat at Skerricha and the sun shone. He showed me the telegram I had sent him from Galway, 'We made it – see you soon,' it said. Coming home to Ardmore meant everything.

Hugh had continued the improvements on the croft all through the summer, confident that we should return. Now the little house on the hillside above the wood at the far end of the loch was pale blue with bright white, gable ends instead of the grim black I remembered. Life seemed wonderful.

We stayed for ten days and the weather was fine for the time of year; perhaps the Atlantic had seen enough of storms for a while. Each day when I looked up at the clouds, I imagined I was still with Chay and *Rosie*. Those clouds, they used to tell us so much.

Walking alone through the wood, I looked at the ripening hazel-nuts and the blackberries. I reached out to touch them, and to feel the green leaves between my fingers – I was still alive. My shoes were stopped short by the rocky path, where I stamped them to make sure it wasn't all a dream. I determined to keep stamping my feet and looking at the trees and clouds; they are life, the very stuff for which I had struggled so hard to stay alive.

The water in the loch rippled gently far below; no angry surge ever penetrated this sheltered arm of the sea; still it was the same dangerous element waiting patiently for me to make just one mistake.

One day, at teatime, 'Willy the Post' brought a letter from America. The thick manilla envelope contained the draft proof of an article to be published on twelve pages in the *Saturday Evening Post*; also a request for me to check it over, and then telephone New York with any corrections. The red telephone kiosk below the house rings in the little croft, but it is hardly ever used and the line is never good even in the best of weather. It was dark by the time I had read the article through, and as I stumbled down the slippery path I was clutching a flickering oil lamp in my right hand. I booked the call to New York, and returned to the house for supper just as it came on to rain. Ten minutes later the bell drummed damply from its position over the inside of the front door: my call to New York. I grabbed the draft story in one hand and the oil lamp in the other and set off through the heavy rain. As soon as I reached the slope I fell flat on my back and the lamp went out. I groped my way back to the house and set off again with the spare lamp – it blew out as soon as I left the front door. Marie Christine handed me our torch, smiling quietly to herself. It was very dim, but I made my way to the kiosk and lifted the receiver before the operator rang off. It was New York.

'Is that you, John?' drawled the voice of Jim Atwater, senior editor of the *Post*, from his office high up in a skyscraper somewhere along Madison Avenue. It was still daylight and office hours in New York.

'Yes, it's me,' I stuttered wearily, covered in mud and soaked through. 'You won't be able to understand the situation here, but just believe me it's rather difficult to read clearly, with this dim torch.'

I read the story over the telephone. There were few alterations. It was the only good objective description of the voyage ever written.

'Thanks, John, I'll call you next week.' Jim rang off. I crawled up the hill for a hot bath and a change of clothes; Jim moved on to the next item on his agenda.

Marie Christine and I walked and fished a fair bit, but soon I was laid low by the eighth boil of the summer on my backside, which meant several days lying on my side. Recovery was hastened when Jim rang from Philadelphia and asked us over for a week to do T.V., and radio shows, to help publicise the story in the *Saturday Evening Post*.

We returned to Aldershot and embarked on a daily round of lunches and dinners; Chay and Maureen were just as excited as Marie Christine and me over the prospect of a week in New York and Cape Cod. The revelry was interrupted when, on the 15th October, just six weeks after our landing, the *Puffin* was found by a frigate of the Royal Canadian Navy, abandoned and capsized near the middle of the North Atlantic, David Johnstone's log and some film were recovered. T.V. men flew to Lisbon where the frigate landed the *Puffin*, and a gruesome inquiry into the fate of the little boat and the tragic loss of her crew was enacted on various radio and T.V. programmes. How easily the situation might have been different, how lucky we had been.

We flew across to New York in a Pan American Boeing 707. It didn't take long, and I recalled the fast-moving jet trails we had seen high above us on some fine days during the rowing. Maureen and Chay went up to Cape Cod to revisit all the people who had been so kind to us while we prepared for the voyage. Marie Christine and I were booked into a hotel where one boiled potato cost a dollar; in four days I did fourteen radio and T.V. shows in New York and Philadelphia. Before the end of this I realised that our voyage was just another item in the ceaseless quest after material for the entertainment business. Before one network T.V. show it was explained to me, 'This is a light frothy show, but sometimes we like to get down to the "nitty-gritty" and that's you!'

We were quite ready for our visit to Cape Cod when the week-end came at last. Driving through the flaming leaves of the famous New England fall, I remembered the straightforward sincerity of the fishermen. Captain Johnny Stello, for example, who had himself been washed from the deck of his fishing boat, been given up for lost, and then picked up by another boat which happened to pass through the same area an hour later. These men know little of 'frothy' and 'nitty-gritty'; they simply know the sea and life. There were tears in the eyes of some of the old dorymen when we met them in Kenny's old boatyard. Our lives had depended on the skill they had acquired in another century. In that desperate seven-day storm, it had been their instinctive feeling for design which had kept *Rosie* from being crushed by the mighty crests as they broke all around, but never on top of our little dory.

On our return to London I found I had put on two stones in weight in two months; I went to bed with another boil, and with waves of bitterness and cynicism washing over me. 'To travel hopefully is better than to arrive' – how true it seemed; after action there had come the reaction. Now I felt I had betrayed everything and simply taken the easy course, which was to agree with everybody and everything. As a child I had often wondered how it would be to live the life of the rich and famous, a 'star of stage, screen and radio' as they used to say, a friend of everyone. For a short time I was living just this kind of life. We were treated very well by everyone we met. Sometimes there was acrimonious discussion between promoters and our agent, but wherever we ourselves went we found nothing but kindliness. It was as if people really wished to believe we were something special, out of the ordinary; but I could never believe that I was any different from the man who had counted cars just two years before, after a time in the dole queue. Just one cold wave could extinguish any flame of arrogance which might be kindled by the publicity.

Already I was beginning to feel the need to return to the sea, to think out the future for myself. Single-handed sailing seemed the best kind of challenge and Francis Chichester was already on his way to Australia. The one thing left untried was a single-handed voyage from Britain right round the world and back to Britain without calling at any port: The trip I had dreamed of in 1961. I now believed that an attempt was within my grasp; my good fortune seemed unreal.

The kind of spirit that would be required in such a venture shone clearly in Alec Rose, when I met him after a talk I gave at a yacht club. He asked me to the cocktail party he was giving in Portsmouth Town Hall, for all the people who had helped him in his attempt to follow Chichester in 1966. Standing on an empty beer crate in the middle of the ornate civic room, with a drink in one hand and tears in his eyes, this deceptively mild figure told the sad tale of his attempt. He had been hit right at the start by an escort boat which had damaged the self-steering gear; he was then run down in the Channel by a steamer; and finally, while undergoing repairs in Plymouth, *Lively Lady* had crashed from her stocks and cracked her side. Friends from all walks of life were gathered round him; I suppose few would have thought he could overcome the handicaps and start again the following year.

Throughout my own preparation, and the voyage itself, I used this example to help me with the inevitable difficulties I encountered.

The night after Alec Rose's party, Chay, Maureen, Marie Christine and I were guests of honour at a charity ball in London. There was an auction to raise money, and one of the items was a navy blue silk evening purse. When this item came up for sale, Dennis Miller, owner of *Firebrand*, one of the leading British ocean racing yachts, said he would take the buyer of the handbag with him on the Fastnet Race in August 1967.

'He thinks a girl will buy it,' I thought, 'but here is a chance to gain some experience on a really great boat.'

'Ten pounds,' I called.

'Fifteen,' came another voice.

The bidding went on, but I secured the handbag, which Marie Christine never used. It was a start. I would sail in as many ocean races as I could in the summer of 1967, compete in the Single-handed Trans-Atlantic Race in 1968, and attempt a non-stop circumnavigation in 1969. After that Rod Liddon and I planned to start a school of adventure at Ardmore. We decided that we would both try to join the Special Air Service Regiment for a three year tour of duty in the autumn of 1967. I just hoped the army would back me with the sailing, in the same way that the Royal Navy was backing Leslie Williams with his huge *Spirit of Cutty Sark* in the Single-handed Trans-Atlantic Race.

My confidence in this programme sprang from the realisation that while I knew I was in myself no more extraordinary than the man who counted cars in 1964, I believed that the other competitors would not be extraordinary either. Endless dinners, speeches and lectures had brought me into contact with many people whom I had long admired; I was shocked to find that some of them admired me. I came to believe that as long as my health held, I would stand a level chance with other people. It stands to reason that in the short spell allotted to a man on this earth, he cannot hope to become invincible; no one is.

Christmas came, and Marie Christine and I drove up to Ardmore. Somehow the paler colours of winter are more realistic than the brightness of summer. The local people, uncluttered by tourists, appear more real. Everyone is friendly, and there is time to stop and pass the time of day, a pleasant custom sadly not much practised in the rush of sophisticated modern living.

Marie Christine had joined a Christmas club at a Farnham grocery during the autumn. Now we had with us the fruits of all the weekly subscriptions, including the turkey, pudding, mince pies and cake. We asked Hughie over for dinner on Christmas evening; we planned to celebrate a pretty good year.

Looking from our window in the dark, down the loch towards the looming mass of Foinavon, there was not a light to be seen; it was a white Christmas and the wind of the day had fallen at dusk. Shadows danced on the white-panelled wooden walls of the tiny living-room as the peat fire burnt warmly in the hearth. The crack under the front door was sealed with old curtains, and the smell of the roasting turkey wafted in from the kitchen. The table was laid for three, and the candles and crackers were all set. Marie Christine was wearing a long red skirt and white blouse, with her long fair hair piled high on her head in my favourite style. After a hot bath, my dinner jacket felt good after the rough working clothes of the day.

There was a knock on the door and Hughie came in dressed to kill in his best suit; the snow had muffled his approach along the narrow path through the wood and past the low stone byre to the blue front door. He was smiling as he changed into the warm pair of slippers I keep for visitors. Soon he was sitting in the rocking-chair sipping a preliminary 'drop of the Crawfords', as they say in these parts.

The dinner started at eight and finished at two in the morning; we sometimes fell asleep between courses. The candles burnt low and we continued the everlasting discussion about how it might be possible to make a living at such a remote place. The more names we could recall of those who had failed, so the more of a challenge it presented; we had failed in 1964 but we had learnt from that failure. It must be something new; none of the established methods proved practical in this land of rock and heather. A School of Adventure was by far the most attractive idea, but the capital required seemed beyond our means; it would be a risk in any case, because if people failed to come, then the buildings in such a remote situation, would be worthless from a resale point of view.

Our one week of peace passed too soon, but we were glad to escape the serious celebrations of the Scottish New Year. Hughie assured us that he would be at the Boat Show in London, where *Rosie* was seen by 310,000 people, most of whom, it seemed, shook hands with Chay and me. But Hughie never came – the New Year festivities lasted for nearly a week and he took to his bed to recover. How different it must have seemed for *Rosie*, the focus of so much attention, compared with her inconspicuous debut as a varnished open dory at the same show the previous year. Then nobody showed any interest, and she was taken home to Bradford in disgrace, to await my purchase in the spring.

When Donald Campbell was killed at Coniston, it was clear to both Chay and me that a quest to continue trying to beat succeeding achievements would probably end in disaster. The challenge was clearly to live a long life, and to resist the temptation of excitement.

Towards the end of the show Dennis Miller came to see *Rosie*. He offered me a place on *Firebrand* for the coming ocean-racing season. I was delighted; as number seven or eight in the crew my main duty would be making the tea and cooking, but I would have an opportunity to learn fast.

After another visit to New York for a T.V. show, and a weekend in Montreal to discuss a possible film of the rowing, I returned to Farnham and went down with 'flu. I had not felt physically in good shape since we landed, but little condition was required to stagger from one appearance to another.

All four of us were asked to a reception for the Soviet Premier at Lancaster House. Chay and I wore special rosettes; as the guest of honour made his way down the centre aisle of the vast and lavishly decorated room, we were called forward and introduced to Mr. Kosygin. He beamed and gave us both a bear-hug embrace.

'If you and I could get in a rowing boat together perhaps we could come to an agreement,' said Mr. Wilson. This was translated into Russian by the expressionless interpreter. There was a pause and then a short smiling reply.

'If we didn't fall out,' said the interpreter. The party moved on – our moment of glory was 'only a memory'. I smiled to myself at the thought of challenging Mr. Wilson to a duel.

We returned to the plates of scampi and the friendly waiter we had met at other engagements in London. We were able to assure him that he would have a longer run than us at these places, but that we had enjoyed ourselves.

Although the public engagements continued, Chay and I became primarily involved with a six months' lecture tour of schools for the Army. Chay toured grammar and state secondary schools, and I spoke at the ten top officer-producing public schools in the various Commands. I found it a valuable if arduous experience; there were usually two and sometimes three lectures on each day of a five-day week. As I had hardly visited any schools since my Pangbourne days, I found it most interesting to compare my reception at these famous schools. Also I would try to run twenty laps on each athletic track, if I could do this while the boys were in class. Slowly I began to regain some semblance of physical fitness; running against the clock, it was encouraging to watch the steady improvement in my times. Of the schools which I visited, I was most impressed by Ampleforth.

At the end of February, the four of us attended a small cocktail party at Buckingham Palace. This was given by the Queen for about twenty people in pairs from different walks of life including politics, the Services, acting, education and rowing, and each guest brought one close relative. Although much younger than all the others present, we were not too nervous because the four of us were able to talk among ourselves, and this was a great comfort. Maureen and Marie Christine were dressed impeccably. We were led into a small room which seemed distinctly palatial; the walls were hung with a large number of what were probably priceless paintings. In a subdued fashion everyone made small talk. The Queen entered, and the various pairs of people, with their relatives, were brought forward in turn, while the remainder continued with the small talk.

We were about sixth on the list, and I noticed that each pair spent perhaps ten minutes in conversation with the Queen; clearly this was likely to be my only chance ever to speak in any coherent fashion with a reigning Monarch. I had better have something to say, and not simply stutter and stammer.

We were approached by an equerry and led across to the corner of the room in which the Queen stood. I was relieved to find myself taller than Her Majesty; somehow I had never imagined it this way. I had gone through a period of total worship for a beautiful young lady who always appeared on the screen at the end of a night at the cinema, inevitably dressed in uniform and sitting side-saddle on a horse while taking the salute at a big parade. During the National Anthem I would long for someone to move so I could attack them in Defence of the Queen, but I was always too shy to do any such thing. Now I was actually standing before the lady who seemed rather older, but no less beautiful, than the young lady who had appeared on all those screens. She was twisting an enormous diamond ring in her left hand, and she knew all about us.

'Would you do it again?' I was ready for the question.

'Only for you, Ma'am,' I smiled, feeling like Sir Walter Raleigh.

'Oh, I wouldn't ask you to do anything so foolish.' I smiled weakly but could not think of anything to say.

I can't remember any more of our conversation. Soon the party was over and we went home. No matter which way life led in the future, there could be no beating that first visit to Buckingham Palace.

One day at the end of March, during a week at Ardmore, 'Willy the Post' brought an invitation from Mrs. Mirabel Topham for the four of us to watch the Grand National from her own box at Aintree; first-class rail tickets were enclosed in the envelope. Since the failure of my 'system' in 1960, I had managed to avoid horse-racing altogether; Chay had never been to a race meeting. We wrote and said we would be delighted to come.

It was raining steadily when the train drew into Lime Street station in the Beatles' home town. Double-decker buses with destinations like Penny Lane, growled past us, spraying grey water as we tramped the pavements searching for a way to Aintree. At last we found a bus which set us down in the rain right opposite the main entrance to the course. We showed our tickets and soon found ourselves immersed, once again, in the world of the rich and famous as they milled around the main grandstand on National Day.

Mrs. Topham, a large and friendly lady who seemed to move in an aura of pink and lavender, made us welcome and entertained us to a fine luncheon.

During the meal the distinguished guests discussed prospects for the race, but it seemed that no one had any clear idea who might win. Most of the ladies liked the idea of a horse owned by Gregory Peck. I could foresee my usual racing loss approaching fast.

After lunch we made our way to the Tote to place our bets. The rain had stopped but the sky was grey and threatening. The ground was muddy, but the huge crowd seemed filled with excitement and enthusiasm.

'Chay, you put something on Foinavon,' said Maureen. We had talked of this mountain all the way across the Atlantic. Chay had named his house Foinavon. I had thrown too much money away on horses to back a hopeless outsider, the worst prospect in the whole field.

'You can, Chay, I'm not,' I said. Marie Christine backed a few more likely prospects. Chay looked unhappy as we left him standing in the queue to carry out Maureen's instructions.

The race had started by the time we met up in the stand, but we found a good place to watch the field come round for the first of the two circuits of the treacherous course. In a nearby box was the Duchess of Westminster. She owns the estate on which stand the mountains Foinavon and Arkle, after which the horses are named.

Foinavon was still running as the horses came past for the first time, but far behind and out of contact with the rest of the field. The Duchess smiled, having sold Foinavon for a fair price some time before the race. Chay said little, but there was a stony look in his eye. Maureen was careful to say nothing at all. Marie Christine and I were hopeful that our horses might come in, as they were well placed. We made our way indoors to watch progress on a television set.

Suddenly there was a roar from the crowd. The whole stand seemed to erupt as everyone stood up, people dashed around us trying to get to the television set. At the far end of the course, out of sight from the stand, there had been a bad fall; this was followed by a pile-up in which practically the whole field either fell or were dismounted.

Eventually, Foinavon arrived on the scene, and calmly moved through the chaos, cleared the jump and ran on alone. With barely a mile to run Foinavon seemed at least a quarter of a mile in the lead – the horse only had to stand up to win the Grand National.

Maureen and Chay seemed to be on fire as we ran back to the front of the box. Out of the murk lurched a very tired horse, still clearly in the lead. The loudspeaker system boomed out the situation – it was going to be a close-run thing. With only the last fence to clear one of the favourites was closing the gap fast. Foinavon brushed the top, staggered and then cantered steadily on; Honey End soared over and thundered after Foinavon. The gap narrowed down to yards and then feet, but the finishing post

Chay and I had to parachute into the sea off Jersey for B.B.C. TV News a year after the rowing. For amateurs we achieved a remarkably united splash-down.

(*Above*) At Buckingham
Palace, 1967;
(*left*) Rebecca Louise
Ridgway, christened at
St. Paul's Cathedral.

flashed by on the left of the struggling horses. Foinavon had won
– just.

When Chay reached the window reserved for tote first place
winnings there was only one man ahead of him in the queue, and
none behind. But there were long queues at the windows reserved
for place winnings. After a lengthy pause while the odds were
calculated, the shutters went up and paying out began. The man
ahead of Chay was trembling as he thrust his ticket across the
sill to the cashier. When he saw the pile of notes he collapsed.

Foinavon had won at 500–1. We have happy memories of
Aintree.

As spring turned to summer the ocean racing began. I discussed with Blondie Hasler my intention of entering the Single-
Handed Atlantic Race in the following year; as usual he was
encouraging. The lecture tour became more of a strain, as we
lost count of the talks we had given and the nights we had slept in
the back of our cars.

I felt nervous when, at Cowes, I presented myself aboard
Firebrand for preliminary sailing trials. She is a mighty boat
built with strength for speed; every detail is immensely powerful
and tuned to win. The crew of seven were dedicated, seemingly
impervious to cold and discomfort. I was an unnecessary extra
and I felt it. In the Solent we practised changing sails and ten-
sioning the backstays to achieve a perfect rake with the mast.
Gybing, tacking, running free, hoisting and dropping spinnakers,
all these manoeuvres were rehearsed as if life depended on it.
Dennis Miller, a powerful figure with jet-black hair, reddened
his face with abuse as he drove his crew. Split seconds were
pared from the times, but Dennis was not a man to be satisfied
unless he had won, and we were only racing against ourselves on
that Saturday afternoon.

Next morning we beat *Noryema* and *Quiver*, in a short practice
race from Cowes to the eastern end of the Solent and back, an
encouraging start. Crouched on the foredeck, I helped the genoa
go across before the mast when we tacked. Sometimes it went
over with a tremendous crash, and on one of these occasions,
unfelt by me, the snaking sheets snagged on the metal strap of my
precious Rolex watch, wrenching it off my wrist and overboard.
It was a sad loss of an old friend which had been on my wrist for
five years. I said nothing until we had tied up. On *Firebrand* no
one but Dennis complained of anything, and he complained of

L

everything until we won. Winning was really a form of relief. Although possessed of a sharp tongue, his outbursts were nearly always justified, and the anger short-lived.

I enjoyed myself and learnt much which was to come in useful in the future. Although my duties seldom exceeded tea-making and writing up the log, I was able to watch the crew at work and note how the smallest variations of rig sometimes produced startling results on the speedometer. They were a happy crew and we won several long weekend races. Comfort was never a consideration. I felt sick on every race, particularly when beating into the wind; the slamming was remarkable but the boat was never spared and showed no sign of the strain.

After six races, I realised that the time had come to sail on my own if I was to enter the Single-handed Trans-Atlantic Race in the following summer. I had seen the sinister black hull of Eric Tabarly's *Pen Duick*, which ran away with so many ocean races in 1967; it seemed presumptuous even to think of competing with this man, but life is short and I had to go ahead. At the end of June I met David Sanders of Westerly Marine who was keen to have a standard thirty-foot masthead sloop raced in the Trans-Atlantic Race. I took to sailing alone, on their demonstration model out of Gosport. Regretfully I wrote to Dennis Miller and asked if he would release me to concentrate on single-handed practice; he was very good about it and agreed that the crew should be able to make their own tea for the rest of the season. Tom Richardson was a twenty-three year old helmsman of *Firebrand*, and a qualified boatbuilder; he worked in the leafy boatyard owned by his father at Bursledon on the Hamble River. He came out on the *Westerly 30*, and offered to help me fit out the boat to be used for the race when she was built.

In early July Chay and I were involved in a different race; Maureen and Marie Christine were both expecting babies on the same day, the 8th July. Marie Christine won and Rebecca Louise was born on the 3rd July, much to the delight of the newspapers who knew her name before I did. Samantha Fiona Blyth arrived on the 19th July. All this must have had a effect on my lecturing, because after I gave a talk to a Preparatory school in Salisbury, one of the little boys said to the matron as he was getting into bed, 'Did you know that Captain Ridgway didn't go to the loo for ninety-two days?'

As soon as Marie Christine was all right I took a week's leave and sailed in the Solent with my brother Michael on the *Westerly 30*. Michael is in the Metropolitan Police and at the time, he was on sick leave with bronchitis; it seemed to me that some sun and sea air would be just the thing to cure him. He agreed to come, although he had never been on a yacht and had little regard for my navigation, knowing full well the trouble I had had at Pangbourne to pass the subject in G.C.E. at O level. We sailed together on four consecutive days of sunshine, timidly at first, with much use of the fifteen-horse Volvo-Penta engine and echo sounder. Even these aids could not prevent us from running on to a sandbank on the first evening near Fawley Oil Refinery. Fortunately, the rising tide soon lifted the bilge keel yacht from an embarrassing situation. On the second and third days Mike and I circumnavigated the Isle of Wight, gaining confidence in perfect weather. On the fourth day Mike had to return home and we managed only a short sail in the morning. He was sunburnt and looked fit again, but this might have been because he knew he was getting off the boat in a few hours' time.

'You're not really going to sail across the Atlantic alone this *next* summer are you?' he said, clearly still unimpressed by my navigation.

'Oh yes I am, only it will be a new boat and she won't have an engine.'

After a day at home in Farnham, with Marie Christine and Rebecca, Alec Larkman joined me at Gosport and the pair of us set sail for Cherbourg to repeat the voyage of the ill-fated *English Rose II* in 1961. During the night, we cut across the busy shipping lanes in the Channel dodging the speeding ships; a Force 4–5 easterly wind made conditions rather choppy. I was delighted to see the hero of the 1961 crossing discreetly being sick over the side, while I only felt a little rough myself. After a day and a night in the familiar harbour at Cherbourg, Alec grumpily agreed to return, having failed to buy any duty-free liquor because he was without the necessary green card. We made a fast passage home, on a broad reach with a south-westerly wind. The time had come to sail alone. My next voyage would be the 500 miles alone from Plymouth around Land's End to the Fastnet Rock on the stormy south-west corner of Ireland, and then back to Plymouth.

My week's leave over, I returned to the lecture circuit feeling refreshed; it was nearly at an end. After the summer leave in

August I was to take a six-month Special Air Service selection course at Hereford, along with Rod Liddon.

Soon after the Cherbourg trip, I returned to the Channel Isles with Chay, this time by parachute for the benefit of television news. I always worked on the principle that the fewer jumps I did the smaller my chance of getting hurt; this theory pandered to my endless fear of parachuting. After posing for a few fancy shots in our equipment and life-jackets, we climbed into the ancient Hastings aircraft and took off from R.A.F. Odiham. I fixed a determined smile on my face for the yawning telescopic lens on the T.V. camera, which always seemed to be focused on us.

A friendly R.A.F. parachute dispatcher, dressed in a pale blue jump suit, sat down beside me for the short flight across the Channel to Jersey, where he was going to dispatch me into the sea.

'Do you know they cleared one of these crates out the other week, and found half a ton of coal dust under the floorboards, from the Berlin Airlift back in '48. Shows how old they are,' grinned the dispatcher.

'Oh yes.' I clenched my teeth to keep smiling; air-sickness beginning to make itself felt. The T.V. cameramen were joking happily with the soldiers, zooming their lenses up and down the fuselage. Soon we neared the Dropping Zone. The dispatchers stood up and began to shout their orders above the roar of the slipstream, which boomed continuously once the doors were removed on the port and starboard sides of the aircraft.

'Stand up.'

'Hook up.'

'Check equipment.'

'Call off, for equipment check.'

'14 O.K., 13 O.K., 12 O.K. . . . 3 O.K., 2 O.K., Number 1 O.K., Starboard stick O.K.'

I was No. 1 starboard and Chay No. 1 port; we should leave the aircraft simultaneously from opposite doors. My helmet was jammed tight on my head by the chin-strap, and the main and reserve 'chutes strapped over my airborne life-jacket. Still I contrived to smile, although now even the cameramen looked serious.

'Action stations!' We all shuffle-stepped towards the doors near the tail of the plane. The aircraft made a drumming noise over the DZ, banking sharply at the end to turn and then turn again, for the final run in, we swayed awkwardly, hanging on to our parachute strops. All eyes were on the twin red and green lights on either door, waiting for the red light to come on. I glanced across the fuselage at Chay; he was grinning happily and gave me a mock, 'thumbs up'. I responded weakly. The telescopic lens zoomed at me from the after side of the doorway.

'Red light on, stand in the door.' The sticks shuffle-stepped the remaining paces forward. I let go of my strap and held on to the door-frame, the sea far below my feet. The dispatcher braced my right elbow. I smiled foolishly to myself – 'here we go'.

'Green light on, GO!'

I made what is known as a forceful exit and hurtled down the slipstream, gritting my teeth, holding my breath. My whole body was tensed as if I had cramp, waiting for the 'chute to open to stop the sickening falling sensation in the pit of my stomach.

The canopy developed with a snap, and suddenly I was swinging with my head forced hard down on my chest.

'Twists,' I cursed myself, a thousand feet above the sea. The rigging lines were twined up from a poor exit. I must free myself before reaching the water or I might be unable to get out of the harness. The wind could catch the canopy and drag me along or, worse, under the surface. I kicked out of the twists, frantically trying to keep calm. Once free I looked all round me to make sure I wouldn't get entangled with someone else in the air. Chay was a long way off. I could see the rescue boats on the blue water below, nearer now.

Judging the height above the sea is difficult. It is necessary to unfasten the harness and hang from the straps, in the last few feet of the descent, in order to get free from the 'chute when it starts to drag across the surface. A Marine did this a little too hastily on one occasion, and fell 200 feet to his death. I unfastened the reserve 'chute on one side, twisted the harness lock, hit it with the heel of my right hand, and freed my leg straps, holding the harness with my left hand all the while.

Suddenly I fell with a lurch, grabbing at the harness with my right hand. I hit the sea and let go of the harness.

'Ahoy! We'll pick you up.' A little cabin cruiser steamed up and I crawled over the side into the cockpit while one of the crew heaved my parachute aboard with a boat-hook. They handed me a cup of tea. I smiled confidently and we headed for the next man in the water.

Soon I rejoined Chay on the control ship and after a few more photographs, the news item was concluded. It was all a memory. We spent a pleasant weekend starting the first of the annual Sark to Jersey rowing races; all we had to do was present the prizes, make a speech and enjoy ourselves.

The last of the lectures was finished in the following week. I made my way down to Plymouth to stay at the Joint Services Mess where Alec Larkman was stationed, until the *Westerly 30* arrived by road from Portsmouth.

I sailed alone at ten in the evening of Friday, 28th July, bound for the Fastnet Rock and back to Plymouth, on the 500-mile qualifying sail for the Trans-Atlantic Race. In under a year I planned to leave the same breakwater, in company with the fleet of other sailing boats, bound for America. Now I was alone, and it was getting dark; on top of this I was unfamiliar with the self-steering gear which had been fitted only that day. The wind dropped almost calm and by six in the Saturday morning I had hardly reached Eddystone Light, barely a dozen miles from the harbour entrance. It was not an auspicious start. I had hardly slept at all.

After breakfast the wind picked up, bringing dark rain clouds scudding from the south-west. I held the boat as close to the wind as I could, and the familiar slamming started. Soon it was blowing Force 5–6 in gusty rain and I crawled along the deck, attached to my safety line, to shorten sail. Pitching and heaving out on the bow I lowered the No. 1 jib and lost the pin of the D shackle over the side. Cursing my carelessness, I returned to the cockpit for another, and then ran up the No. 3 jib.

I reefed three rolls on the boom and then let fall the one and only roller reefing handle. I almost cried with fury as it clattered noisily over the side. The next port was Falmouth, it was a Saturday and the shops would be shut by the time I started to inquire after another reefing handle. I just knew there wouldn't be one in Falmouth, and the manufacturers were bound to be closed: I felt so sea-sick that if I went into port I couldn't trust myself to start again, so I just kept going. If the wind got up any more I planned to lower the mainsail and run before it up Channel under a storm jib.

At six-thirty in the evening I rounded the Lizard and headed for Land's End. The wind dropped to Force 4. At six-thirty on Sunday morning I saw the ghostly beam of Wolf Rock light on the starboard side, as it shone through the white mist. Using my simple radio direction finder, I made my way north towards

Fastnet Rock; we were on a broad reach with the wind again Force 5-6 from the south-west; it was another day of sea-sickness.

I wrapped up warm with several pullovers inside my oilskins, and lay gazing up from my bunk at the grey sponge-backed material which covered the bulkheads in the cabin. Everything was wet – the demonstration boat was hardly fitted out for a single-handed cruise – but we were getting along at a good rate. All the following day we sped along and I began to think that Blondie Hasler's self-steering gear was the best invention since sliced bread. Gradually the miserable sea-sickness left me.

At one o'clock on the Tuesday morning, three whole days out from Plymouth, I saw the loom of Fastnet Rock Light. I then made a nonsense of the tidal stream problem, and spent the whole day tacking up to the lighthouse on its sinister rock in a gentle Force 3 wind from the west.

The sun shone warm on my back, and the wild Irish coast glowed green beyond the thin white line of surf. Romantic names like the Roaring Water River, Baltimore, Skull and Skiberean Light Railway and Badger Island covered the large-scale chart. It was glorious, and as I lay on the deck basking in the sun, it seemed the day of a lifetime. Everything seemed rosy. How I wished Marie Christine and Rebecca were with me to share the fun.

After we had rounded the Fastnet Rock at seven in the evening, the wind veered north-west and gradually blew up to Force 5-6 again. Goose-winged now, we romped towards Land's End once more. Running before the wind next day the sun continued to beat down on us; how different it was from the oilskin misery of the first few days. This voyage was quite hazardous from a navigational point of view, because the coast was never far distant, and I was always worried about the shipping. A battery of alarm clocks ensured that I never stayed below for longer than one hour, night or day.

Running along in the warm sun, it was easy to lie on the foredeck and think of the Atlantic race and the non-stop circumnavigation beyond. But I knew the cruel sea had not changed.

At three o'clock in the morning it was cold and dark. I longed for sleep but was worried by the proximity of Round Island. Alone in the night, close to a rocky shore with only one person's judgement to rely on, doubts are constantly crossing the lone

sailor's mind. We were being driven fast towards the Scilly
Isles and I could not afford to relax. Once more I longed for the
dawn, and the warmth of the sun on my back to help the sleep
from my eyes. My head nodded forward and I tried a hundred
squats in the cockpit to keep me awake, then a cold drink of
water, then press-ups, then a trip on to the bows to trim the sails
at the winches.

Slowly, very slowly, the sky brightened in the east to herald a
new day. The air was chill and everything covered with dew; now
for a cup of steaming hot black coffee to keep me awake. The
north-west wind should carry me clear between the Scillies and
Land's End, hard by the notorious Seven Stones Lightship
where the *Torrey Canyon* was wrecked. At last the sun came out
and I started my limited repertoire of songs to fend off the last
assault of fatigue.

I made a good square breakfast of more coffee, scrambled eggs,
toast and marmalade, then I had a wash and shave. We cruised
past an open launch from which two men were ripping for
mackerel just off the southern tip of Land's End, and then we hit
the tide just nicely, to push us up the Channel towards the Lizard.
There was not a cloud in the sky and the sea reflected its deep
blue. It was good to be alone at sea after the hectic months
following our landing on Aran. I followed the coastline for several
miles, and was surprised time and again by the beauty of little
coves and headlands.

It appeared likely that we would make Plymouth during the
early hours of Friday morning if the north-west wind held at
Force 4, I dozed in the sunlit cockpit all through the day; there
would be no sleep again in the coming night.

A number of men were making their 500-mile qualifying
voyages that summer; one unfortunate sailor was returning along
the South Cornish coast and went below for a sleep leaving his
boat on self-steering. Apparently his alarm clock failed to awake
him; the wind changed and the self-steering gear continued to
keep the yacht on the same course relative to the wind. As the
wind backed to the west, so the yacht turned towards north and
the cliffs. The poor man awoke too late – his proud new yacht
went on the rocks in almost calm conditions, but before it could
be floated clear a gale sprang up and the beautiful boat disinte-
grated before her owner's eyes. I must stay alert for just one more
night. The Horlicks curry tasted fine; I cooked it as if it were to

be my last meal, making the whole project last as long as possible to help to keep me awake.

The lights of Plymouth came into view not a moment too soon. At four-thirty on Friday morning we passed the breakwater. All was quiet; I thought I could understand something of how Drake must have felt when he returned to Plymouth.

It had been a valuable six days and a few hours alone at sea; I would take several reefing handles on the Atlantic Race!

After a good breakfast with Alec I left the Joint Services mess for Farnham. David Sanders, of Westerly Marine, was as pleased as I was about the trial, and he agreed to send a crew to collect the yacht from her berth in Plymouth Docks over the weekend. Plans were laid straightaway for the building of a new boat for the Atlantic Race in the summer of 1968.

From Farnham Marie Christine and I drove up to Ardmore with Rebecca. Rod and Jeannie Liddon arrived three days after us, and we settled into the blue croft for our three weeks' leave. Rod and I managed a fair bit of walking, to prepare ourselves for the rigours of the Special Air Service selection course to come, on our return south. Long days of fishing for sea-trout on Loch Hope, and walking along the high ridge of Foinavon overlooking the majesty of the North-West Highlands, came to an end far too soon. The Liddons left to finish their packing for the move to Hereford, and we were left with three days on our own.

Marie Christine agreed to come up to the little hut on the shores of Loch Dionard. It is six miles from the narrow coast road, and Robert Mcleod of Gualin Lodge had kindly reserved it for me, for a day.

We left the road at the southern tip of Loch Eriboll, which is a big sea loch running inland some ten miles from the north coast: It seemed that Rebecca might be the youngest visitor to Loch Dionard for many years. She was all of six weeks old, and lay in a long straw basket strapped across the top of my Bergen rucksack, quite oblivious of the bumps as we picked our way up a long unused footpath through Strath Beg. After four miles on the valley floor beside the burn, we started to climb through the purple heather, up 800 feet on to a long ridge studded with grey boulders. It looked as if they had been tossed from the palm of some ancient giant, but in fact they were left stranded by dwindling glaciers a long time ago. From the top of the ridge we could see the loch, a lead-grey strip, reflecting the dull sky above. Perhaps a mile long and a quarter mile wide, lying north-west to south-east, it feeds the sinuous Dionard River as it burbles glee-fully to the Kyle of Durness, a dozen miles to the north by way of a gentle bow out to the west. The southern side of the shallow loch is bounded by the north-west flank of the Foinavon massif, rising 2,500 feet sheer from the water's edge. Prehistoric corries cut deep into this haunt of deer and golden eagle.

We scrambled eagerly down the scree to the tiny wooden hut on the other side of the river, which we forded without difficulty as the water was low. The door creaked open and there, exactly as the year before, were the two timber bunks, the table and little gas cooker. It was as if we had only been away for the day – except for Rebecca that is. Tea was quickly made, and soon we were pushing the old wooden boat out into the rippling water. The party on the river would have gone home by now, and we were half a dozen miles from the nearest house; it was time for the evening rise. As I pulled at the grey oars, the breeze dropped away and the water turned to glass around us. This silver mirror dimpled as the sea-trout nudged the surface by the weed beds, and shattered where the salmon rolled to quieten the sea-lice still nagging at their fresh-run skins.

Rebecca, cuddled into her basket, was wedged safely on the floorboards; a contented smile played on her face as she sucked quietly at her thumb. Marie Christine stayed in the stern and I moved up to the bows. We took up the trusty split cane rods and flicked false casts through the air until the flies reached twenty feet from the boat. All was peace; the mountains towered high above and little waterfalls splashed gently in the dusk.

I dropped my team of three wet flies by the edge of the weed bed and let them sink, then slowly I drew in the line hand over hand watching the point where it broke the surface. It flickered and I struck instinctively. Ten feet of tempered split cane took up an urgent curve, black against the setting sun.

'I've got one too,' cried Marie Christine. Both fish skittered across the surface, exploding the silence.

'Try and keep them at opposite ends of the boat.'

Reels screeched, the boat rocked, Rebecca slept peacefully on. My fish ran deep, the line snagged the bottom of the boat and then fell slack. I reeled in, watching Marie Christine fight for our breakfast. Slowly she tired her catch. Quite soon he strayed over the waiting net, and I scooped him into the boat. He lay beside Rebecca's basket, a glittering bar of silver, nearly two pounds of fresh-run sea-trout.

'Time for cocoa.' I took up the oars and rowed us back to the little hut. Pleasantly tired we soon fell asleep on the wooden bunks.

Next morning, while breakfast fried, I came out of the hut for shaving water, and immediately crossed into bright sunlight. A pair of red deer hinds grazed peacefully at the water's edge, a few hundred yards downriver on the far bank. I looked up to where the line of cliffs, still in shadow, cut across the clear blue sky, and I saw a pair of golden eagles scribing lazy circles in the air. But the midges were out, there was no wind, and a cloud of these minute insects soon gathered round my head. I scooped up a saucepan of loch water and rushed back to the hut, slamming the door behind me.

After breakfast we daubed ourselves with midge repellent and hung a piece of muslin across the basket to keep them off Rebecca. We dashed for the boat and I pulled rapidly for the middle of the loch – the midges don't come far out over water.

The day passed, with frequent breaks for knobs of cheddar cheese dipped in Branston pickle, in a contented haze of casting and rowing. We caught only one fish, a sturdy three-pounder hooked on a teal blue and silver deep in the middle of a bay; but it wasn't a day when catching fish was really necessary.

Next morning we walked happily back to the car, and I thought of all the walking to come in the weeks ahead. I wondered if the thirty miles Rod and I had done through the mountains would prove sufficient training.

Four weeks later, and rather thinner, with the most arduous part of the selection passed, I drove from Hereford to collect Marie Christine from Farnham. We met Maureen and Chay at London Airport and flew Aer Lingus to Shannon. We were to be guests of honour at the annual Galway Oyster Festival. It was a wild weekend at the end of September, and we stayed once again in the unaccustomed splendour of the Great Southern Hotel.

On the Saturday morning we were at the pageant when the Oyster Queen disembarked from her ancient hooker boat to present the Mayor of Galway with the traditional platter of oysters. From here the festivities really got under way and the irresistible Irish revelry took over; under the marquee at Paddy

Burke's it seemed all Ireland was gulping oysters and Guinness. In the evening a great ball in Galway made it a night to remember.

We awoke with splitting heads next morning to find a gale roaring down Galway Bay from the Atlantic. The *Naomh Veanna* could not sail for Aran. The planned Irish coffee reception aboard the steamer was cancelled, and it seemed that we might not be able to return to the Aran Isles after all.

However, after numerous phone calls and a mad drive along the wild coast road towards Connemara, we found ourselves bucking a heavy sea, aboard a small fishing boat.

Once out of Cashla Bay the swell grew longer and conditions in the tiny wheelhouse became unpleasant. The smell of fish and engine oil soon transfigured the four intrepid merry-makers – our rosy complexions drained through white to pale green. Chay retold the tale of the parachutist who pretended to be sick in his brown-paper bag, then swilled it round and made as if to drink the foul contents, and of the dire consequences among the other parachutists aboard the plane. Maureen rushed out on deck, luckily to the leeward side. Marie Christine and I made some forced conversation about the proximity of the Kilronan breakwater, and grimaced at Chay.

We landed at three-thirty in the afternoon. The tourists were long gone from the islands; only the people of Aran remained to face the winter gales. It was better that way. We walked the couple of hundred yards along by the harbour wall to where the narrow road curves to the left and towards the island. Here the backlash of the dying gale broke weakly on a little beach of yellow sand. Just above the high-water mark on the verge of the road stood a granite monument some twelve feet high, its upper half draped with a white sheet.

A small crowd gathered as Father McNamarra held a simple ceremony in Irish and then in English. Chay and I pulled a piece of white string and the sheet fell away. A fine plaque of Connemara marble, embedded in the granite, bore the details of our voyage and a short line of Irish, which translated means, 'May God not weaken them.' The same line is on a bronze plaque on the rock just off the beach at Nauset Inlet, Cape Cod, many miles away.

I looked at the friendly faces and felt warm.

We had a celebration lunch at the school house and were hustled back aboard the trawler for the return voyage to the mainland. It was just a memory.

10

Golden Globe

IT was teatime on a snowy Saturday afternoon in early January 1968. We were sharing a flat with the Liddons, on the ground floor of a big house on Quarry Hill in Hereford. The Special Air Service Regiment's selection course was nearly finished. We had spent a happy Christmas at Ardmore, and in just under three weeks' time Rod and I were due to fly to South-East Asia for a month in the jungle.

The future appeared settled. I expected the Single-Handed Trans-Atlantic Race to involve about six weeks of 1968. I would then attempt a non-stop solo circumnavigation of the world between July 1969 and July 1970. Rod and I planned to leave the army in 1970-1 when our S.A.S. tour came to an end; both families would then move to Scotland and build a School of Adventure at Ardmore.

'I see here that Commander Bill King, a retired submarine captain, is to attempt a non-stop solo circumnavigation this summer, sponsored by the *Daily Express* – it's just been announced at the Boat Show,' Rob read from the newspaper. The cup of tea stopped half-way up to my mouth. The future was no longer settled.

'Let's have a look.' It was right enough, the details were there, high capital outlay and revolutionary boat.

'I bet he's regretting they made this announcement,' I said.
'Now it will be a race; a whole gang of people will come forward –
including me.' My mind went back to *The People* article in
February 1966 which outlined the *Puffin* plan for rowing the
Atlantic.

'What do you think, Johnny?' asked Marie Christine.

'It seems cut and dried. It's such an expensive venture that it
will require sponsorship. Sponsors will come forward only for
the people who can show they stand a chance of being the "first"
person to sail the thirty thousand miles non-stop. The public is
tiring of sailing epics; sponsorship won't be easy. Sadly it's 1968
or never.' I was thinking aloud.

'What about the S.A.S., they won't like it?' said Jeannie
Liddon.

'No, I don't suppose they will, we'll just have to see.' I pictured
a painful interview with Lieutenant-Colonel John Slim.

The rest of Saturday was spent with pencil and paper on the
inevitable 'Military Appreciation of the Situation'. The conclusion was 'now or never'. I had three weeks before we flew to
the jungle; plans must be laid for me to sail in a *Westerly 30* in
five months' time on 1st June, the starting date of the Single-
Handed Atlantic Race. The Atlantic Race would provide a useful
cover – it would allow the preparations to be carried out in peace
and quiet.

Next day Rod and I drove down to the Westerly factory at
Waterlooville, near Portsmouth. A photographer did some
pictures for the *Daily Express*, of the yacht which was being built
for the Atlantic Race. On the way home, we called on David
Sanders at his house in Winchester. He liked the idea of the
circumnavigation – it would help the Westerly export drive if a
production boat could complete the 30,000 miles non-stop. He
was prepared to put up the boat, if the Yachting Panel at the
Boat Show agreed that she could, theoretically, take the strain of
such a voyage.

Three days later I visited the Boat Show and made some dis-
creet inquiries of the panel of experts; in principle the *Westerly
30* should be able to weather any conditions. I walked across the
floor of the exhibition to the Westerly Stand.

'They say the boat could go anywhere.'

'All right we're on,' David replied.

'We'll use the same hull with the same list of modifications I made after the five hundred-mile trip last summer. Can you launch her by the end of the first week in March?'

'Yes.'

'O.K. I'm going abroad for a month. Tom Richardson has agreed to fit the boat out at the Elephant Boatyard on the Hamble, I'll see you at the end of February.'

At Hereford, Lieutenant-Colonel Slim agreed to arrange a year's unpaid leave, and release me from duty on 24th February when I returned from the Far East.

Tom Richardson came to dinner with his wife Rachel, he was the ideal person for the fitting-out, a young man equipped with modern ideas and an open mind. At all costs I must avoid the snags encountered by Chichester – too many cooks all disagreeing and delaying.

English Rose IV would be nearly as simply equipped as had been *English Rose III*. No holes in the hull, which would be built in one strong piece; this meant no engine, no loo and sink water pumped over the side. There would be heavy teak drop boards, rather than a cabin door, and strong portholes in place of the usual windows along the cabin sides. To avoid charger motors, liquid batteries, the bulk of the expensive Marconi Kestrel wireless set and the attendant problems of fuel stowage, I planned to use the hand-operated Clifford and Snell Lifeline set we had used on the rowing trip.

Archie de Jong, of Horlicks, agreed to plan and deliver to *English Rose IV* 400 days' rations, packed in Arctic sledging boxes, and weighing a total of 1,100 pounds. Michael Sissons, of A. D. Peters and Co., my new literary agents, set about preparing contracts with *The People* newspaper, whom I had found good to work with after the rowing trip, Independent Television News and Hodder and Stoughton the publishers. Hugh Belayse-Smith, having left the sea, was studying to become a civil aviation pilot at the London School of Flying. Unselfish as ever, he started on the navigation problems.

As the giant V.C. 10 lifted off from the frosty airfield on the night of 22nd January, 1968, I nestled back into my seat; at least there was a good team working on the venture.

Next day Rod and I were in the jungle. For a month, with small groups, we plodded in the semi-darkness beneath the jungle canopy, carrying our food on our backs; I grew thinner and thinner. The tea trolley of Quarry Hill was far away. The only good place was in my hammock, made from parachute silk, which I slung between four trees every night. Every morning before dawn, there was the misery of changing into stinking wet marching clothes in the dark, stowing dry gear and hammock into a rucksack, and then marching off for an hour before a brief halt for breakfast. It was all part of the 'hard routine'.

Gradually the past receded, and life became bearable again, as our bodies grew used to a simple way of life. Picking bloated leeches from my skin – carefully to avoid them bursting, and so splashing myself with my own blood; nursing the curry over the tommy cooker; scratching the filthy beard on my unwashed face; tramping endless miles through trackless primary, and worse secondary jungle, in four-man patrols; scratched and bleeding from the grasp of sticky, thorny plants and bushes. . . . No cutting was ever allowed in the dense undergrowth, as we eased, pushed and pulled our way along, moving on a compass bearing.

At nights we shivered fearfully as the trees, some 200 feet high, occasionally crashed to the ground out in the eery darkness. A few months earlier, one of the men had been crushed when one night one of these giants, after standing for perhaps a thousand years, tumbled over on to the jungle floor. The soldier died slowly, trapped underneath it.

Sometimes we followed tracks left by elephants; sometimes we walked along the numerous small rivers and on the sandy bars saw the huge paw marks left by tigers. More often we would move across the grain of the country, up and down, across the steep-sided valleys; gasping for breath as the sweat formed rivulets on our bodies.

One day of rare blessed relief, when we were lying-up just below the crest of a mountain ridge, I lay in my hammock and watched a million ants pick their way along a network of branches. Beyond this tracery, formed by the upper branches of the small trees along the ridge-top, the cruel sun boiled the humid air above the blinding green of the jungle, spread out below as far as the eye could see. Monkeys screamed and chattered, and a squat heavy-shouldered deer-like animal crashed through the undergrowth, unaware of our presence. When eventually it did see me, it stopped and we stared at each other, then it bolted down the slope. I must have looked and smelt gruesome. I lay back and smiled, life was so simple; eating, sleeping, marching, these basics replaced the cluttered problems of civilisation. In my hand

(*Left*) Chay and I unveil a plaque at Kilronan in the Aran Islands, 1967; (*right*) training to sail alone around the world non-stop, I ran up Trig Hill on seventy-one consecutive days; (*below*) dressed to round the Horn, padded hat and all, before leaving the Hamble River for the Aran Islands and the start.

The Single-Handed
Round the World
Non-Stop Race, 1968
Rebecca and
Marie Christine come
say goodbye.

lay a slim volume, not of Keats, but of Mary Blewitt's *Celestial Navigation for Yachtsmen*, thoughtfully waterproofed by the publisher. I read it four times through during the month.

Life and death are stark and simple in the jungle. A helicopter crashed into a stream-bed – we had to carry a putrefying corpse strung along a bamboo pole, out to the road. A soldier disappeared on a river crossing; Rod and I saw the blackened body bob up to the surface from a deep pool next day, when the expanding gases gave it the necessary buoyancy.

I looked at the sky and the trees and stamped the ground. I thought of the *Puffin* and how life raced by. It was time to fly home and prepare to sail.

From my seat in the V.C. 10 on my way back to London, more than five miles above the Indian Ocean, I could see the blue sea far below; it looked hot and calm. Perhaps it would stay that way for a year, perhaps it wouldn't.

We refuelled at Gan Island, and there I said goodbye to Rod. He was going on to the Middle East for a period in the desert, and then high altitude free-fall parachuting in France. After a quick snack, we took off from that lonely atoll, and flew on across the sea through brilliant sunshine and cloudless sky. Suddenly, in a stark line, the blue water turned to pale yellow sand, as we crossed the coast of the Arabian peninsula and the high peaks of Oman. Far away near the horizon I could see the blue margin of the Persian Gulf. I thought of Bahrein.

We had to follow the 'corridor' for R.A.F. aircraft, and quite soon we were above the desolate snow-capped mountains of Turkey; on the Russian border I saw Mount Ararat where Noah rested with the Ark. From an astronaut's point of view there seemed to be no reason why the blue shouldn't have covered the brown down below. Time was hurrying by; from the Ark to the V.C. 10 was, I suppose, a comparatively short time. We refuelled again at Cyprus, and soon touched down in England.

As soon as I had handed in all my equipment at Hereford, I turned the blue M.G.B.-G.T. for Farnham, to deliver my usual priceless gifts to Marie Christine. Next day Tom and Rachel came to dinner at the old terraced cottage, and we got down to the details of planning once again. Everything was proceeding to schedule, which seemed miraculous.

I had a physical training programme, arranged to ensure that my fitness would not suffer if snags should occur in the final stages

M

of preparation; I wanted no recurrence of the Boston hospital period. Besides my usual daily exercises, I ran three miles across the tank tracks of the log race-course in Aldershot for the next seventy-one consecutive days.

Archie de Jong, at the Horlicks factory in Slough, assured me that the rations would be delivered by 14th May. He also told me that he would be visiting Fortnum and Mason's in London, to select special treats for high days and holidays during my year at sea.

Hugh Belayse-Smith had bought eight pilot books and eighty charts; the navigation was now reduced to a simple exercise of revision and stowage.

When our small team visited the *English Rose IV* at the Westerly factory in Waterlooville, we found her gleaming white in a long shed with twenty or so other yachts. They were all undergoing the finishing touches before dispatch to ports all over the world. It seemed odd that a young Army officer should be able to help with the export drive. Wally, the works' foreman, was well pleased with the progress on *Rosie*, and forecast her launching within the week. Tom Richardson nodded satisfaction, the long list of modifications was complete. *English Rose IV* looked as strong as a battleship; the simplicity of her design and the lack of sophisticated fitments was precisely what we required.

David Sanders, the managing director of Westerly, had agreed to start a subscription list to ensure that the £4,250 basic cost of the boat was paid for by the time I sailed from Aran on 1st June. Makers of glass fibre, resin, sails, fittings, masts, paint, rope and all the many other items which go into the building of a yacht, would be asked to subscribe towards the cost of this particular boat. In return for this the manufacturers would be given unconditional rights to free advertisement should the voyage prove successful.

I agreed to pay for the fitting-out at the Elephant Boatyard, and I expected this to cost something under £4,000. I hoped Michael Sissons would be able to raise £4,000 in advance, from newspapers, T.V. and publishing contracts.

My aim, financially, was simple. I required to sail in a yacht which I owned and which was fully paid for; the basic £4,250 by manufacturers, and a further £4,000 worth of fittings and equipment by me. I was not willing to embark on a voyage, untried by anyone before, with the added mental strain of financial worry. If the worst came to the worst, then there must be no question of Marie Christine's having to face creditors. After prestige gained by the rowing venture, this arrangement appeared feasible. Should it prove impossible I determined not to sail.

The idea of sponsorship is alien to the British ideal of sport and amateurism. Quite clearly the British public is interested to read of endurance, and the establishment of new records by Britons. If they were not interested in this form of innocuous entertainment, then sponsorship would not be forthcoming; the British would then disappear from this field of progress.

Shortly after *English Rose IV* was launched, with the Atlantic Race number 28 painted black on her white sides, *The Sunday Times* newspaper announced its Golden Globe Race. Hearing that various people were preparing for an attempt to make the first single-handed non-stop circumnavigation of the world, they offered a Golden Globe for the first boat home, and £5,000 for the fastest voyage completed before the autumn of 1969. This seemed a clever, and inexpensive, policy to corner the field of ten yachts, many of whom would be contracted to other newspapers. They would have a weekly story for at least fifteen months and could well repeat the triumph of the Chichester story.

One wise business magnate whom I visited explained the economics of the venture plainly, when he said, 'If you really wish to undertake this voyage, then like any other young man you will require financial backing. This can be arranged, but you should realise that is simply business. Any firm putting money into the venture must gain publicity in return, to justify the expenditure to its shareholders. This publicity can be achieved in two ways, firstly, if you succeed; and secondly, if you fail gloriously. In the second case it would be preferable if you died – slowly and over the radio.'

I visited a senior army psychiatrist with a view to offering my services as a guinea pig to the American space programme. A year on my own might yield some interesting personality changes, if I were to undertake a series of mental tests at various stages during my isolation.

In the remains of a vast Victorian hospital near Southampton, I completed numerous tests to determine a variety of things concerning my personality.

After lunch the psychiatrist showed me round the hospital graveyard. The spring sunshine touched brightly on the daffodils and fresh green grass, and in the distance a man was mowing the narrow verges. The graves were laid out with military precision in long neat lines. Train-loads of wounded men had arrived at this hospital from the trenches of the First World War; many of them had ended their journey in this cemetery. Each headstone proclaimed number, rank, name, age, regiment and date of death; the whole cemetery was planned in chronological order.

As we walked along the neat gravel paths, I wondered what the psychiatrist was thinking, and if this was just another test.

Later we visited the mental wards and then I completed more tests. As I drove away, the psychiatrist promised to let me have the results, and any progress he made with the N.A.S.A. people in America. But he never did. Ever since then I have looked in the mirror at least twice a day.

Towards the end of March, Marie Christine, Rebecca and I drove to Ardmore. In peace and quiet we compiled detailed lists of one man's every requirement for 400 days. Also we planted a small rhododendron bush just outside the little blue house, carefully encircling it with wire netting to deter the hungry sheep. I photographed the Ross family by their front door; the picture was destined for the bulkhead over the chart table in *Rosie*.

When the time came to return south, I cast many a lingering glance over the little wood along the loch and beyond to the timeless bulk of Foinavon and Arkle. I felt the words of a song Chay used to sing during the rowing:

> *There's peace worth more than gold,*
> *At my haven under the hill.*

At Bursledon, on the Hamble River, *Rosie* was now in a mud berth alongside a floating catwalk. Boat-owners, busy with their spring overhauls for the coming season, often asked inquiringly after the fine new yacht in the Atlantic Race, the race No. 28 on her sides stopped any further thoughts about her future.

Tom and Rachel live in a converted old fishing boat, the *Morwenna*, also in a mud berth but on the other side of the catwalk from *Rosie*. By day Tom worked in the yard and by night he worked aboard *Rosie*. With ever-increasing frequency I visited the yard, and Tom patiently listened to endless 'points' I had to make. We discussed problems late into the night; steadily Tom's fine workmanship produced more strength and greater simplicity.

My principle problem was to ensure that delivery dates were

met by the many companies who were providing equipment for the voyage. While I found it easier to persuade firms to donate materials with the rowing behind me, the sailing required a far greater range of equipment and a delay on any one item could hazard the entire venture.

Camping Gaz, the agents for the Bleuet Gaz we had used on the rowing trip, were enormously helpful. They supplied all my clothing requirements, from their Pindisports firm, in addition to the heating and lighting provided by the small Gaz cartridges.

At a talk I gave after dinner, to the Anchorites at the Café Royal in London, I met Captain First Rank Beledev, the Russian Naval Attaché. We had had a long talk at the Boat Show, in January of the previous year, but I had not seen him since. His predecessor had returned to Moscow during the Profumo Affair, but Captain Beledev, with his thin face and rimless glasses, always presented a sober, rather severe outlook. He seemed interested by the talk I had given, and promised to send a bottle of vodka for me to drink during the Atlantic Race, if I sent him a copy of *A Fighting Chance*.

On my return home, I dispatched the book duly signed, but no letter of acknowledgement ever arrived, still less the bottle of vodka, which I had thought of drinking after rounding Cape Horn. I wondered what the psychiatrist and Captain Beledev had in common.

By the end of April Michael Sissons had settled two major contracts with *The People* newspaper, and the publishers Hodder and Stoughton. I.T.N. and Wilkinson's razor blades had also come in. I should be able to meet my £4,000 bill for the fitting-out costs. David Sanders of Westerly assured me that the subscription list for the basic £4,250 cost of the yacht was coming along well. The deliveries were to schedule and there were no major problems with the preparations. It seemed all too good to be true.

One day the phone rang, just before lunch, in the little Farnham house. I leant over from the small green armchair where, in the tiny sitting-room, I was going through the 'lists'. I picked up the receiver expecting to hear a delivery problem, but the voice was a cool American drawl.

'I work in London for John Houston, the film director. You flew with him from Shannon to London, after your rowing trip in 1966. He often talks of you, and he would like for you and Chay to be in a film of his this summer. Could you do it?'

In an instant I knew the ecstasy Marilyn Monroe felt at her first film part.

'Er . . . what kind of part would it be?' I replied, trying to sound nonchalant.

'You would be knights in a film he is making about the middle ages in Vienna.'

'I am rather tied up this summer on a sailing voyage.'

'Well, John will call you next week when he comes to London.' He rang off. I saw myself spread across the silver screen, 'Walter Mitty comes to Town'. But John Houston never rang, and I wondered what *he* had in common with the psychiatrist and the Russian Naval Attaché.

On 5th May, Marie Christine and I went to dinner at Chay's and Maureen's house, Foinavon, in Waterlooville. We were on our way back to Farnham from a busy day at the Elephant Boat Yard. By this time we knew of several entrants for the round-the-world race, Bill King in *Galway Blazer*, Robin Knox-Johnson in *Suhaili*, Nigel Tetley in *Victress*, the Frenchmen Moitessier and Fougeron. Tom and I planned to sail *Rosie* to Galway on 18th May, and then I should leave Aran alone on 1st June. Only Robin Knox-Johnson had declared an intention to start in June. The remainder were expecting to sail in August, September and October; they were relying on much larger boats and greater speed to overhaul Knox-Johnson and me on the way round the 30,000-mile course.

We were half-way through the inevitable prawn cocktail of our rowing dreams when Chay put down his teaspoon and said, 'Well, it's time to put all the cards on the table – I'm going to join the race!' The eating stopped. Nobody said a word. Marie Christine and I just looked at each other, stunned. Maureen and Chay looked anxiously at us both.

Tom Richardson had told us he had seen Chay, looking very workmanlike, aboard a red yacht moored in mid-stream a few hundred yards down the Hamble River from the Elephant Boat Yard. I had seen quite a lot of Chay myself, until Christmas, but since returning from the jungle I had been preoccupied with planning the voyage; only at the back of my mind did I have an idea that he might enter the Atlantic Race.

'Why didn't you tell me, Chay? I've been quite open with you, in fact I have told you all my arrangements, and now I find you are a competitor.'

I felt as if I had been hit with a hammer. In my life I had come to believe that a few people would never let me down; Chay was among them. The rest of the world owed me nothing, and I freely accepted this, but with these few I felt a certain bond of affection. I suppose I was more annoyed at my own inefficiency than hurt; I had been so involved that I hadn't foreseen the possibility, and kept more in touch with Chay.

'There were two reasons why I couldn't tell you until now,' said Chay. 'First, the company making the yacht is a rival of Westerly and they asked me not to say anything. Secondly, I knew you would try to stop me, because of my inexperience; you would feel responsible for Maureen and I believe you might have persuaded me not to go. Now I am committed and so I can tell you. I am to sail from Portsmouth on 1st June.'

Although I could follow his reasoning I felt betrayed. It was many weeks before I could realise that he was right; it would have simply created another worry for me, and Chay was perfectly entitled to make his own decisions.

Human relationships are always complex, if they have any depth. It is interesting to see the individuality of human beings even after ninety-two days of near total reliance upon each other, time moves on and situations change.

Fortunately the competition didn't worry me; I couldn't grasp the idea of a race lasting a year. The ocean is no race-track; the struggle is between the man and the sea. In this case, it was rather like putting a number of dice into a cup, shaking them, and spilling them on to a table. Someone would come up with a six. Whatever happened no one, not even a computer, could guess the right permutation of the nine boats. A race might develop in the last few thousand miles back up the Atlantic, and if it was between Chay and me, then it would be great fun. But in reality, there would be only the sea and me, and that was the best way.

With under a fortnight left before Tom and I were to sail to Galway from the Hamble River, life became hectic. I still managed to run every day and felt relaxed and confident; everything moved according to plan. It was difficult to believe that I should be having such luck compared with the difficulties experienced by Chichester and Rose.

The Sunday Times carried a story each week, as entrants flocked to join the race; no rules had been published. I hadn't made a formal entry: *The People* kindly agreed not to print the preparation story until the Sunday after Tom and I left for Galway. This enabled work to proceed in peace and quiet down at the Elephant Boat Yard. Chay was still keeping quiet, but it seemed that Knox-Johnson really would leave some time in June. There would be three small thirty-foot yachts at least two months ahead of the six big ones, all spread out over millions of square miles of ocean. Truly it would be the gigantic event I had dreamt of in 1962. The penniless subaltern now felt like Cinderella at the ball.

At last Saturday, 18th May, arrived, grey and forbidding. I kissed Rebecca goodbye, as Marie Christine took her into our kind next-door neighbours, Cis and Syd Towns. We then drove down to Bursledon in the blue M.G. The Richardson family gave us a fine lunch, and a little pennant with a white elephant on a blue background to fly on the top of the self-steering gear.

At five in the afternoon, Tom and I stepped aboard the trim little yacht; she was gleaming white and teak, everything was new. The trials were almost over; now she had to leave the host of little yachts and sail the 500 miles to the start line. *Rosie* seemed tensed and ready to spring, as she lay deep in the water. She was carrying sixteen sails, 1,200 pounds of water, 1,200 pounds of food, and all the other requirements for a 400-day passage.

It was a dull day; the fresh green leaves of summer, although there on the trees, were not much in evidence. Rain threatened, and the wind blew fresh from the east, Chay shook hands and gave me the St. Christopher medallion he had kept from the other *Rosie*. He smiled and his blue eyes laughed. 'I'll be thinking of you.' *The People*'s cameras flashed; only half a dozen people knew what was happening.

'See you,' I grinned.

Marie Christine and Rachel were aboard John Horsburgh's sturdy little yacht *Cruineag* as she towed us down to the mouth of the Hamble. Ian and Jane Pelling waved goodbye from the catwalk and then drove down to the road's end on Southampton Water. As we weaved our way between the lines of craft moored to the trots all the way down the river, I thought of the last time I had come down the Hamble River in 1962, aboard *English Rose II*. I caught a glimpse of old Charlie Middlin leaning on his stick by the hard; if anything did go wrong, it would not be the fault of his hours of work on the boat. His battered old seamanship manual had pride of place in the rack of nautical books.

At six in the evening we slipped the tow rope, and hoisted the full main and genoa. Tears came to my eyes as I waved goodbye to Marie Christine aboard the *Cruineag* as she turned for home, even though I knew I'd see Rachel and Marie Christine in Galway, for they were driving over in the M.G. during the following week. I knew how Marie Christine would feel, driving back to the empty house in Farnham, after all the rush of the last few weeks. Without her organisation, the trip wouldn't have been made.

A fresh wind swept us down the Solent, and we were helped by the tide. Soon it grew dark and I began to feel sick, but Tom cooked us a big supper, and my spirits recovered. It was cold on the open sea, and only one person could sit or lie on the bunk; the cabin was full of gear. We did two hours on, in the cockpit, and two hours off, in the cabin, alternately through the night.

Next morning, after a hot breakfast, we rigged the trade-wind booms, and ran fast down Channel, under twin No. 1 jibs. In the first twenty-four hours we logged more than 100 miles despite failing wind in the afternoon. Tom was well satisfied with *Rosie*; I was delighted.

After four days of light airs, we had rounded Land's End, crossed the Bristol Channel, and were abeam of the Fastnet Light. The wind climbed steadily all day from the south-east through Force 8 to severe gale Force 9, just as the forecast had said. The sea roared angrily, snatching at the rigging. I felt distinctly queasy, but Tom was luckily unaffected by the awkward motion as we jilled along across the wind. Conditions were cramped – there was ample space for one but not for two. Foolishly, in the rush we had not brought enough food for the trip; we found ourselves growing hungry, while at the same time being surrounded by food we dared not open. I was glad the gale was pushing us out to sea, instead of threatening us with the gruesome west coast of Ireland which we had so dreaded on the rowing.

Two days later at six-thirty in the morning and six days out from Bursledon, the Earagh Light at the western tip of the Aran Isles was abeam to starboard. I could see the narrow channel through which the other *Rosie* had passed, nearly two years before. We were not going to risk trying that with the yacht, at this stage.

The day turned fine and cloudless, with a light westerly breeze. We ran slowly under sun and blue skies towards Galway, the

islands to starboard and the Irish mainland to port. A small
fishing boat, crossing from Aran to the mainland, stopped to give
us a huge lobster which we later boiled up in the cockpit for
lunch; the crew seemed pleased to see us.

At Galway, Joe Herberts, our companion at the Oyster
Festival, had arranged our accommodation at the Ardilaun
Hotel. The incredible Irish hospitality started all over again.
What a place to begin or end a voyage. The Irish are kindness
itself.

After four days of final preparation, including coats of anti-
fouling paint on the bottom and changing all the drinking water.
Rachel, Tom, Marie Christine and I sailed down Galway Bay
under the grim cliffs of Black Head, to Aran for two days of
peace before I sailed.

A letter had arrived from David Sanders, enclosing the bill o
sale for *English Rose IV*. I owned the yacht. All my bills were paid,
so there was no need to worry about the money side. We were all
vastly relieved.

In Aran we stayed with the Conneeley family once more, Colin
Thomson arrived to see me off. The Aran Islanders were
delighted I should start from Kilronan; everywhere we went we
were greeted with Irish smiles.

Two nights before I sailed we visited a tiny bar at the back of a
little old house near the harbour. It was full, so Marie Christine
and I sat on a wooden bench under a narrow window. Suddenly
the crowd parted; there stood a great ginger-haired islander, with
a tumbler-full of whiskey in his stubby right fist.

'Here,' says he. 'Good luck to you.' A hush fell and I recalled
that great western film, *Gun fight at O.K. Corral*. Everyone
looked on. Slowly I got to my feet.

'Cheers.' I knocked it back in one long gulp like water. A cheer
went up, and night fell like a black velvet curtain.

Next day the press and T.V. arrived in strength; Michael
Sissons enjoyed himself and kept them all happy at the same time.
Marie Christine and I walked to the cliffs of Dun Aengus. As we
looked down at the endless surge, 600 feet below, from the stone
walls of the prehistoric fort, one year apart didn't seem very long.

On our return, Father McNamara blessed *Rosie* and gave me a
small bottle of holy water. That night the islanders gave a farewell ceilidh in the Kilronan village hall and Father McNamara
presented me with a fine hand-knitted Aran jersey and a local

tam-o'-shanter to keep my ears warm. Whenever Marie Christine and I danced, the T.V. cameras danced too; the islanders must have thought it as odd as we did. Around midnight we all drove back to the Conneeleys at Kilmurvy and tucked into a great feast of fried mackerel which had only just arrived at the house.

It was late when we went to bed, and I couldn't help thinking of that first night ashore from the rowing, under the same roof. Now I was off again and my next night ashore, in a year's time, should be again under the same roof.

The Saturday morning of my departure dawned fine and dry, with a gentle breeze from the west. The warm sun made it all seem so easy – just get in the boat and sail away. Over breakfast a number of telegrams arrived, among them one from Chay. 'Last one home's a cissy. Who cares who wins.' The last sentence is a modification of the S.A.S. motto, 'Who dares wins.'

We arrived down at the little harbour just as the steamer arrived, bearing the Mayor of Galway and many other friends who had kindly come all the way to the far side of Eire to see me off. Somehow, there was an air of magic in the sunlight, on that Saturday morning.

At eleven a.m. there was a final press conference, and then I kissed Marie Christine goodbye. I clambered across the row of boats alongside the harbour wall and dropped on to the deck of my little home. The lifeboat threw me a line and I made it fast to the bow and then cast off fore and aft. Slowly the gap widened as the lifeboat took up the slack, and gently eased *Rosie* from the yacht alongside which she had been moored.

As we slid silently through the calm water towards the end of the harbour wall I glanced back, just once, at the lonely granite monument by the sandy beach. 'This is it.'

At first all went well; the lifeboat crew kept everything under control. We moved steadily out into clear water surrounded by a little fleet of small craft. I could see Colin Thomson, standing with Marie Christine in the bows of the green I.T.N. trawler.

Quite soon, a conflict arose between the B.B.C. T.V. launch, and the larger I.T.N. boat. The B.B.C. men cut inside, obscuring the I.T.N. vision. I knew both teams were at each other's throats, as a result of a problem over the filming of a heart transplant patient in a London hospital the previous week.

The I.T.N. crew created a fuss, and the B.B.C. men dropped astern to try to come up on the port side instead. They went across our stern so close that the bow caught the pushpit a glancing blow, only narrowly missing the self-steering gear. I was furious, all my pent-up self-control evaporated, and I screamed abuse at them. At the press conference I had taken great pains to point out the need for care while we were at sea. I knew this to be one of the most hazardous phases of the entire voyage. Both Chichester and Rose had been hit.

Luckily I could see no damage, and I made a conscious effort to calm myself. This was a great occasion for me, the first person ever to set out on such a voyage. I could see the brave little figure of Marie Christine, in her pale blue coat, still waving up in the bows of the I.T.N. boat.

In open water I hoisted the mainsail and the big genoa. I then slipped the rope from the lifeboat, and felt the gentle breeze belly the sails as *Rosie* dipped slightly to starboard. The lifeboat crew, who had brought us in at the end of the rowing, waved farewell and turned for home.

One by one, the other little boats dropped astern sounding their horns. The wind stayed steady and I set the self-steering gear. Only the I.T.N. boat stayed with us, Marie Christine still forcing herself to look cheerful.

'Sit up on the bow, will you, John,' someone called. Under contract the best thing is to be as co-operative as possible, so I moved forward and the cameras whirred. Dressed in my Aran jersey and tam-o'-shanter I waved confidently, feeling desperately sad for Marie Christine.

The trawler seemed to be coming too close, in on the starboard side. 'Look out!' I ran aft, trying in vain to reach the helm.

We collided as the battered green trawler rolled up on a swell, on to *Rosie*'s starboard side. There was a horrible crunch. Everything and everybody shuddered.

The trawler veered away to starboard, I rushed along the side of the yacht to examine the damage, my stomach tied in knots. When I looked up I could see Tom signalling that he would come aboard; the trawler turned in a big circle to come alongside.

'It's too dangerous,' Tom shouted changing his mind. He waved to the helmsman to keep clear. 'It doesn't look too bad; it's only the rubbing strip, isn't it?' he yelled.

I looked down at the splintered strip of wood, that masked the bolts joining the deck to the hull. I felt that awful sickness; defeat filled my mind. The bloody despair of trying to do anything with anyone – all that mattered to them were their blasted pictures.

'I'll sail south. If the damage is worse than I think, then I'll make for Cornwall. There's no chance of repairs here.' I pointed to Aran, and tried to sound cheerful.

Thirty thousand miles and I must start off damaged – it was ironical that we should come 500 miles to ensure a quiet start.

The trawler hooted goodbye, anxious to leave the scene. I blew some kisses to Marie Christine and felt the tears hot on my cheeks. My world had come crashing down. I went below and turned on the radio – full on, to drown everything in music. I checked the stern again, where the B.B.C. boat had hit and then stumbled, cruelly twisting my ankle. I sat in the cockpit and got a grip of myself, forcing my mind and body to relax.

We would have to tack ten miles north-west, up the sound between Aran and the mainland, before rounding Eeragh Light on its rocky little island, and then heading south. The sun was warm, the breeze failing. Aran lay long and green to port, and the spectacular Twelve Pins lined the sky on our other side. It was no day to feel broken.

Unpacking the lunch Mrs. Conneeley had prepared for me, I could just see the house, high up near the top of the cliffs which form the other side of the island. Inside the packet was a letter which must have arrived just as we left the house, with yet another St. Christopher. The letter described how lucky the medal had proved for its owner. How kind poeple are, I thought tears of self-pity streaming down my face, how kind people are.

At eight thirty in the evening we rounded Eeragh Light after a frustrating day in a near calm. I was promptly sick and this made me feel better. Looking back I could see the way we had come in from the rowing and I wondered how the coming year would work out. A huge swell was running in from the Atlantic, the remains of some distant storm. With the freshening north-west breeze on my cheek, I set the first part of our course, to clear the south-west corner of Eire. Fastnet Rock lay thirty miles to westward.

Rosie moved smoothly across the swell; I had shut her damaged side from my mind. There was no indication that she could not reach England if necessary, for the sophisticated glass-fibre repairs unavailable on the west coast of Ireland.

For two days the wind failed. The sails slatted noisily to and fro, while I looked gloomily at the Irish coast. Bob Conneeley as assistant keeper on Earagh Lighthouse had told me all the keepers would be watching for me. At one time it seemed the tide was driving us ever nearer to Inishtearaght Rock Light. The radio played endless sentimental music; it seemed to express my homesickness perfectly. Even the toothpaste tasted of home.

Then the wind came out of the west. I changed the big ghoster foresail for the strong No. 1 jib, and reefed the mainsail a couple of turns. 'Ah'm on ma way,' I said to myself.

Rosie raced south; every day the weather grew warmer and the going more easy. I was scheduled to meet Bill Gardner, the chief reporter of *The People*, off the north-west corner of Maderia around 15th–16th June. He would take a canister of my diaries, tapes and film for his newspaper and I.T.N.

One evening with a blood-red sunset, 240 miles west of the French coast at the northern end of the Bay of Biscay, I was lying back on my bunk with the long army notebook I used for the detailed planning of the School of Adventure at Ardmore. At the foot of my bunk, the clock on the bulkhead over the chart table said 2200 hours; I rolled out to check the log and the main steering compass. Far out on the port side, a catamaran seemed to be coming our way. A quarter of an hour passed and there was no mistaken his intentions. The number 12 on her side meant she was in the Atlantic Race, which had started from Plymouth on the day I left Aran. My competitors sheet told me number 12 was the *San Giorgio*, a giant fifty-three-foot catamaran, sailed by Alex Carozzo, 'the Italian master navigator' as the *Observer* newspaper had called him. Our meeting was quite a coincidence.

As he closed with *Rosie*, a black-bearded figure at the wheel raised a megaphone to his lips.

'Hello there, can you give me a position?' I smiled to myself – the supreme accolade for one who passed O level Navigation at the fourth attempt.

'I'll try. I'm not in your race, you know. I'm sailing south – round the world.'

'What is your name?'

'Captain Ridgway.'

'Oh, I have read about you. I hope to be joining the race when I return from America.' He wheeled the big multi-hull around *Rosie* with typical Italian verve and élan. I dreaded a collision.

From the position at three-thirty that afternoon, I quickly

calculated our present position and called it out to him over my own powerful Tannoy hailer. He wrote busily on a scrap of paper.

'Thank you, goodbye and good luck.' He swung away to starboard, and headed for the crimson sunset. I returned to my bunk and the plans for Ardmore.

'Hello there.' Ten minutes had passed; he was back again, sweeping his acrobatic circles around us.

'I lost the paper! Can you give me another position check?'

It was like some kind of pantomime, two madmen screaming at each other in the gathering dusk, way out on the ocean. We could have been the only two men left alive in the world, for we both spoke with sufficient gallantry, savouring the moment.

I gave him the position again, and this time I stayed in the cockpit and watched him go over the horizon, feeling a strong bond with this man I had never met. 'He who would greatly win must deeply venture.'

Alex Carozzo did in fact join the Golden Globe race. Returning to Plymouth he abandoned the Single-handed Atlantic Race, and built a new sixty-foot yacht. When the time limit ran out for the start of the Round the World race, he lay at anchor to finish stowing his gear and supplies before setting sail. Sadly he had to give up when he developed stomach ulcers off Lisbon.

When I went below it was too dark to read and I soon fell asleep. 'Charlie', the self-steering gear fitted by Old Charlie Middlin, kept us on the right course while I slept. The little elephant pennant fluttered bravely on the lead counterpoise of the wooden vane, all the while indicating the direction of the wind. H.M.S. *Elephant*, Nelson's flagship at the battle of Copenhagen, was built at Elephant Boat Yard in 1786; I couldn't do better. The old paraffin lantern, lent by Bill of the 'Jolly Sailor' at Bursledon, flickered through the night to warn passing shipping, although I was well off the main lanes. Every couple of hours, the battery of alarm clocks called me to check the log and the main steering compass against the little auxiliary compass rigged over my bunk. I had a good look at the sea and listened to the noise of the wind in the rigging for anything wrong, and then returned below to fill in the written log with the details.

The days passed and we found a steady north-easterly airstream. The water turned a deeper blue, and the sun blazed. *Rosie* romped south at six knots, under her trade-wind sails. The supply of avocado pears given me by Jane Pelling ran out, and also Mrs. Conneeley's scones and marmalade. Sardines, 'hard-tack' biscuits and army cheese, all eaten al fresco in the cockpit, became the order of the day, the inevitable curry the order of the night. It was quite like old times.

Every three days, in order to conserve water, there was the pleasure of a shave with a brand new Wilkinson's Sword Edge blade. An everyday chore became a work of art. A good shave is worth a hot meal.

Stretched out on the foredeck, basking in the sun, I thought of how much Marie Christine would enjoy this kind of sailing; but it wouldn't last – soon we should be in the southern winter. This trade-wind sailing, running with a foresail poled out on either side, foreward of the mast, and no mainsail, meant that the strain came on the backstays. There was no real way of telling if the collision had strained the shroud plates. There were, however, some rather worrying hairline cracks in the white surface coat of the glass-fibre deck, where it surrounded the mainstay shroud plate on the port side. The foot of the mast, mounted on the deck, seemed to have shifted slightly in its shoe. Unfortunately, the sea was never calm enough to work on the damaged area of rubbing strip, because spray always kept it wet, thus making impossible such glass-fibre repairs as I could attempt under way. Perhaps after Madeira, in the doldrums, I would be able to make a good job of it; until then I would wait my chance.

Slipping south, at 100 miles a day, I could still hear the radio programmes from home. Each afternoon I remembered 'Woman's Hour' territory in Broadcasting House, those powerful 'ladies' luncheons' before the programme, in their special dining-room. Kindly, motherly Marjorie Anderson, responsible for the smooth flow of the programme when on the air, with her cigarettes and stopwatch. And the edgy-looking faces behind the glass panel.

As we began to close Madeira, I had a dream that Tom was still aboard, and that I must return to Aran, and start again. This was something of a nightmare to me. The distance to the island narrowed, and I thought of Bill Gardner, from *The People*, flying out to Funchal from London. Even now unsuspecting radio hams on the Island would be his target; they would all be cajoled into listening out for my signals. Thirty miles long by twelve miles wide, Madeira is well named the Pearl of the Atlantic; with sugar-cane and bananas on the coast it rises dramatically to 6,000 feet

ean rendezvous off Madeira
eeks out of the Aran Islands
Bill Gardner on his whaler.
kies in the early stages soon
I to despair, and I felt my
had crashed as I turned for
and failure.

Dunrobin boys (*above*) help move the roof sections for the John Ridgway School of Adventure at Ardmore. Rod Liddon and Hughie Ross (*left*) worked all through the winter of 1968–69. The 90-foot building looked like a spider's web in the snow.

with vegetation altering all the way up. To me it would look like Bali Hai, after two weeks alone with the sea.

I read several of the books by Colette, but found these sad and I didn't want to read sad books at this early stage. The 120 paperback books had been presented by Michael Sissons; his assistant, Petra Lewis, had gone to great trouble arranging for a panel of authors, all clients of A. D. Peters, to list the books they would recommend for a year alone. Quite clearly, I would emerge an intellectual giant if I read the complete library. Kingsley Amis, Gavin Lyall, Nigel Balchin, even Bernard Levin had been among those to contribute lists, but sadly I doubted if I should ever even start some of the books.

Nigel Balchin had suggested the Colette books; they are wonderfully descriptive, but so sad in the way they highlight the brevity of life. Given time to contemplate, it was painful to think of those near and dear to me, some of them growing old when for many years I had thought them ageless. I felt grateful to the rowing for at least making me aware that time was passing, and that my life was NOW, not in the future or the past.

I began signalling to Madeira for ten minutes in the hour, three or four times a day, using the yellow 'Lifeline' set and the backstays as the aerial. Sweat dripped in the confined space of the cabin as I cranked the handle to provide power, but something was wrong inside the set: it was not charging. I tried every combination of test and aerial, and I tried night and day; something must have gone wrong on the way round from the Solent to Galway. It had worked perfectly when it was fitted at Bursledon. I had great faith in the set as we had used a similar one on the rowing. It was hard to expect it to work in this new role, completely different as it was from its normal emergency operation. I was relieved to see it would still function perfectly on the automatic distress frequencies.

As the north-east wind gathered strength, and *Rosie* rolled along at seven knots, so ominous creaking sounds began to come from the area of the collision. Lying in my bunk the noise was not far from my feet. I began to worry, and reduced sail accordingly. The noise disappeared and I put it down to carrying too much sail; in such a situation it is easy to accept such reassurance.

Gradually I came to believe that the collision had upset me more seriously than I cared to admit. The loneliness tied my stomach in knots. I found myself far too tense after a day in the

N

cabin; only active physical work on deck could ease the tension. If the weather was particularly hot I just lay reading and this became irksome; in an odd way it was all too easy. 'Charlie' kept the boat moving steadily along, somewhere between 120 and 140 miles each day. I had little or nothing to do but my daily round of maintenance, everything was new and it was quite easy to keep it that way. I always rubbed candle-wax on any possible point of chafe for sails and ropes, and my red oilcan poked into every nook and cranny of Charlie's works; there was no trouble with any part of it.

My problem was that, after the collision, it was as if I had a kind of mental bruise, which I forced myself to ignore. The result was that I just could not relax and recharge myself; somehow I felt off balance.

Although unable to raise anyone on the radio, I knew Madeira was not far away. After fourteen days at sea I calculated that we were seventy miles north of the island, and the Funchal area beacon sounded loud and clear on the direction finder.

Next morning I spoke, with my loud hailer, to the S.S. *Duquesa* of London, and they promised to report my position to Lloyds; the word would soon get to Bill Gardner in Funchal. For Marie Christine it would be the first 'sighting' of this trip and would surely bring back memories of the rowing. For me there was the same excitement on seeing the ship turn towards us, the same pride in my voice when I said I was fit and well, and the same sad loneliness as she dipped below the horizon.

During the afternoon, the wind fell flat, and we slatted round and round in circles until I felt my head would burst. A yellowish brown turtle drifted by, then a shoal of green-backed fish, six to eight inches long, took station by the stern. They rippled in unison when I waved my hand over the water; they were like a burnished phalanx fading into the indigo sea. Soon I had a visitor, one small housefly; he buzzed inside the cabin, scribing tight figures of eight round the huge aerosols of fly-killer thoughtfully provided with the rations. I smiled, feeling omnipotent – it was like a Greek fable. He could travel with me, heaven knows, there was enough food for one rather droopy man and a fly. But he soon pushed off somewhere, and I wondered if he made it to the shore.

Next morning I could see the outline of the mountains against the sky, although it was hazy. I saw several fishing boats, and they waved frantically, as if they were expecting me to appear. The island turned beautifully green as I grew close; soon I could make out the delicate tracery of the little terraced fields, and the terra-cotta roofs on the white houses. Above, just where the mountains turned to brown rocks, all was covered with fleecy white cloud by the time I drew close. The whole vision, gave the appearance of a green volcano rising sheer from the ocean bed . . . a last vestige of legendary Atlantis.

A squall piped up sharply from the south as we closed the rocky north-western corner of the island – it was just as the admiralty pilot had warned. Here was the rendezvous, but no sign of Bill. Darkness crept in and I decided to stand off for the night; it was Sunday and not a good day to meet anyone off a foreign island.

It blew half a gale all night, and I jilled along under a scrap of storm jib. After breakfast, I edged inshore to Porto do Moniz, the little fishing village nearest the rendezvous. Still no sign of Bill. I moved in until I was only half a mile from the rocks, hoping for some sign. No sign. It was too rough to go any closer so I tacked out to sea and left it to 'Charlie' – it was lunchtime.

The tea was just boiling when I heard the familiar bleep of the Tannoy hooter. I peered through the little porthole over the cooker and saw an ancient-looking grey boat, about the size of a small coaster. By the harpoon gun mounted in her bows stood Bill, frantically waving a Portuguese flag. I dropped every-thing and clambered into the cockpit, clutching my own loud hailer.

'I've been waiting ten days,' laughed Bill.

'I'll bet you have. Sunning yourself on the beach.'

I dropped the grey Schermuly canister over the stern; it con-tained my diaries, films and tapes. We moved ahead, the grey container floated astern, and I paid out the buoyant red line to which it was tied, while the whaler turned to pick it up with a boat-hook. Bill got it first time. Deftly he unclipped my container and fastened another he had ready by his side. It splashed into the sea and I hauled in the line.

We had a brief chat about the next rendezvous off Tristan Da Cunha, far down in the South Atlantic. Although he couldn't get there himself, he was in touch with the island by radio from the Science Museum in London, every Thursday afternoon. Every-one at home was concerned about the collision, but I said I thought it would be all right. Bill told me Chay had started a week after me, and Robin Knox-Johnson a week after Chay.

'*The Sunday Times* have come out with some rules.'

'About time,' I said.

'What's wrong with your radio?'

'I don't know, I've tried everything – I must have damaged it on the way round to Galway from the Hamble.'

'Well, the rules prohibit your taking anything on, so we'll just have to judge the rendezvous.'

'O.K.'

'See you off Bluff, New Zealand South Island, some time in October.'

'See you, Bill. Give my love to M.C. and Rebecca.'

The *Persistencia* headed east along the north side of the island; Bill waved for a long time. I hoisted the genoa and shook out all reefs from the mainsail. *Rosie* romped along in the wake of the whaler, running free. It would be easier for us to get round the eastern end of the island, according to Bill, who had asked everyone, so it seemed.

I undid the red screw-top of the grey polythene container, and eagerly thrust in my hand to pull out its contents. There was a lot of mail and a roll of recent newspapers, including *The People*, which led with an article on the Glasgow gangs written by Bill. He had kindly put most of his packed lunch in the container – there was fresh bread, a tin of local sardines, a chunk of cheese, some cherries and a bottle of Portuguese beer.

In a special envelope I found the rules of the Golden Globe Race. I was already disqualified for taking on the lunch it seemed. 'To hell with their race,' I thought. 'Who wants rules two thousand miles after the start?'

We made thirty miles in five hours, and by nightfall we were turning south again, to round Porta da Barlavento Light at the eastern end of the island. Soon I had us moving nicely south-south-west in a gentle breeze. In the dark I could see the bright lights of Funchal, some way along the coast on the southern side of the island.

I noticed a cargo ship coming round the Barlavento Light; she was moving at about half speed. 'Making for Funchal,' I thought. I went below and picked up one of the trusty Bardic torches; for several minutes I played the light on the sails, just to give a warning of my presence in case she had failed to see my navigation lantern. The ship came close; I could hear the thud of her engines. Again I flashed the light, fearing another collision. Still she came on. I held the torch beam on the sails, and felt for the life-raft straps with my free hand. The ship passed only a few yards from our port side.

Suddenly a rasping voice bellowed foreign abuse from the starboard wing of her bridge. I could understand some of the more colourful words. They weren't complimentary – he thought we were the pilot boat for Funchal and that I was 'attracting' him with my torch. The ship went to 'Full Ahead', and left us alone in her swirling wake.

There is a twelve-mile channel between Madeira and Ilha Deserta. We were in the middle when it dropped flat calm, at eleven that night. I dropped the slatting sail and trusted myself to the care of Smith's alarm clocks. Every hour I checked our position, by cross-bearings from three lighthouses.

The next day broke hot and calm. I fixed the damaged side with glass fibre, and whistled for wind just half a dozen miles off Funchal. The radio played, but Jimmy Young's recipes couldn't help me much. I watched the planes coming and going from the small airport. Just across the water holiday-makers would be basking in the sunshine, easing away the tensions of their lives. I was baking in the sun, and tension was winding me up like one of my alarm clocks.

'What do I have to worry about?' I thought. 'Things are going well, I'm on schedule,' But I couldn't relax.

I heard the Queen's Vase Race on the radio from Ascot. I knew Marie Christine would be there with Ian and Jane Pelling. She would back 'Hurry Hurry' – so would I in this bloody calm.

'Hurry Hurry' came second. The commentator said he was 'all at sea' in the final straight. Still, he finished.

At noon the North-East Trades returned and *Rosie* soon dropped Madeira far behind. I checked the glass fibre when the spray came on; it had set all right. Five feet of ribbing strip had been removed from the base of the starboard cap shroud, forward. In all, six of the bolts which served to hold the deck to the hull now stood clear – the wood had acted as a form of washer. Of these, one had sheered off flush with the side of the boat, three were bent up and two were perfectly straight. To the eye there was no sign of distortion at the joint. None of the bolt-holes had been unduly enlarged, the overlap of the deck on the hull appeared perfectly flush. This was good news – I was looking for reassurance. *Rosie* must be very strong.

Our next landfall should be the Cape Verde Islands, 1,000 miles south down the Trade Winds. Tristan da Cunha was 4,500 miles south from Madeira, via the various dog legs I would have to make to allow for the differing winds.

Rosie rolled down before the Trade Winds, maintaining six knots for day after day. 'Charlie' had quite a job keeping her on course, because there was a fair bit of yawing about, as each big following swell overtook us. This became so severe that I had to change the twin No. 1 jibs for the really high-cut running sails. The poles could then be raised to make quite certain they would not be dipped into the sea by an exceptionally heavy roll.

The days passed and my only tasks were oiling the self-steering gear, candle-waxing the ropes and sails, and oiling the teak woodwork outside. Every twenty-four hours, Rosie covered around 140 miles. We had been lucky with the weather ever since leaving Aran. Each evening I listened to the B.B.C. World Service on short wave, on the expensive Zenith radio my parents had kindly given me for the voyage. The test matches were a source of great interest; John Arlott's beautiful word pictures took me back to my prep school days – the annual visit to Lord's for the Gentlemen v. Players match, and great bags of cherries eaten very slowly in the stands, while white figures dashed about the green grass, far below. The pigeons, muted applause, the scoreboard – I could see it all.

There was far too much food – I had never travelled Rolls-Royce before. If I grew weak, I knew Archie de Jong of Horlicks would blame me for not eating, so I forced myself to consume a fixed minimum diet each day, and then tried to eat over and above this set amount whenever possible. Normally a compulsive eater, I found it needed an effort of will to eat at all when the cabin temperature climbed into the eighties and nineties.

My staple lunch was a packet of 'hard-tack' biscuits with butter (half a pound in a sealed packet per week) and Marmite. Also I had to eat a packet of rye bread or pumpernickel every week; I found this went best with butter and marmalade. A couple of vitamin pills and salt tablets were washed down with a pint of glucose drink.

The exercise of knocking all this back, while swaying in the narrow cabin of a little boat as she rolled down the wind, enabled me to practice one of my few talents. It seems to me that at some time in my family history I must have been related to the McVitie biscuit family, for my mouth is precisely the right size to take one chocolate wholemeal biscuit. This talent has spelt FINIS for thousands of biscuits. Now, with a little adaptation, I found I could destroy a piece of crumbling pumpernickel, butter and marmalade, while at the same time balancing and bending my neck backwards, as the cabin headroom was not quite my six feet.

On the longest day of the year we were 27° north of the equator, as against the sun's 23½'N; soon we should overtake it. The nights were drawing in as we progressed farther south; I dreamed of Ardmore, where there would be twenty-four hours of daylight; of trout-fishing with Hughie Ross, and coming home with the dawn chorus at three in the morning. Ardmore was a sheet anchor for me; on the bulkhead among the instruments were photographs of Marie Christine and her rhododendron, the view from the front door and the Ross family outside their little white croft. My book of plans for the School of Adventure was filling with pencilled notes. Sometimes I would tell *Rosie*, 'There's a sheltered little sea loch, not far from Cape Wrath, which never feels the Atlantic surge. All we have to do is wait one more year and cover another twenty-seven-thousand miles. We'll play it cool and easy, chipping away at the miles with old "Charlie". Then you can bob at anchor below the little wood under the croft.'

Each morning I had that vital cup of tea, the apple flakes, sultanas and Bemax for breakfast. Then the daily round. The team must proceed with caution, every sinew must be checked and rechecked, we must look after each other. The damaged side looked strong enough, but the foot of the mast which had moved in its shoe seemed to mean that the shock of the collison had affected the rigging. We would just have to wait and see what happened south of the equator when we started to beat into the South-East Trade Winds.

At night I thought of Chay, and how he would be getting along a week behind me, and of Robin Knox-Johnson a week behind that, and of all the other competitors preparing to start. I wondered what it was that had driven the various people to undertake the voyage. For myself it meant living – each day was an achievement, something real, progress which could actually be measured. Instead of the training which had started at primary school and continued endlessly in the army, I was once again involved in reality. My attempt was probably the result of frustration, my weakness was probably that I was not 'hungry' enough for success. Because of the rowing, the achievement was not worth enough to me.

By the time the flying fish appeared I was beginning to realise I could do with an even larger stock of candles than I already had aboard. The twin headsails used quite a lot of wax, where they draped over the steel pulpit on the bows on their way out to the poles. I thought of all the candles burning passionately round intimate little dinner tables in London restaurants.

I planned to pass some ten miles west, and clear of Pointa Mangrade, the westernmost point of the Cape Verde Islands. All night I worried about making the landfall in the dark, after 1,000 miles of my own navigation. The admiralty pilot says that visibility is very bad, and that the breakers are often heard before the land is seen. Every hour or so, I rolled out of my bunk before the alarm clock sounded, and went on deck to scan the horizon for the light, which has a range of fourteen miles. I knew the 'loom' would show considerably before the beam itself.

At five-thirty in the morning, the wind piped up from the north. As the dawn slowly lit the eastern horizon with an angry pink flush, it framed the towering 6,500-foot peak on Santo Antao. A north-bound ship passed far out to the west.

The wind whipped the crests of the waves and I 'changed down' to smaller headsails. No sooner were these set than 'Charlie's' braces slipped, and we nearly broached before a particularly large wave. The twin headsails went aback and the rising wind slashed at them. One was ripped right off its forestay, and all the hanks were torn open; also the outhaul snap shackle burst open. In other words the sail thrashed about, secured only at the top and bottom.

A bitter struggle began on the foredeck as I fought to recover both sails; the wind shrieked with glee. In the end it was down and I crept below and burst into tears; for some reason I could not shake off the emotional strain of the loneliness. I noted that I had cried at some point on each of twenty-seven consecutive days. Something must surely be wrong – I was just unable to relax.

By seven I had had a good breakfast and we were scudding along south-south-west at four knots, under bare poles in a full gale. All day we tramped along. As the wind abated so I raised canvas from a spitfire jib, through twin running sails, twin No. 2 jibs and on to twin No. 1 jibs. I renewed the piece of shock cord, which holds 'Charlie's' worm screw in mesh with his main gear wheel. After this I cut off nearly all my hair. It was a busy day.

A few days later, the trades began to fail and we were entering the Doldrums. The wind became flukey and our progress slowed. I altered course, and we headed due south under mainsail and genoa on a broad reach, and in some ways it was better, if not faster. It had been pretty scary sometimes, up on the foredeck alone in the dark with both headsails crashing madly at the ends of their poles in a squall.

One morning I awoke to the all-too-familiar sound of the slapping noise made by the mainsail tugging on the boom in a near calm, with an oily swell rolling in from the south-east. Automatically I reached for the black and yellow comfort of the plastic Bardic torch, clipped eighteen inches above the head of my bunk. I flashed the light on the instruments over the chart table at my feet, six in the morning B.S.T. five G.M.T. Daylight would be shining across the old churchyard and into our bedroom window at 2 Middle Church Lane in Farnham.

I heaved head and shoulders over the bunk lee-board, and found myself staring at a full page advertisement in a colour supplement. It had fallen on to the little two-foot square of floral carpet I kept on the cabin floor. A pretty girl in a nightdress clutched a huge teddy bear on the balcony of a smart town house. 'Today, just for the hell of it, take a picture before breakfast,' the caption read. I smiled, weakly rubbing the sleep from my eyes, and tottered the pace and a half to the 'garden gate', as I called the cabin entrace to the cockpit. The main steering compass read south; *Rosie* and 'Charlie' were still taking the party in the right direction at three knots. An enthusiast would change the genoa for the ghoster to stop the slatting – this would give a smoother and marginally faster passage through the water. I decided to catch up on more delightful sleep and change at dawn, perhaps an hour later.

At eight-thirty I awoke. It had been light for two and a half hours; we had covered seven miles since five-thirty, less than two knots. A cup of tea would cheer the spirits.

I was on the foredeck, later in the morning, when I smelt the old familiar cod-liver oil tang of our days on the Grand Banks of

Newfoundland on the rowing. It was the plankton, the old dory-men said, watch out for whales. I looked all around. Yes, there they were, about a quarter of a mile ahead, a large school of average-sized whales. Soon we were up with them, shiny jet black with vertical foreheads dropping straight down to their mouths. They all decided to follow *Rosie*. Like small submarines they would surface and dive; passing right under the yacht they assumed a beautiful brown colour, but they would never surface closer than twenty-five yards. I was sad to leave them behind.

The Doldrums called for much patience; each day we covered only short distances, and this was achieved in short hops whenever a zephyr of breeze sprung up. It was a time for reflection. Each evening I would eat my curry, wash out the pressure cooker and scrub my wooden spoon. I would watch the short sunset while leaning on the 'garden gate'. The sea sometimes turned into a cloth of rippling gold; occasionally the great silence would shatter, as a silver fish arched into the air.

Too soon the show would be over, and I, returning to my bunk, would have the Zenith radio give me the news of the outside world, as the short wave programmes came to life in the new darkness. The horrors of the Biafran war, just over the eastern horizon, made me wonder how God could have any sympathy left for one fool like me, voluntarily isolated as I was in a tiny boat on the edge of the holocaust. Days came and went and the sea went on for ever. Sometimes I could almost believe there never had been any other way of life for me, but alone on the sea. Nobody in the world knew exactly where I was; I could turn left to Africa, or right to South America. I could sail a long way, in any direction, and simply disappear from the endless round of bad news; Vietnam, Biafra, Bobby Kennedy's assasination. . . . Landing on some remote coast I could invent a new personality. . .

During the day, with long hours to while away, I toyed idly with my future. I even considered the idea of simply resting in the sun for a year and then returning home to say that I had been all the way round the world, but that was illogical on two counts. First, I doubted if it could be carried off, too many people would see through the story. Second, and more important, it would not be possible for me to live with such a fabrication.

Always my mind returned to Ardmore. For me, the search for an aim in life was over; travels with the army had convinced me that Ardmore would always be home. It seemed important to contribute something to life, in return for the pleasure it had given me. I felt that if I could spend six months at Ardmore, running the School of Adventure with Rod Liddon, then I could have a large part of each winter free. During this free time I could work at whatever came along, and remain in the mainstream of life, and thus offset developing a narrow-minded attitude to things. With the rapid improvement of air travel. . . . My mind raced with all sorts of schemes for expeditions during the Southern Hemisphere summer. It was really a question of contacting like-minded people who had time to spare in the British winter. South America, Africa, Australia, there are plenty of places.

I viewed the 30,000-mile voyage as a ladder with ten rungs. After covering 3,000 miles I had my hands firmly on the bottom rung; within the short period of just one year I would haul myself up each rung to the top of that ladder. After Australia, I would be pioneering longer distances than anyone had ever achieved before – what a wonderful way to spend one year of my life.

I spent very little time in considering the likely improvement of reputation and financial gain. Our experiences after the rowing had convinced me that the branch of the entertainment business dealing with 'sagas of the sea' was uncertain, to say the least. The public was always looking for something new, and it seemed they had had enough of the sea for a while. Another imponderable was timing – a serious new development in world affairs, such as the assassination of Verwoerd, the South African Prime Minister, which had wiped everything from the headlines on our return from the rowing, would seriously affect the financial results. Sitting alone on the timeless sea, it is easy to regard the machinations of the news industry with some amusement. A clash of personality, a change in public taste, a more newsworthy event – any of these could dramatically affect the impact of landing. If it was anything like the rowing, life would become an anti-climax. To travel hopefully is better than to arrive.

The important thing is that nothing can remove the mental effects of the experience of the voyage upon the individual voyager. Here is the gain.

Early in the morning of 8th July I tacked to the west. We were through the Doldrums on my thirtieth birthday. By eight in the morning, we were close-hauled to a rising south-east wind, the start of 1,500 miles against the South-East Trade Winds which blow free from Capetown to the equator.

Now we would soon see how *Rosie* had fared in the collision. The familiar slamming into the seas soon had me feeling pretty sick, as I opened the birthday presents. A silver pencil 'to cover the world' from Colin Thomson, a rare book of seabirds from the Gouldings. A fine fruit cake, two small tins of shrimps and *A Book of Comfort*, poems by Elizabeth Goudge, all from Marie Christine.

Next day I had just turned on the Zenith for the shortwave news when I heard my name mentioned. Marie Christine had requested a record for me on the B.B.C. World Service at quite short notice. 'Born Free' came over the air on the African Service and cheered me up no end – they had missed my birthday by only one day.

Now that the wind had returned, the daily maintenance became more intense. I replaced the elephant burgee with a rough one I made of red bunting. I read up the literature on my Czechoslovakian grease-gun, assembled it and proceeded to 'shoot' 'Charlie' – it seemed more professional than an oilcan somehow. All six portholes and washers were regreased and sealed, in readiness for the rough weather ahead.

We crossed the equator some 840 miles off the most easterly part of Brazil. *Rosie* was moving steadily at a daily average of some five and a half knots towards Tristan Da Cunha about 2,250 miles to the south.

Daily the south-east Trades gained strength and the accompanying sea grew in proportion. I reduced sail to a No. 2 jib and heavily reefed mainsail. We crashed on into a huge swell with fine sunny Trade-Wind weather, and a steady headwind of force 5 and sometimes 6.

Rosie lifted sharply to the heavy sea on her port bow, cutting through each breaking crest. As a wave moved along the hull, we would be left 'floating' on air, and then the bows would fall like a lead balloon, plunging into the trough with a bone-shaking crack. In the bright sunlight, whenever I went into the bows for rations from the cabin, I could see the black curtain of the sea outside, through the glass-fibre hull. At times like this I felt that the onus was on *Rosie's* designer, and I hoped he had catered for the slamming, or we would soon be making our way to the bottom, two miles away below the twin keels.

With little manual work to be done on the deck I exercised my mind by culling through the ten years of diaries I had written every day since half-way through Sandhurst in 1958. It was interesting to see the changes. Too much of this led to eye-strain, and this affected my balance on deck, which was not good at all.

After a few days, the occasional vicious rain squall came along on the wind, heralded by fierce black clouds. These brought gale-force winds sometimes, but also rain. If there was not too much spray, I was able to replenish the water tanks with the rain off the sails. I could hitch the after end of the boom up a little with the topping lift, then a turn of the reefing handle would twist the boom to form a gutter. When the rain came on, it ran down the sail and then along the gutter until it reached the forward end of the boom; here it spilled into a large red polythene bucket, with a sink fitting in the bottom. Because of the heavy weight of rain, I ran a three-quarter-inch clear polythene pipe along the deck and into another bucket. Even with this large bore of pipe quite a jet of water came out. At first the water would be brackish, but soon the salt would be off the sail, and clean water gushed from the pipe, which I then inserted into the water tanks. The brackish water in the bucket could be used for washing clothes or cooking. Rainwater does not keep as well as tap water, and so I always used it first.

For some time, I had been keeping a close watch on the hairline cracks around the after shroud plate on the port side. This is the plate on the deck from which the steel wire runs about halfway up the mast and prevents it from falling over to the starboard side of the boat. We were on the port tack, and most of the strain fell on this wire.

We were about 600 miles south of the equator and some 600 miles east of Brazil: This was no time to lose the mast, for we had no engine. With a small No. 2 jib and heavily reefed mainsail we were making nearly four knots.

The seas were long and high, the white crests sparkling in the sun. Every so often *Rosie* would stumble, taking a sea awkwardly, then she would shudder to a halt, decks streaming. I was horrified to see the deck bulging around the damaged shroud plate while the cracks opened and closed, bubbling spray.

Something would have to be done, and quickly.

I dropped both sails and we rode broadside to the sea. Trusting to the capshroud, I lashed the mainstay to the nearest strong point. I then removed the deck plate, and replaced it with a new one. When its two bolts projected below the deck, through my larder roof, I fitted on a stout piece of marine ply fifteen by six by seven-tenths inches and bolted the plate through it to strengthen the deck. It seemed to do the trick, and we sailed on again.

Next morning I noticed that the plywood had taken on a curve and was creaking ominously. I checked the situation from every angle. There were at least 700 miles of trade winds ahead and it was the southern hemisphere's equivalent of January. I thought for several hours on the predicament. One thing was sure, if the deck plate went, then the mast would definitely go with it.

The only way to avoid the strain on the plate was to turn and run downwind to some South American port. The strain would then be transferred to the twin backstays.

If I did this it would mean the end of the voyage, the end of the chance of a lifetime.

To go on meant the Roaring Forties in winter; no one in his right mind would go there with a damaged boat.

No engine, no shipping, no aircraft, no long-distance radio.

I tried to puzzle it out all day. I had photographed the cracks on 1st July. I recorded then, 'I do not believe these too ominous.' But at the back of my mind I had begun to wonder why there should be cracks on the port side, and not the starboard side. The conclusion I reached was that when the trawler hit the starboard bow, on the first day of the voyage, the impact must have caused a sudden 'whip' in the mast, which could have strained the plates on the port side. Whatever the cause of the damage, the result had been a steadily increasing bulge in the deck round the chainplate. Had I not replaced this plate on the previous day, I am convinced that it would have pulled out during the night with disastrous results. The piece of wood only slowed down the inevitable process.

As night came on, I sat in the light of the Gaz lantern. Somehow I could not bring myself to give up. After all that time; the thought, planning, worry, cost, energy, hopes, fears and a thousand other factors. . . . I couldn't imagine giving up. One half of me said, 'Go on, it'll work out if you try,' the other half said, 'Give up, be sensible. There is no point going on until the mast comes down in some lonely storm in the Southern Ocean.'

Eventually, at nine-fifteen in the evening of 16th July, I went on deck and altered course for Recife, 570 miles downwind on the east coast of South America. Then I went below and cut the first slice of my thirtieth birthday cake, and lay down to try and work out what I had done.

I couldn't sleep, and by four-thirty in the morning I knew I couldn't give up. I stumbled out and altered course again, to beat south once more instead of running north-west before the wind. I went below again and tried to sleep; every now and then I flashed the torch across the cabin to the bit of plywood on the opposite bulkhead. It had the familiar curve in it, and it was flexing up and down, up and down, with the motion of the boat.

By eight-thirty I could stand it no longer. The spray was finding its way into the cabin; *Rosie* sounded as if she were being bounced on a concrete road. There was no point in leaving her to pull the shroud plate through the deck and lose her mast. I altered course again for Recife, and had breakfast. Then I boomed the No. 2 jib out of port in place of the No. 3 and left the mainsail, reefed well down, over the starboard side. During this I was careless – the boom swung viciously across and hit the back of my head; it gave me a headache, but then I probably had one already.

For two days I relapsed into a dangerous state of mind, while we ran 260 miles downwind. Listless and dejected, I lay on my bunk, my mind crowded with all the thoughts of misery and self-pity which from time to time engulf every human being. I failed to make any entries in the log, I did no cooking. The great dream had folded before my eyes. I thought of all the work and hope so many kind people had put into this grand design. Now I had let them down. In an awful fatalistic sort of way, I looked forward to my return home; I would feel more suited to the inevitable denigration and contempt than I had with all the embarrassing praise after the rowing. I imagined the glint of pleasure in the eyes of the editor of the smart yachting magazines, as they reached for their 'editorial' pens in their London offices. I had done the right thing. Far better to disappoint people and bear the ridicule than disappear gloriously. At least there would be no awful search and rescue operation to endanger other people's lives on my behalf.

I had picked Recife from the *Admiralty Pilot* for South America, because it was the nearest port in my path with a British Consulate. It was necessary to draw a map of the harbour and buoyage system from the descriptions in the *Pilot*, because my chart of the South Atlantic included both Africa and South America. Recife was just a little word, marked on a coastline thousands of miles long.

We covered 130 miles a day, despite my inattention. After three days I picked up the reassuring 'Dit da dit, dit dit da dit', the call sign of Recife aero beacon, dead ahead although we were still 250 miles off the Brazilian coast. I would appear quite literally 'out of the blue'. There could be no hope of hiding the bitter disappointment. If only I would wake up and find it just a nightmare.

I wrote in my log: 'I don't think I have ever given up in my life before. Now I feel debased and worthless. The future looks empty and, and, and, I won't write any more, there must be something to fill this vacuum.'

I decided that 'while there's life, there's hope' and set about looking for something interesting to eat. A long face would achieve nothing.'

Archie de Jong had provided a special box of 'goodies' from Fortnum and Mason's for 'high days and holidays'. Scotch grouse! Picking the lead shot from my mouth, I wondered if the poor blighter had ever thought it would end up on a battered aluminium plate, ninety-nine miles off the coast of South America.

I picked up the loom of Olinda Light, smack on the bow, at five-thirty on the morning of Sunday, 21st July. Soon the sky-scrapers came into view, with the dawn. With little wind and no engine I had to be careful.

We sailed over a bamboo pole which was anchored to the sea-bed; it snapped the safety wire of the self-steering oar with a *crack*. The blade shot up horizontal with the surface, as if vastly relieved to be rid of its burden. It would be needed no more; I took over the helm for the last five miles.

We passed a rusty Liberty ship which reminded me of the *Clan Kennedy*, the S.S. *Couer de l'Aigne Victory* was lying at anchor near the line where the pure blue of the ocean changed starkly to the yellow brown of the muddy river flowing from the harbour entrance. I held my breath as we covered this line, fearing a sandbank, but we moved steadily ahead at about two knots.

We cleared the grey concrete breakwater over the muddy current and entered the harbour. A few men were fishing with long bamboo poles under the hot sun. I was impressed by the vivid green of the foliage, and all the other colours of the city, after weeks of blue and grey. We sailed to and fro, awaiting clear-ance for health, but when it became clear that nothing would happen, I tacked up the river, looking for a British ship among the dozen or so cargo boats lining the wharf. There was only one, the smartest of them all, the M.V. *Rossini* of Liverpool. I hailed some of the crew who were on deck and they said I should come alongside.

A ladder was lowered and Captain John Souter, clad in tropical white uniform, came aboard *Rosie*, then we had a chat in the cabin. I shall always remember with gratitude the kindliness shown to me by the crew of the *Rossini*, and in particular by Captain Souter and the chief officer.

After ten minutes I followed the master up the ladder, turning at the top to look back at the wonderful, game little boat which I had let down.

It was all a memory.

11

Building at Ardmore

I SPENT ten days in Recife, trying to sort out my affairs. Captain Souter arranged with the Lamport and Holt line to let him ship *Rosie* home as deck cargo to Avonmouth. Bill Gardner flew out from London via Rio de Janeiro, wrote a story for *The People* and took a film for I.T.N. Everywhere people were kind and helpful. Dr. Fernando Barbosa solved the Portuguese language problem by translating for me – he became 'Muy Amigo'.

South America impressed me. My trips abroad with the army had usually been to places where hatred was never far away, yet in Recife I found little hatred, and it was a welcome surprise.

From the luxury of my seat in a Comet of the Royal Flight, the Atlantic seemed only a pond. We spent the night at Dakar and then flew on to London with a refuelling stop at Lisbon. I had been lucky – the plane was returning from a proving flight for the Royal Tour of Brazil, and they gave me a lift home in my capacity as a serving officer in the army.

During my first few days at home, Marie Christine and I talked long and hard about this unexpected turn in our future. While I was happy to be home, we had to decide what to do next. There were three possible courses: first, I could set off again in a much longer boat; second, Marie Christine, Rebecca and I could set off round the world to write articles for a newspaper; third, we could begin the dream of a School of Adventure at Ardmore. I had to make a move; I needed to expend the store of energy I had built up for the circumnavigation.

One large company tried in vain to lease the *Cutty Sark* or the *Sir Thomas Lipton*, two successful giant yachts of the Atlantic Single-Handed Race. By now it was early August, and I was doubtful if I could achieve a planning success in the eight weeks left before the time allowed for starting in the Golden Globe Race ran out, and another winter set in. *Rosie* could not be returned to her makers and repaired in time, and she was too small to reach Cape Horn during the Southern Hemisphere summer of 1969. Sadly I shelved the idea of circumnavigation.

Marie Christine was keen to sail in *Rosie* with Rebecca and me. It would mean leaving the army and sailing in the early summer of 1969; a newspaper was half interested in the idea, but in the end we decided it was not really a good thing at that time in our lives.

The third course was nearest my heart. I longed to return to Ardmore where we had failed in 1964, to make a living against the odds. To this end I visited various people with whom I had become acquainted during the army lecture tour of schools after the rowing. The most optimistic of these was the Rev. C. E. Johnson, headmaster of Seaford College. Many people felt Ardmore was too far from London, but he felt that its very remoteness might count in its favour as an adventure school.

We had made some money from the rowing, although much of it had gone in income tax, as accruing from one year. There was enough left to give me just one chance to achieve the freedom and independence I had always wanted. If I made a mistake, then the money would be gone and I would have to take a job where I could.

I had the energy; now was the time to make a great effort.

Rod and Jeannie Liddon came to 2 Middle Church Lane for a weekend in mid-August. We had both served for several years with the Parachute Regiment, we were both married with one child; careers and pensions were at stake.

There could be no guarantee of success at Ardmore; so many people had failed to settle on the West Coast of Scotland, including myself. If we were wrong this time there could be no return to the army and we had no qualifications for civilian life. Our affairs could turn rather grim.

All the plans were rethought late into the night round the kitchen table; the four of us attacked the problems from every angle. It seemed risky but none the less worth while.

My own experience of various aspects of life, since the rowing particularly, led me to believe that there is an increasing demand for quality. If we could establish a small school from our own resources, with no outside commitment to charities, trusts, religious groups, sponsors, partners or any other institution, then I believed we could make a go of it. Quality must be the main principle; we must keep the school small. Rod and I must instruct ourselves, not disappear into an office. We aimed to build something small, independent and better than anything that had been done before. If we could produce the quality, then people would come.

Next morning Rod and I settled down in the green armchairs in the tiny living-room. In true army style we got it all down on paper. We decided that I must resign my commission on the following day, and immediately visit Ardmore to look for a site to build the school. On my return at the end of a week Rod would then decide whether or not he should resign. If we did not go to Ardmore, Marie Christine, Rebecca and I would sail round the world in *Rosie*, trying to pay our way with magazine articles. The Liddons would remain with the Special Air Service for the time being.

It was a glorious summer morning as the Royal Highlander pulled into Inverness station. I made my way straight to the Crofters Commission, the Highland Development Board and the estate solicitors. They all knew me pretty well by this time, and I suppose they must have wondered what my next scheme was, and only hoped that it wouldn't involve them.

Fortunately, their response was as favourable as might be expected in the circumstances. By mid-afternoon, my business completed, I took another train on north to Lairg. My good friend Dick Donaldson met me at the station; he is a retired major who lives in a little croft some two miles across Loch Laxford from Ardmore at Foindle. As he got out of his gleaming Sunbeam Rapier I could tell by the firm grip and smiling face that he liked the idea. As we drove the fifty miles from Lairg across the mountains to the West Coast, Dick, a lithe figure in his sixties, with close-cropped hair like steel wool, told me all the news. Just an hour and a half after leaving the station, we were tucking into the usual Donaldson feast, prepared by Helen, his pretty dark-haired wife. From the window I could see the entrance to Loch a Chadh-fi and Ardmore.

Next morning, Dick put me ashore from his boat below the wood at Ardmore. I climbed the hill and called on the Ross family at croft No. 77. They were pleased to see me safely home from the sailing trip to Brazil. After a cup of tea, I walked the three miles round the sea loch to see old Bill Ross at Skerricha. Where the narrow coast road runs down a steep hill to the eastern end of the sea loch there is a small house and a cluster of low out-buildings – this is Skerricha. Bill and his burly son, Donald Hugh, readily agreed to help with the idea of the school. They agreed to renounce about an acre of their out-grazing, by the shore along the southern side of the sea loch, on the conditions that the proprietor should feu this site to us to build the school.

Later, I walked out to the proposed site, and sat alone on the stones of the old ruined croft house. The afternoon sun warmed my back. Many years before, a family had left this place and sailed to Canada, during the notorious Highland clearances of the nineteenth century.

Sheep, the cause of their eviction, had grazed on the tiny green headland in front of the ruined home ever since their departure.

The tide flowed in and out, the heather purpled and faded, the bracken sprouted, turned green and then reddened and died. Only the timeless hills of bare grey and pink rock stood sentinel on the shores of this sheltered sea loch.

Now, once more, laughter would return.

Six days later Rod resigned his commission. We were committed. Marie Christine, helped by John Ford of Horlicks, designed a brochure for 1969. We had it printed in Farnham and began the long task of attracting young people to Ardmore, while there was still nothing on the ground.

In mid September Rod and I drove north in his Land Rover. Sixty miles short of Ardmore I caught a glimpse of a long new-looking cedar building beside the road.

'Hang on, Rod, let's go and have a look at that. It looks just what we need for the school. We'll be able to find out what it cost to build here.'

He turned the vehicle round, and we soon found a farm worker near the building.

'It's for sale, three years old, but never been occupied. It was to have been twelve offices but the firm went bust. The auction is at Dingwall on 2nd October.'

The man showed us round. It was in new condition except for the floor, which would have to be renewed. Ninety feet long by twenty-four wide, it was just what we needed. Rod thought he could dismantle it. I was worried about the cost – this sort of construction would cost £6,000–£7,000 in the south of England, and I couldn't afford that much. We decided to go to the auction and see what happened; offers were not allowed as the matter was in the hands of the receiver.

At Ardmore we walked the ground with Donald Hugh. The site we had chosen would mean a half-mile track from the road end to the building, but this didn't deter Rod. The water for the school would come from the source of a burn which entered the sea beside the ruined croft house. Four 500-gallon tanks, and a few hundred yards of alkathene piping from the hills just behind the site, would soon see that working. The shallow sea loch is only 200 yards wide, and completely protected from the ocean swell; it would be fine for dinghy-sailing and canoeing. The timber building would fit snugly along the pebble beach, only a few feet from the high-tide mark. But there would need to be considerable excavation to make a hard foundation for the forty-eight concrete piers on which the building would stand.

Rod hired a J.C.B. earth-mover and set about the long task which lay ahead.

We had nine months. Rod, helped by Hughie from Ardmore, would build. I would try to persuade people to come on the courses.

After three days at the Mountain Safety Exhibition in Glasgow, during which the Scottish T.V. did a short piece on the school, I returned to Ardmore in Hughie Ross's green mini-van. I was tired and none too cheerful. It was dark and blowing a gale from the west as I turned off the road down the gravel footpath to the little driftwood shed which serves as a garage. As I closed the shed door and picked up my rucksack, I could see the dim yellow light of Rod's torch, bobbing towards me from farther down the path. It was not raining, and a half moon just lit the hills sufficiently to make them look like the bones of some prehistoric monster scattered by the seashore.

'Hello, how did you get on?' There was Rod, powerfully built, beaming enthusiasm. Clad in parachute smock and combat trousers he was a most reassuring figure.

'O.K., O.K.,' I replied. But to myself I thought, 'I've picked the right man; if anyone can build this in time, Rod will.'

We walked the three miles along the winding path, through the hills and over the burn, towards the little croft. As we drew near the final gorge, I could see the Tilley lamp shining through the window high up on the opposite hillside. Soon we were in the warm kitchen; Rod had cooked a fine steak and onion stew and this was followed by tinned peaches and cream. Over steaming mugs of hot cocoa, Rod spoke optimistically of the progress.

'The track is coming along O.K. I'll have got it right to the site by the time of the auction in Dingwall.'

'I hope we can afford it.' Depression, following the failure of the sailing voyage, seemed to dog me whenever I was tired. My self-confidence was shaken and I found it hard to be optimistic about life.

Shortly before the auction of the timber building, Rod and I drove down to Inverness where I was due to give a talk on the rowing voyage to Findhorn Yacht Club. We stayed with Donald Davidson, the vice-commodore of the club; his optimism, coupled with the warm reception for my talk, helped immeasurably to restore my normal good spirits.

I felt my luck was about to change.

On the morning of the auction we bought five more small timber huts from a builder near Inverness, one of which was planned to be Rod and Jeannie's home during the first season. For these we only had to build the concrete foundations – the builder would deliver and construct. We had lunch in Inverness with Donald Davidson and drove to the auction twenty miles away.

The atmosphere in the Dingwall Cattle Market on that afternoon was decidedly professional.

The sawdust ring inside the severe auction building is surrounded by tiers of brown wooden benches, on which the canny farmers sit. When the cattle come into the ring, the fiercely efficient auctioneer, in spotless white coat, mounts a rostrum. He then conducts proceedings just as if the buyers were an orchestra. We felt out of tune.

'I'm trembling like a leaf here, I can't understand a word he's saying.' I looked at Rod, hoping for reassurance from the decidedly agricultural looking, ruddy faced figure seated beside me.

'Neither can I,' he grunted, puffing on his pipe, trying to look calm. The grizzled grey hair above his ears looked odd on a man of twenty-nine.

Horribly wealthy-looking farmers raised and lowered shrewd eyebrows in response to the staccato calls of the white-clad auctioneer. Cattle came and went. We tried hard to understand the procedure and the jargon.

'The sale of a ninety by twenty-four-foot, superior wooden building will take place in the adjoining building at ten minutes past three,' pronounced the auctioneer at last.

We scurried for a good place at the other ring. We found somewhere that would command a view of the expensive farmers stalking in after us, all dressed up with studied nonchalance, in their fine-quality tweeds.

Doubt, panic and defeat spread through my mind. We didn't stand a chance. I pictured the building converted to a piggery or battery chicken house, tucked away in the corner of some isolated farm.

Worse, I could hear my voice bidding me into bankruptcy.

I glanced nervously at Rod. 'Why doesn't he suggest we leave,' I thought. 'It's all his fault, what the hell does he know about money? We'll be ruined in ten minutes' time.'

The auctioneer mounted the rostrum. The gavel cracked a warning. The talk stopped.

'This superior wooden building must be sold today. It is divided into twelve compartments and two toilets, and fitted with Flexel Ceiling Heating and electric wiring throughout. It is of very sound construction and is suitable for use as a dwelling, sports pavilion, offices, workshop or chalet. It must be removed from the present site by 1st November.'

Silence. I licked my lips nervously, feeling like a rabbit hypnotised by a snake.

'What am I bid?'

Silence.

'Come along, gentlemen, come along, who will start the bidding?'

Silence.

'Now come on. Who will give me two hundred pounds?'

A hand raised in the crowd; to my rapid glance he seemed a slight, pale figure not at all like a farmer.

'Two hundred pounds I'm bid. Who will give me two hundred and fifty, two fifty?'

I watched my right hand, in a detached sort of way, as it went up into the air. I could hear the blood thudding in my ears.

'Two fifty. Three hundred, three hundred? Two seventy-five, then?'

Silence.

'Two seventy-five then, two seventy-five?'

'Two seventy-five, sir.' The pale man's hand was up; nobody else seemed interested. It was between him and me, a battle of wits.

'Three hundred, now come along, gentlemen, who'll give me three hundred?'

I smiled and raised my hand in an expansive gesture. This was meant to show the pale man that I could go on for ever, he might as well give up.

'Three ten,' the pale man murmured.

'Three ten, three twenty, three twenty?' The auctioneer looked grim, his mouth twisted up at the right-hand side, in a way that reminded me curiously of Corporal Harwood, back at 'Stalag IX'.

'Come on, who'll give me three twenty?'

I raised my hand again as if stung.

'Three twenty. Three thirty, three thirty?' The pale man looked hesitant but raised his hand.

'Three forty,' I said as clearly as I could.

'Three forty. Three fifty, three fifty?'

Silence.

'Three hundred and forty pounds, going at three hundred and forty pounds. Going going, gone. At three hundred and forty pounds to you, sir.' The auctioneer nodded in my direction.

It was over. Rod and I stared at each other in disbelief. We had bought it.

I was signing the cheque in the outer office when the pale man came in. My hands were trembling; I felt generous, every man was my brother.

'I only wanted half for a house. Nobody thinks it can be dismantled, you know,' he said.

'I do,' was all Rod said.

We drove down south jubilant.

At the florists in Inverness, I bought old Mrs. Ross a dozen chrysanthemums. 'To be delivered to croft No. 77 Ardmore,' I said smiling. That would fix Interflora – it's fifty miles from the railway. I thought of 'Willy the Post' carrying a bunch of chrysanthemums four miles along the footpath in the rain. It was a day to celebrate.

Home at 2 Middle Church Lane in Farnham, I set about trying to contact Mrs. Yvette Brown whom I knew owned croft house No. 76 at Ardmore, on the other side of the wood from the blue croft, No. 80, and next door to the Ross family in No. 77. After some difficulty, I reached Mrs. Brown on the phone at Loch Torridon. She very kindly sold me the house and the three acres of land running down to the sea for £400.

My luck had changed. Although the house had been empty ten years, and had no running water laid on, the walls were of stone and four feet thick. It would be a better place for the Liddons to spend the winter than the caravan they had bought. The sooner we all moved north the better.

One frosty morning in the middle of October, Marie Christine, Rebecca and I drove into Lairg on our way to make a permanent home at Ardmore. We bought a paraffin stove and some other winter gear at Mr. Bielecki's store. Then, after a cup of tea, the three of us set off into the brittle winter sunshine and headed for the snow-capped mountains and the west coast.

My heart was singing as we drove along the narrow road running by the northern shores of the great Loch Shin. After twenty-five miles without seeing another car, we reached the watershed at the western end of Loch Merkland. At this point the road winds through a pass in the North-West Highlands, and then falls steeply down the Kinloch Brae to Loch More. Here we saw any number of red deer feeding close by the roadside, brought down from the heights by the winter frosts. Soon the lofty peaks of Ben Stack and Arkle came into sight. I recalled the despair I used to feel, driving along this same road in 1964, when I worked on Kinlochbervie pier.

Now we were back, with a chance.

Next evening, when we were well settled into the blue house, Rod and Jeannie, with Jamie their baby son, arrived at Skerricha. Their Land-Rover towed a huge trailer bearing all their belongings. They have come to stay, I thought as I climbed out of the boat to meet them.

As we made our way back in the little blue yawlie, along the loch towards the landing place under the wood, we could see a bright shaft of light shining down from the Tilley lamp in the window of the blue house up on the hillside. It seemed to be guiding us in through the dark.

The Liddons were tired from the 700-mile drive, but at last we were all set to get started.

After a good night's sleep Rod and I started the long business of ferrying luggage across the loch and up the hill to No. 76, the whitewashed stone house which was their new home.

The chimney needed sweeping and so Hughie showed us the Highland method of performing this task. The basic equipment required is a length of stout string, with a flat iron tied to one end. A couple of feet up from the iron, a good bunch of heather is tied on the string. Rod perched on the gable end and gently raised and lowered the iron in the chimney. All the soot gathered on old newspapers below. Soon the driftwood fire roared in the fireplace for the first time in ten years. The Liddons were in.

Rod and Hughie set off next day to start dismantling our new building, sixty miles away at Bonar Bridge. This was no easy task. In the evenings they sat round a fire in the local pub, and sang songs while the fiddler played. At the weekend they returned and we moved the remainder of the Liddon equipment across the loch from Skerricha to Ardmore.

Meanwhile I made use of the planning experience gained in the rowing and sailing ventures. Marie Christine hammered away at the typewriter all day, and Rebecca, with remarkable consideration, played quietly around the house. For exercise, I dug a potato patch forty-five yards long and ten yards wide; it was hard work turning the turf for the first time in years, but it served to clean the soil and kill the rushes.

The days passed all too quickly. The dismantling process was completed just before the end of October, and returning fish lorries began to bring the sections to the waterside, ready for rafting across to the site. Not one of the windows was broken.

Endless financial calculations seemed to prove that we could just afford to build and equip the school, but periods of depression were frequent. If we failed to fill the courses in our first year, we would be unable to continue, and all the work would have no resale value, because of its isolation. I was worried.

At weekends Rod and I talked late into the night. With poor radio reception, no T.V. and newspapers only on Sundays, there was plenty of time for work and thought.

Although I had had an initial offer to start on the Scilly Isles, and there was some vague correspondence regarding the starting of a school on the Isle of Man, we were determined to avoid any assistance which would involve outside control of the school. Above all else we wished to do it our own way, with complete independence.

The North-West Highlands had seen the best summer in living memory, and the weather held dry and cold, thus enabling Rod and Hughie to finish the track and start on the foundation in quick time.

Our luck held. We hired a large raft from the County Council in readiness to float the heavy roof sections on to the site when the concrete piers were prepared.

It was with transport that we were particularly handicapped; 200 concrete blocks cost fifteen pounds in Inverness, but the transport for the 100 miles to the road end cost a further ten pounds. After this the forty-pound blocks had to be carried on our backs 200 yards to the edge of the loch. There they were loaded into the dinghy which could carry thirty-five blocks, or 1,400 pounds – one precarious load. After a quarter-mile sea trip, the blocks would be unloaded and carried up the shore to a stock-pile on the site. Six hundred of these forty-pound blocks went into the foundations alone; after that many more were needed to build the foundations for the other buildings.

Because we had not been able to cut peat during the early part of the year, we had to burn wood on our fires. Twigs from the birch trees made good kindling. The branches are cut during the early summer and left to dry where they fall. When the first frosts come the brittle branches are dragged up through the trees and piled high in the old stone byre with its black felt roof.

For logs we went to sea, out round the end of Ardmore Point and along the open Atlantic coast. On tiny beaches above the high water mark there lies a harvest of firewood, the remnants of deck cargoes of pit props and pulp logs washed overboard in long-past storms. Who knows, perhaps we burnt some of the logs we passed on the rowing trip.

Our fourteen-foot, clinker-built, blue wooden yawlie, powered by the big Seagull 102 outboard, could carry quite a load of wood and tow the eight-man life-raft fully laden at the same time. Sometimes the wind would get up suddenly while we were on the wrong side of the Point; then we would have to hurry back, abandoning part of a load on the beach. When the north-west wind blew, and long seas ran in from Greenland, there was always the threat of snow to blot out the Point, while the yawlie rolled across the swell sweeping into Loch Dughaill. We kept the sparking plug only finger-tight, twisting the cable round it to give a good grip; if the engine failed or was swamped, there was always a dry plug at the ready.

Later in the year two lobster fishermen were recovering their creels from the edge of a reef off nearby Handa Island. It was blowing up from the west, and they knew their gear would be lost in the storm if they left it. As they neared the marker floats, the sea sucked back, exposing the sinister black hump of weed-covered rock. The next swell lifted the little open boat and set it down on the waiting jaws, where it overturned throwing father and son into the cold merciless sea. Within a few minutes they were done for.

In November I had to go south to London – an advertising firm had asked me to pick the winner of a nationwide competition. I was greatly attracted by the £100 and expenses they offered; also I thought it would be an interesting experience as I had not done such a thing before.

The night train from Inverness rushed me to London by seven-thirty on the morning in question. At precisely eleven o'clock I took the lift to the fourth floor of the glittering steel and glass office block in Knightsbridge. Dressed as smartly as I could muster – for my suit suffers from hanging in the damp wooden garage at the Skerricha end of the loch – I smiled nervously at the pretty receptionist. Within seconds an immaculate young executive appeared and greeted me as if we were old friends; I became increasingly unhappy about my damp unpressed suit.

In the 'Presentation' room, I couldn't fail to see the black rubber dinghy, piled high with the 133,000 coupons returned from an issue of 4,000,000. Other people soon came and filled the room; the cameras flashed while champagne flowed.

After a while I was escorted to another room, and there left alone to choose the best ten of thirty slogans selected from the

133,000 entries. I spent half an hour on this because I felt I was
the last of the 4,000,000 pieces in the jig-saw puzzle. My decision
would link a £10,000 'dream home' with some lucky person.
Looking out of the window, high above Hyde Park, I felt a
sudden urge to pick up one of the phones at my elbow and ring
the winner, but there were no names or addresses on the pieces
of paper.

As soon as I had chosen the sequence I returned to the Presentation room and handed them to a pretty young secretary with
shoulder-length brown hair. We all went down one floor for an
elegant lunch; it seemed everyone was pleased, particularly the
'clients', who talked of starting another competition with places
on courses at Ardmore for prizes. After a fine lunch, I was just
hoping to be asked to do another job of this none too strenuous
work, when the secretary with the long brown hair came into the
room, this time with a white face. She whispered something to
the immaculate executive, and his face fell a little. I wondered if
I was responsible.

The coffee was served and the lunch ended somewhat sooner
than I had expected. The 'clients' were shown to the lift, over
which the word 'Down' glowed in red. Everyone shook hands. I
went with the immaculate executive in the up lift; he explained
what had happened. When the brown-haired secretary had made
up the list of the top thirty slogans she had failed to note their
corresponding names and addresses. Had I got anything on
during the afternoon? Could I possibly help them sort through
the mountains of 133,000 cards for the ten top slogans?

It was a long afternoon, and a far cry from Ardmore.

That night the Royal Highlander carried me back to Scotland.

Walking alone along the footpath back to the blue house,
because the boats were at Ardmore for the weekend, I looked
around me at the pinks and greys in the rocky hills, the brown
heather and the red of the bracken, the whole bordered by the
blue of the loch. Somehow the country seemed much more
friendly towards me than I had remembered in 1964. Then it
had been a war of attrition, the weather and rocks conspiring to
wear down my resolve; now they were welcoming.

We bought an ex-R.A.F. mooring launch, fitted with a 60-h.p.
Perkins diesel engine. This proved ideal for towing the county
raft, laden with heavy roof sections, from Laxford Pier some four
miles away. One of us had to stand on top of the sections as they

moved through the water, acting as mobile ballast, while the other two handled the launch.

Steadily the stockpiles on the site were mounting. Fish lorries returning empty from Aberdeen picked up the materials on their way through Inverness, and brought them to the road end at Skerricha. From there, Rod and Hughie man-handled them to the boat, or carried them by Land Rover along the rough track if absolutely necessary. The launch towed the heaviest sections on the county raft. We were up to schedule.

I helped on the site whenever possible, but most of my time was spent on planning; the rowing and sailing ventures had been good training. Marie Christine typed letters to all and sundry in an effort to bring people to Ardmore in 1969. From our experience of the improvements done to the blue croft, we knew very well the difficulty of buying things in the Highlands – delivery dates are notoriously inaccurate. It only needed delays with certain items, such as cement or timber, to bring the whole construction to a halt. If the building was not finished on time, we would be in real trouble.

One night, old Hector Ross, Hughie's father, was taken off Ardmore by boat. At eighty-one he had a recurrence of the stomach trouble he had suffered twelve years previously. This time it was cancer and a serious operation; no one but old Hector himself believed he would see Ardmore again. A truly wonderful old man, he was slight of build but straight as any of the hazel branches he cut from the wood under the hill. These were for walking sticks when out gathering with the dogs. Hector Ross had the most peaceful face I have seen in any man. A true shepherd who loved his flock, his clear blue eyes shone in a tanned face under soft grey hair when he talked of them. Nearly all of his life was spent on Ardmore, far from the road. To everyone who visited him in the Inverness Hospital, he spoke only of one thing, his return to Ardmore.

Perhaps in the smallest way, I knew what he felt.

With his father away, there were pressing demands on Hughie to help in maintaining the family's crofting way of life. He was unable to spend as much time on the site. Old Hector had always cut all the year's peat in the spring at Ardbeg, dried and stacked it, and then rowed it across to Ardmore in the autumn. From there he carried it, a sack at a time, up the steep green hill 150 feet to the croft, with its voracious range. Now Hughie had to take over;

Heckie, his elder brother, was involved with the lobsters and the sheep.

On many days Rod worked alone on the site. It seemed an impossible task, but he had set himself to do it and he just kept going. The rain came, and with it the mud. Soon the track was impassable for the Land-Rover.

Work on the foundation piers became a nightmare. The sand for the concreting between the blocks of the piers came from the shores of a freshwater loch, some ten miles distant. The Land Rover could handle only a relatively small amount on the trailer for the cost in petrol of transporting it to the site. Progress became painfully slow as Rod laboured on alone in the ankle-deep mud. It looked as if there was little chance of getting the foundations finished by Christmas, let alone the roof on the building, as Rod had hoped.

On top of all the difficulties his finger joints began to stiffen painfully with a kind of rheumatism. The poor diet of brose for breakfast, cheese and raw onion for lunch, with margarine sandwiches, was beginning to catch up with him. It was a big task for any man to have to build a ninety-foot timber building on his own during the winter in the North-West Highlands. Old Bill Ross was convinced Rod would try and get to the moon in his Land-Rover within the next few months.

Hector Ross returned to Foindle on the other side of Loch Laxford, and Hughie's sister Mary went across to stay with her brother Robert to help look after him. With another person away from home there was still more work for Hughie to do.

Rod and I were down at the shore one day, spitlocking the site for another twenty-foot-square timber building, which was to house *English Rose III*, the rowing boat, permanently at Ardmore. Above us we saw the figure of a young man walking along the path through the wood. He reached No. 76 and Jeannie called down that he wanted to speak to us.

Over hot coffee he told us he was John Greig, a zoologist from Edinburgh. He was dedicated to the preservation of the pure species of wild goat in Britain. He wanted to photograph the goats on Paddy's Isle for a book he was writing, as he believed them to be exceptionally wild.

Some hours later, after a successful visit to the island, he showed interest in the Ardmore wood, which is not only the most northerly on the west coast of Britain but is also completely

Before the snows were gone the main building was nearly complete. When spring came Marie Christine got on with the artwork.

(*Left*) The staff line-up for the business men's one week courses in 1970; (*below*) Marie Christine and Jean show Jamie and Rebecca how to nurse a new-born lamb on the crofts.

wild. It is the home of such unlikely birds as the woodcock and short-toed tree creeper, as well as great tits, coal tits and blue tits. John explained that the wood was really on the edge of the tundra belt, and was therefore made up of the pioneer species of trees such as birch and mountain ash or rowan. The secondary trees, oak, elm and the like, would never come to the Ardmore wood, because of the climate. When he left he took a lump of soil from the croft at No. 80 for analysis.

We learnt a lot that day; he was all for goats, but hated sheep for their depradation of the land. It seems that being selective eaters, the sheep will eat the grass, but leave the choking rushes to grow, and thus gradually ruin the arable land. Goats will eat anything, and cattle will trample the rushes under foot, but sheep will just avoid them, unless snow covers the grass.

Shortly before Christmas we had to drive south for various business meetings. Perhaps the only good thing to come from the sailing voyage was Colin Thomson's engagement to Marie Christine's Irish cousin, Elizabeth. No sooner was I over the horizon on 1st June than Colin, arrayed in my new suit, was pressing another kind of suit with Liz. They were married in Aldershot and I was the best man to Colin, as he had been to me four years previously.

Christmas and the Asian 'flu over, we returned to Ardmore by road. Rod and Jeannie followed, with another Land Rover and caravan load of equipment bought from various London stores.

Although the foundations of the main building were not yet complete, the smaller buildings were actually erected by this time. This meant we were able to store the materials and equipment in the dry. Heavy rain, early in the New Year, reduced the track to a morass and the gallant Land-Rover was unable to manage the last hill, even with chains.

All movement was centred on the little blue yawlie. By this means we moved colossal loads of timber, sand, concrete blocks, sixty iron bunks, life-jackets, mattresses, sleeping bags, blankets, pillows, tents, canoe and sailing-dinghy kits. As well as all this we moved the plumbing and electrical requirements, including a half ton generator.

Rod was beginning to look rather thin.

Disaster struck one bleak Sunday afternoon. In a staunch Free Church area, any kind of labour on the Sabbath is severely frowned upon; we just had to service our domestic arrangements,

P

despite the realisation that 'Anything begun on the Sabbath will come to no good'. One of the Sunday chores was the maintenance and pumping of the diesel launch.

'Give her a shot of the Easystart when I press the button,' said Rod, wiping his hands on an oily rag. There was a deep silence as the launch lay at her snug mooring below the wood.

'O.K.' I held the aerosol ready to spray.

'Brrrrrrrr.' No start.

'I'll give her a longer spray.'

'Brrrrrr. CRASH.' A con-rod smacked through the crank case. In a sense we were lucky. True we needed a new engine – about £300 reconditioned – but at least the broken con-rod had not gone on through the side of the launch, when the 1,000 pounds weight of the engine would have ensured a quick sinking into the black water.

All around there was deep silence.

'Sunday,' Rod muttered.

'I'm afraid this is going to mean another look at the figures,' I replied glumly, pulling the faded green tarpaulin sheet over the ruined engine.

With Hughie unable to work, we tried a new arrangement, whereby I worked on the site during the day and answered the mail in the evening. 'Willy the Post' never arrived before five-thirty in the afternoon and Marie Christine dealt with all the straightforward correspondence. Unfortunately, I found that a long day hauling concrete blocks or the like made me too drowsy after supper to think straight; this rather limited the number of new ideas we were able to think up. New ideas were urgently needed if, with only six firm bookings, we were to raise the further 194 needed to fill the school and save us from bankruptcy.

Our plan for the first year was to run five fourteen-day courses for forty boys and girls aged twelve to fifteen, during the months of July, August and the first half of September. Each course would be roughly divided into three equal groups of boys and girls aged twelve to fifteen years, fifteen to eighteen years and nineteen to twenty-five years. Rod and I would be the main instructors, Rod teaching rock-climbing and I taking groups of eight in the yacht for a day's sailing offshore and around the sea lochs and islands.

From nearly a hundred applications we selected five assistant instructors, giving board and lodging in return for work. John

Coates had just finished a three-year short service commission in the army, and was going up to university in the autumn. Neil McNair was a qualified export representative and also a keen geologist. Peter Haynes, son of a New Zealand cattle rancher, was on a prolonged world tour. Gavin Young had a scholarship to read medicine at Oxford. James Young, a prefect at Dunrobin School across at Golspie on the east coast, offered his services as a general hand wherever needed.

Jeannie Liddon and Rod's sister Sally agreed to do the break-fasts at the school, and make up the packed lunches as necessary. Each evening the launch was to bring the course across to our croft for supper which Marie Christine was to cook; we did this to give the school a family atmosphere.

The fourteen-day programme was planned to cover a set syllabus in such a way that days could be interchanged in the event of bad weather. A forty-seater coach was to meet each new course off the Royal Highlander from Euston, at Inverness Station at eight-thirty on alternate Saturday mornings. On its arrival at Ardmore, the coach was to take the departing course to Inverness in time to catch the southbound Royal Highlander on the same day.

After an introductory talk from me, and the issue of all neces-sary equipment, the course would settle into the three dormi-tories, one for girls and two for boys. During the afternoon swimming tests were planned to 'break the ice'. Wearing swim-ming costumes and buoyancy waistcoats, the students, accom-panied by a safety boat, would capsize a canoe in the sea loch. They would swim with it for a few yards, and then free-swim for the shore accompanied by the safety boat. After supper at Ard-more, the course would return for the night to the main building, probably tired after the long journey from wherever they had come in the world.

On the first Sunday the course would divide into its three groups, and work round a circuit of lectures and practical demon-strations of all the safety methods taught by the school. These would include first aid, hygiene in the field, basic map and com-pass work, the setting up of tented camps, the correct stowage of equipment and rations in rucksacks, and general self-reliance and safety in the hills. Once again the little Bleuet Gaz stoves, used on the rowing and sailing, made the teaching and practice of field cooking a simple task. All students would walk round to our croft for supper and then be shown over the rowing boat *English Rose III*, and told the uses of the various equipment and rations laid out in the timber boathouse.

During the first week, a group would spend two days on each of three main activities, all of which would be taught and practised at a basic level. One group, for example, would spend Monday and Tuesday with Peter Haynes, camping on an island in an isolated freshwater loch, practising canoeing and general self-reliance, far away from the rush of everyday life.

On Wednesday and Thursday, the same twelve or thirteen boys and girls would split into two groups of six, one group spending a day with Gavin Young, learning how to sail the fleet of two-man dinghies in the sheltered waters between Ardmore and Skerricha. The other half-group would sail with me out into the Atlantic on *English Rose IV*, equipped to sail non-stop single-handed round the world. We might do a little fishing for pollack, mackerel and coalfish under the massive cliffs of the Handa Island Bird Reserve. On the second day the half-groups would change round.

On Friday and Saturday the group would make a two-day expedition with John Coates and Neil McNair to the foot of Foinavon. After setting up a base camp, they would be given instruction in local survival techniques. If the weather permitted, they would walk on up to the spectacular ridge at the summit. From here they would see the north and west coasts, the narrow sea lochs, and all the mountains in Sutherland; far away to the south-west, the Outer Hebrides would lie crouched along the horizon. Unrolling at their feet to the north-east, they would see perhaps the oldest landscape on the face of the earth, the 2,000-million-year-old Dionard Valley. At the top of Foinavon it is not difficult to understand the brevity of life.

Returning to the school the group would join with the rest of the course. If wet they could have a hot shower and change their clothes, hanging the wet gear in the drying-room.

On the next day, Sunday, Rod would give practical rock-climbing instructions to those interested, and there would be an orienteering competition within each of the three groups. Neil McNair would give a talk on the geology of the area, and Gavin Young would explain the marine biology of the inter-tidal region in front of the main building. After supper the groups would each be briefed for the main four-day expedition to be carried out from Monday to Thursday. Equipment and rations would also be issued.

Soon after breakfast on Monday morning, the groups would be ferried by Land-Rover half-way along the narrow coast road to Durness on the north coast. From sheltered points along this road each group would make for a different beach; two on the west coast, one on the north coast, five, six and seven miles from the road. John Coates and Neil McNair would take the twelve to fifteen-year-olds, Gavin Young and I would take the sixteen to eighteen group and Rod and Peter Haynes the nineteen to twenty-five group.

At the end of the day, on arriving at their beach, the group would set up a tented camp where the burn runs into the sea. After the evening meal, the rations would be collected and everyone would settle down for the night.

Next day there would be no food.

The survival techniques taught on the first expedition would be put into practice and the instructors would watch the varying shades of self-reliance. By two in the afternoon the group would collect driftwood for a fire and cook up the winkles, mussels, seaweed, brown trout and perhaps frogs if there were French boys in the group. It would be a testing day, the first on which most of them would ever have had to find their own food.

On Wednesday morning the rations would be reissued, and after a good breakfast the group would move out in an orderly fashion across country. Towards the end of the day they would set up another, probably more efficient camp, half-way back to the school. By this time thoughts of the little shop in the Rhiconich Hotel, some four miles short of the school, would be uppermost in the minds of the group. Next day, they would reach the shop some time in the afternoon, and then move on back to the school.

We planned to hold Friday as a spare day, in case the weather forestalled the programme and we had to catch up on activities left undone by this stage in the course. If all was up to schedule, then individuals would have an opportunity to have a second go at whichever activity they liked best. In the evening we would hold a barbecue party on the shore.

The final Saturday morning would see a general tidy up of the school. The course would leave on the coach for Inverness, arriving there around noon.

We hoped at the end of the course to have given an introduction to a wide variety of subjects, and we hoped also to have
developed a sense of self-reliance among those on the course.
Above all, we hoped that they would leave us a little more aware
of the precious gift of life, understanding that living means NOW,
not tomorrow or yesterday.

In addition to free board and lodging and a summer in the
North-West Highlands, we hoped the assistant instructors would
benefit from meeting and instructing a fresh course of forty
individuals every two weeks.

But this was all in the future, we still had to build the school.
At the end of January, with the foundations completed, the sides
up, and the intricate lattice work of the roof and floor joists well
advanced, we had a stroke of luck. The phone bell rang in the blue
house one morning as I was working through the lists of equipment for the thousandth time, recalculating the various delivery
dates. I slithered down the steep path to the bright red kiosk and
snatched up the receiver before the caller rang off.

'This is Graham Williams of the Scottish *Sunday Express*. We
would like to do a story on your school.'

'Would you come up and visit us?' I knew of many who just
wanted a quick glib story over the phone. No one would come up
until the courses were under way; at the present rate of bookings
there would never be a course.

'Yes; may I bring a photographer on Thursday?'

'You certainly can,' I said. Now we'd get somewhere.

It was a foul day, blowing a gale from the west when Graham
came with Farquahar McCechnie. Clutching a bottle of whisky
and several cans of beer, they emerged from a black hire car
bristling with cameras and goose pimples. After a good look at the
skeletal main building, where Farquahar took several photographs, we left the snow-covered site in the yawlie and spent the
day in the blue croft working on the feature. They seemed to
like Ardmore and we waited for the story to appear in the
paper.

In early February the cold weather clamped down. The sea
loch froze whenever the wind dropped, because the fresh water
from the burns lay on top of the salt; and there were days when
the ice proved too thick for the yawlie to push itself through.
Marie Christine was able to ski down from the croft to the sea
on twelve consecutive days.

Graham told us when to expect the story and Rod and I collected the papers from the Rhiconich Hotel by Land-Rover on the Sunday afternoon. We towed Tom Price, a visiting education authority official, on his skis along the path behind the Land-Rover, for the first mile. Rod and I tramped along through deep powder snow towards Ardmore, the bright sun and clear sky reminded me of ski-ing holidays in Austria.

Tom had been sitting by the fire in the warm croft house for some time when Rod and I eventually crossed the sheep fence by the fank, and clambered up the frozen waterfall which marked the path as it wound up the cliff to Ardmore.

Over tea and cakes we read through Graham's excellent story. The phone bell rang and I began the perilous descent to the kiosk once again; it was Marie Christine's mother who had read the story in the London edition of the *Sunday Express*. We were in luck – the cold weather had gripped the whole of Britain, and with the many sports fixtures cancelled, there was little to write about. The feature on Ardmore occupied a half page in all editions of the paper.

As I left the red kiosk and cautiously made my way back up the icy hill I looked up at the little blue house with the white gable ends looking strangely yellow against the snow. Smoke from the log fire curled lazily in the still air from the chimney at the rear end of the house. The oil lamp had just been lit in the fading light of the early winter dusk, but it was light enough to see the sparkle of the brass knob on the front door and the red handle of the brass bell on the door step.

I paused by the door, and looked down over the dry-stone wall between the two rowan trees. A pair of otters were playing on the ice at the edge of the loch. The trees in the wood were tufted white with snow. Away to the east, the last of the sun caught the tops of the mountains, turning them the palest pink.

Inside me I felt sure the idea of the school would work out all right. The ten bookings would soon grow in number and we would win through on our own.

Although Tom Price and Ray O'Connor clearly liked the idea of Ardmore, it seemed certain that no education authority would send children for field-study projects as we had hoped originally. May and June in years to come would have to be devoted to some other form of course. With fine weather, the spectacular colonies of guillemots, razor bills and kittiwakes nesting on

Handa Island, and twenty-four hours of daylight, it seemed a pity that we could not think of a suitable course to run.

A couple of days after Tom and Ray left for England, Hughie knocked on the door to say that one of the young sheep, or hogs as they are called, had stranded itself on a narrow ledge on the cliff some sixty or seventy feet above the sea at Ardmore. With the arrival of the snow, the poor animal had followed the trail of sparse grass and lichen which led down on to the ledge swept clear of snow by the bitter north-westerly wind which carried the snow across the ocean from the Greenland ice-cap.

'I think it's been there a week, it looks awful thin.'

'O.K., Hughie, how do we get there – by sea?'

'Yes, we would be as well, doing that. I'll get the equipment and meet you at the shore in half an hour.' He was gone, back through the snow to No. 77 on the other side of the wood.

Twenty minutes later, well wrapped in the duvet jacket originally intended for Cape Horn, I met him on the shore by the little black shed where, among other things, he kept the 'equipment'. He produced a stout rope, a sea-fishing rod and a much thinner red rope which just fed through the eyes of the rod.

We decided to use his bright blue yawlie, as it was nearer the edge of the ice, on its iron keel-strip. Under a leaden sky with flurries of snow, we started to break through with the ends of the oars to the open water at the mouth of the loch; we had to be careful with the outboard engine because the ice could easily cut through the wooden boat at the bows. Hughie's wiry figure smacked the oar up and down ahead of us for ten minutes, then I took over for ten minutes, and so it went on; soon a crack developed and the wind, helped by the flowing tide, forced one side to ride up on top of the other and form two layers for us to break through.

The wind backed to the west and it seemed a thaw might set in. The huge snowflakes turned wet and melted on touching the duvet; I should have bought oilskins like Hughie. He had offered me a coat and leggings in the black shed.

Soon I could feel the melted snow cold on my back even though I was sweating. It wasn't worth going back to the shore, because we were nearly through the ice now, and it had ridden over itself again in our wake.

After an hour and a half, we had broken the 200 yards through the ice, and the game little Seagull engine pushed us through

rough black water into the snow, and out into the open waters of Loch Laxford. A trim little seine netter was moving up and down the loch, sounding for herring as he headed for Ardmore Point. I sat with my back to the wind, on the thwart amidships, and watched the sharp wind turning Hughie's face pink under the dark-green hood of his oilskins.

When we reached the Point, some twenty minutes later, the starving sheep was moving desperately on the narrow ledge, unable to scramble back on to the top of the grey slablike cliff. The hungry sea surged cold on the rocks some sixty feet below.

We left the boat fastened to the tangle of the weed in a nearby sheltered cove, and carried the equipment with us to the top of the cliff. Strangely the grey sea didn't look as far down from the top, at first, but it was quite far enough when we poked our noses over the top to look at the sheep.

'Let me have a go, Hughie. You anchor the rope for me.' Hughie was already feeding the thin red rope through the rings of the short wooden sea rod. As he fixed a running noose in the end he explained the plan and I fastened the stout rope round my waist in a bowline.

'Crawl down the first ledge, then gradually hang the noose over the sheep's head on the lower ledge, with the rod outstretched. I'll anchor you with the rope from thirty feet back at the top of the cliff – there is no rock to belay to.'

Suddenly I was alone in the snow, Hughie had gone back over the top to anchor himself in a hollow.

'O.K. I'm ready,' his voice called.

I inched my way down the first ledge, and the pitiful sight of the sheep came into view. Bones projected from tight skin where it had eaten all its wool off one side.

I looked at it. It looked at me.

Ragged blue-black clouds hung streamers of snow into the sea on the horizon, the bitter wind made me shiver. If either of us fell, there was a clear drop to the cold sea sixty feet below. I could hear the gentle surge of the waves.

Very slowly, I stretched the dark-brown rod with the dangling red noose out over the ledge, above the bag of skin and bones. It panicked and bolted the four or five feet to the far end of its ledge, four shiny grey hooves scrabbling in the slush discoloured by its droppings. I closed my eyes, feeling sick, as it teetered on the edge. When I opened them again, it appeared to be balanced on its right foreleg, on the very brink, with three legs skidding on the ice. A big black raven flapped slowly through the airspace between the Point and the small green island, a hundred yards offshore.

There was just me and the sheep and the raven.

Hot meals and comfort take the edge off reality; civilisation had lulled my mind into forgetfulness. Here, again, was life and death.

My arm grew stiff with cold. Two or three times the sheep walked up to the noose and returned to the edge. Each time I had to shut my eyes as it slithered on the brink of death. It was slippery on my own ridge and I imagined my feet losing their grip . . .

I made another attempt to coax the noose over its head. Again it turned away and bolted for the edge. This time there was no stopping. As it went over the side it turned in a slow curve, the red dye mark on its left shoulder rolled into view just as it dropped out of sight. I waited a few seconds for the splash and then cautiously turned and levered myself back on to the top.

We moved as fast as we could down to the boat but it took a few minutes. When we reached the spot below where the hog had gone over, there was no sign of it.

'There it is! Just a few yards to the right,' Hughie cried, steering us to the partly submerged patch of sodden grey wool.

'I've got it.' It was so light I dragged it over the gunwale with one hand. It fell warm but dead on to my boots; a stream of frothy sea water spurting from its nostrils.

'Sorry, Hughie, perhaps if I'd been more patient . . .' I knew he had recovered a sheep, on his own, from the same ledge two years before.

'I doubt if it would have survived even if we had got it. I just don't like to see an animal suffer like that, I'd rather see it dead,' Hughie replied.

We motored back along the northern shore of Loch Laxford, the gulls circling overhead.

'Throw it over the side.'

'O.K.' I tipped the soft floppy corpse out of the boat. The gulls left us and prepared to attack the dead sheep. Another life was done.

Back at No. 77 Hughie's mother produced the bottle of whisky from the dresser, and we warmed ourselves. It was all a memory.

February dragged on with snow on the ground for most of the

month. Hughie worked on the site with Rod whenever possible, and building went steadily on. Rod had worked out of doors on every single day of the winter and the strain was telling but he never once complained. One afternoon, when Marie Christine and I had walked to the Achlyness sub-post office, four miles away, with Rebecca in my rucksack, we called in to see the Corbetts at Portlevorchy on the way home. We had a huge tea of Highland pancakes and crowdie, with all sorts of biscuits and cakes to follow. After several cups of tea Ruby produced the bottle of sherry. While old Peter was telling us about life in the Royal Navy during the First World War, his brother Donald came in from the snow with the dogs. He had already caught two foxes in his traps during the winter, and hoped for more prize money from the Kinlochbervie Sheep Club fund; he won five pounds for each fox he killed.

While Marie Christine had another glass of sherry, I left the little grey house on the knoll and tramped my way through the powdery snow for a hundred yards or so, to the dry-stone wall. The rickety wooden gate of fish-box slats, at the eastern end of the croft by the loch shore, had not been opened since the snow came some weeks before. It was jammed tight. The Corbetts use the gate through the wall at the north end of the croft, because it is nearest the Ardmore footpath their only access to the road a mile and a half away. I climbed gingerly over the wall, careful not to dislodge any of the nearly set stones. Once over, I picked my way down to the shore from where I could see the site on the other side of the loch.

In the still air, shadows like long fingers stole another day as the sun set behind Ardmore. The ice floes were only just moving in great slabs on the ebbing tide. I could see the blue yawlie, nosed up on the pebble beach in front of the long, low timber building, the roof trusses showing in a filigree pale yellow against the white snow of the hills which rise sharply to nearly 400 feet, only a couple of hundred yards behind.

For some reason the three figures on the beach were running, the floorboards stacked on their shoulders bounding awkwardly. I was just shaking my head in wonder that they could still manage to be running at the end of a long day, when a movement high above the building caught my eye. There, walking along the sky-line on top of the snow-covered hills, was the black figure of a single stag, his massive antlers held high, fewer than 400 yards from the busy scene on the beach. From the other side of the loch, it seemed to me as if the noble beast was approving our efforts, from his lofty domain.

Another twenty minutes passed, and I threw stones out on to the ice floes to keep myself warm. The light was fading fast and I began to worry about getting Rebecca home in the dark. At last the little blue boat started across the loch. I noticed that Rod was rowing with an unusual vigour for the time of day as he picked his way through the ice.

'We capsized . . . bringing the timber into the beach. It's v-very c-c-cold,' Hugh called as they neared the shore. 'The engine went under, we'll have to row all the way back.'

We called in at Portlevorchy and collected Marie Christine and Rebecca. The delay had meant more glasses of sherry, and clearly Marie Christine no longer felt the cold. Despite chattering teeth and blue faces Rod and Hughie were only worried about the impending wrath of Hughie's mother, when she found out that twelve pounds of dried milk had been ruined in the capsize. Tony Reynolds, the third member of the capsized crew, was a young helper who had arrived unheralded out of the snow only two nights previously. He was clearly having second thoughts about winter work in the North-West Highlands, but he said nothing. It was dark when we landed. The boat was securely moored, and the three parties split up, Hughie to tell his mother about the lost milk, Rod to No. 76 with the drowned outboard, where Jeannie and the driftwood fire waited to revive them. Tony, Marie Christine, Rebecca and I made our way along the snowy path through the wood, back to the blue croft.

Twelve boys from Dunrobin School, with Tim Alexander their headmaster, came to Ardmore the following weekend. They worked like Trojans in the snow, and not only fitted the heavy roof sections in place, each one of which is an eight-man load, but they also shifted tons of stones from the beach into the foundation for the shower-room at one end of the building. With eighteen of us packed in front of the fire in the little blue home, it was probably the greatest concentration of people Ardmore had ever seen. Looking at the laughing faces in the firelight, as the guitar played after Marie Christine's huge fish-pie supper, I felt sure we were doing the right thing at Ardmore.

When John Anderson and Reg Garrod visited us, their black Jaguar, having covered the 700 miles from London without difficulty, just could not make it up the last hill from Loch Laxford towards Skerricha. They left the car just off the narrow road and Rod and I picked them up in the Land-Rover. Although veterans of the Vinland Voyage of 1966, in the sturdy little cutter *Griffin*, it was none the less a stout effort for two men in their late fifties.

From late night discussions round the fire sprang a new idea – courses for tired businessmen. The increasing pressures of modern business methods, with the emphasis on responsibility for men at a younger age than was usual in the past, has created a need for spiritual as well as physical refreshment if a high level of efficiency is to be maintained.

We planned a series of one-week courses, each to be run for only twenty-five men of thirty to sixty years of age, during May and June each year. The dry weather, with twenty-four hours of daylight during these two months, would provide ideal conditions for sailing, hill walking and trout- and lobster-fishing among all the beauty of Ardmore. We hoped the complete break from business and family environment, living with the sea, the lochs and the mountains, would at least give harassed men a new perspective, and at best make them fitter for their work.

John Anderson had helped in the editing of Francis Chichester's *Lonely Sea and the Sky*. This book had made a great impression on me when I first read it in the caravan at Kinloch-bervie, on wet Sundays during our first unsuccessful attempt to live in the North-West Highlands. It was comforting to feel that he should be interested in Ardmore.

When March came there was just a hint of spring in the air, the catkins hanging delicately from the hazel trees in the wood, and the days drawing a little longer as the sun came farther north. Blizzards turned to showers of sleet and rain, and Heckie began to prepare for the lambing season, still two months off.

Rod and Hughie worked down on the green by the sea below No. 76; within a few days the foundation for a small timber museum, twenty feet square, was prepared for *Rosie*, the rowing boat. She was still draped with green tarpaulins at the far end of the loch at Skerricha.

We rafted the sections of the building behind the blue boat on a fine sunny afternoon, down the loch from the road end to Ardmore. In four hours the green-roofed building was up and complete with tongue-and-groove flooring.

The pair of otters which had played on the beach with Rod's two black and white Jack Russell terriers during the winter, now gambolled at the edge of the weed. They were clearly delighted with the new building, but even more interested in the black retriever belonging to the builder. Pairs of velvet scote and mallard paddled about on the loch while small flocks of curlew wheeled about the islands in the middle. Great black-back gulls glided along the wood, unconcerned by the shrill 'kliv-eep' calls of the scarlet-billed oystercatchers as they picked among the rocks on the shore.

Spring was coming, and the easterly winds prompted crofters all along the coast to fire the heather; clouds of soft grey smoke streamed from every hillside, as if signalling the aftermath of a Viking raid.

Unfortunately the same easterly winds gathered strength, until at the weekend we had a gale blowing from the south-east. Another party of Dunrobin boys had come over to help, and we had the usual party on the Saturday evening at the blue croft. During the night the wind grew stronger, until it was the worst I had ever known on the land.

The rare south-easterly wind funnelled up the grey face of Loch a Chadhfi, from Skerricha; for the first time we became really aware of the name of the loch which translated means Loch of the Spindrift. As daylight came during breakfast, we noticed the spray trickling down the window panes, fully 175 feet above the loch.

The outboard motor could not push the blue yawlie up the loch against the wind, so we ferried the Dunrobin boys across to Ardbeg, at the most sheltered place in front of No. 76.

From the top of the hills, on the way to the building, we could see something had gone very wrong. Gaping black holes showed where two complete sections of the roof had been wrenched through the steel bolts holding them in place. The building seemed to be leaning drunkenly towards the sea. One of the sections had landed in the water, and it was pounding against the rocky shore farther down the loch. The other section had not fared so well – a trail of splintered wood showed where it had landed some two hundred yards west, on the beach, and then cart-wheeled its way to destruction against a ruined dry-stone wall.

When I reached the scene, Rod had already hammered half a

dozen timber struts into the walls, and braced them against the floor.

'Another half hour and we would have lost the lot,' he gasped, working with a sort of madness. That building meant a lot to Rod after those murderous weeks alone with the mud; he wasn't going to give in without a fight.

Every blast twitched the building as if it were some wounded giant being struck with an axe. 'Black Sundays again,' I thought to myself.

A master shepherded the boys into one of the other buildings and set about brewing up; the rest of us set about reinforcing the main building. The wind shrieked its scorn.

The main defect was that we had been unable to fit the doors and windows to one end of the building by the time the gale had come. The funnelling wind had built up inside until the two roof sections were carried away. Now it pushed and pulled, steadily weakening the whole structure. If it leant much farther it would simply collapse, and with it would collapse the dream of Ardmore. There were no financial resources to start all over again. Either we held the building as it was until the storm passed, or we lost everything.

Three hours later, only the plate-glass window panes flexed with the wind. Inside, the building looked as if it was prepared to bear the assault of a tidal wave: four-by-two timber joints propped the walls at intervals of a few inches on all four sides.

The Dunrobin boys left early – there was nothing to be done. But the wind continued. In all we had lost a total of five doors, two roof sections and many yards of roofing felt. The little hut for the generator, which had been stacked on the shore for rafting over on the next tide, had disappeared completely. The struts held and we walked home round the loch hoping for the wind to drop. From the path we could see the missing generator hut stranded on the seaweed in a sheltered corner of the loch. The air was filled with a white mist – this came from the tops of the small waves when they were sliced off by the wind.

Marie Christine and Jeannie had also seen the missing hut, and we met them down by the shore. On their way over, they had been lifted off their feet and blown into the ditch beside the path. The wind seemed to fill everything with its shrieking and tugging. We kept looking across the loch, but the main building held firm.

Next day the wind had gone, and Rod and Hughie used the

Land-Rover to tow the building upright into true once more. Very soon the roof was repaired, and nobody would have believed that anything had ever happened. The remaining windows and doors were fitted in double time in case the wind should return.

Easter came and went and the sun showed some strength at last. Rod and Philip Carte, a friend from London, were able to work on the roof of the main building stripped to the waist, as they laid new felt. The work was only just up to schedule for the planned opening date on 5th July. Hughie was needed to cut the peat and Rod worked alone – he had not missed one day outside throughout a bitter winter.

Spring heralds the arrival of the pert little pied wagtails and wheatears. They come to share the bird-table with the robins, chaffinches and the great-, coal- and blue-tits which live in the wood all year round. Other little visitors are the tiny wrens, the dunnocks and the short-toed tree-creepers. The bullies are blackbirds and thrushes which eat far more than the smaller birds; they can be outwitted, however, by hanging fat from a string which the tits love to peck from aerobatic positions. The plumage of all these birds is always in beautiful condition when contrasted with the scruffiness of town birds. Above the wood on most days soars the broad-winged buzzard, circling to wait for the little shrews to poke their noses out for the sun.

In the spring the otters and seals tend to leave the sheltered sea loch, the otters to roam far and wide among the scattered hill lochens (little lochs) and the seals for the open Atlantic coast at Ardmore Point. There they can breed, and bask in the sun, on the flat rocks surrounding the Glas Leac, or Green Island, made emerald by the droppings of countless breeding great and lesser black-back gulls and eider duck.

With the onset of lambing towards the end of April, Hughie and Heckie make their twice daily rounds of the peninsula to tend the new-born lambs. The numerous foxes make savage raids and take their toll; with fewer crofters to hunt them down the foxes annually grow more numerous. On the hilltops, Heckie dresses up the scarecrows to ward off the marauding golden eagles when they quarter the foothills at dawn and dusk before returning to their lofty mountain eyries.

Rod and I planted all the potatoes on one Saturday afternoon, in the long strip I had dug in October. The bookings were coming along steadily, and it seemed as if we might reach the

(*Above*) Ardmore in summer. The Atlantic is over the hill which protects the crofts from winter gales; (*left*) the need for mobility and co-ordination is as great as ever. Each morning before breakfast I try to make the punchball lie down.

Restored to a new condition, *English Rose IV* now carries boys and girls from as far away as Yokohama and Seattle.

The 12-15-, 15-18- and 18-25-year-olds learn how to use the equipment. In May and June 20 men between thirty and sixty come for a complete change or environment.

total of 200 boys and girls for the summer after all. If we did, it seemed certain that we could hold out until the following year. Then we planned the six one-week courses for twenty-five thirty- to sixty-year-old men, in addition to the five two-week courses for forty boys and girls aged between twelve to twenty-five.

As well as the two major types of course, we set about trying to arrange one ten-day course for forty-five preparatory school boys, aged twelve to thirteen, during the Easter holidays of the following year.

In order to keep ourselves mentally alert we approached Shell Mex and B.P. Ltd., to see if we might run a special two-week course for them, during September of each year. Our idea was to run a stiff physical and mental course for thirty high-potential young men in the management sector in industry. The syllabus was to be specified by the companies involved, each of which would provide volunteer students in their early twenties. The staff of this course would include training officers from the companies concerned; they would have ample opportunity to get to know the students, and at the same time preside over the various business problems to be introduced while the students were under stress.

We hoped that the company would benefit from a better knowledge of the motivation and potential of its students. We also hoped that the individual student would gain from an assessment of his character from some ten different angles. Rod and I expected to benefit from the mental stimulation of mixing with a group of ambitious young men.

We were lucky when Tom Glyn Jones, the manager of the Personnel Development Division of Shell Mex and B.P. Ltd., showed interest in the idea and came to Ardmore to see the school for himself. He liked what he saw, and offered to set about arousing interest in other companies from different sections of industry.

The progress on the building began to improve with better weather. Four boys from the sixth form of George Watson's College in Edinburgh came for a week and quickly the bare shell was transformed into a dining-room, three dormitories, a drying-room, hot showers and lavatories. In three days Marie Christine and I stuck 2,200 polystyrene tiles on the ceiling each one a foot square.

Q

Gavin Young appeared in the middle of May. A fresh-faced, athletic-looking boy, who had recently left Rugby School and was waiting to take up a medical scholarship at Oxford, he had just spent a month protecting the ospreys, farther south in the Cairngorm Mountains. His idealism and quiet enthusiasm served to help us on just when our spirits were flagging with the much longer hours of work allowed by more daylight in May.

Gavin worked tirelessly by day, and practised with his bagpipes after supper. Each evening he listened to 'Music at Night' on the wireless with Marie Christine and yet he still managed to be the first up each morning. It was refreshing to find someone younger than me who seemed to possess all the qualities of tolerance and humility which I found so lacking in myself. With Gavin around, somehow it didn't seem possible that we would not be ready on time. Once more 'luck favoured the bold'; he came from nowhere just when we needed him most.

Another stroke of fortune came when Dick Donaldson of Foindle introduced us to Rowena and Kenneth Crabbe, who have a house farther down the coast at Scourie. On a fleeting acquaintance, they offered to lend us their fine new dinghy and outboard motor for the summer. Knowing full well that it would receive hard wear, they insisted they would rather see it used than lying idle at Scourie. This kind of gesture is hard to beat when people are really hard-pressed.

In early June, with twenty-four hours of daylight, everything started to happen at once. We had four weeks until our opening on 4th July. Long sunny days provided us with drought conditions.

Rosie, the yacht, arrived on a huge truck and we hired a mobile crane to lift her gently into the water at Kinlochbervie. Then we rigged the tall gold mast above the white and teak hull.

'My, but she looks bonny,' everyone said around the little fishing harbour. Repaired to a new condition, she symbolised our confidence and pride.

Hughie and I sailed her down the coast to Ardmore on the first Saturday in June. First we tacked far out to sea and looked back at the majesty of the North-West Highlands; what a wonderful landfall it would make after a long voyage.

We managed to make the broad entrance to Loch Laxford on the return tack. The wind dropped to a gentle breeze from the south-west; warm sun and blue sky made us close our eyes and smile. The silence enveloped everything but the tinkle of the water along the hull; we were heading straight for the Matterhorn-shaped peak of Ben Stack. Half-way along the four-mile loch we turned to port and *Rosie* ran free up into Loch a Chadhfi, the little sheltered sea loch I had told her about while we were alone in the South Atlantic.

High up on the western side of the loch, by the edge of the wood which sweeps down to the sea, I could see old Mrs. Ross and her family waving handkerchiefs as we ghosted by. Jeannie was waving from the other little white croft.

There was a feeling of 'peace worth more than gold'.

Soon *Rosie* bobbed gently to her anchor under the wood. Rod and Gavin came alongside in the sturdy launch and we began unloading a years' supply of rations intended for the circumnavigation. *Rosie* floated higher on the water; the sixty-horse diesel in the launch throbbed and bore the stores to the shore by the little timber museum below the two white crofts. *Rosie*, the rowing boat, now rested in state on a special platform inside the building, after one last row down the loch laden with Dunrobin boys. There was plenty of room in the neat cupboards Rod had built to store most of the equipment and rations from *Rosie*, the yacht.

Rod, Jeannie and baby Jamie moved house from No. 76, to one of the small timber buildings we had built on the site by the main bunkhouse. A small burn ran a few feet from their new home and Jamie sat for hours playing in the pools with toys which were not always waterproof.

'Car, car,' he murmured happily, his round face beaming with pleasure as he ran toy cars along the smooth rocks on the bottom of the little stream.

Taff and Pippa, the two little black and white Jack Russell terriers, regretted leaving Ardmore because it meant no more games on the beach with the otters, and because it put old Mrs. Ross's pet chickens out of reach.

Marie Christine, Rebecca and I moved sadly from the blue house down to No. 76. Gavin stayed with us and worked tirelessly during the move, which was essential both for communications with the school and to provide a dining-room for the courses when they came over for their evening meals. We could have fed everyone in the timber bunkhouse, but it was important to us to reduce the institutional atmosphere of the school to a minimum.

We laid on a supply of drinking water for the white-stone house, No. 76, for the first time, running a pipe 1,100 yards from a hill lochan above the crofts, Marie Christine faced the prospect of cooking for fifty each evening – it was going to be a busy summer.

On the site, work forged ahead. The magnificent vinyl flooring generously supplied at cost by the Marley Tile Company, was laid immaculately by Gordon Whitehead, the area manager, and Gavin. Morag, Gordon's wife, made the bright curtains for the long plate-glass windows. The walls and doors were painted by unskilled workers like Jeannie and me, while the showers, drying-rooms, lavatories and wash basins were fitted by that talented plumber, Rod Liddon. He also built a damn across the burn near its source in the hills and piped drinking water to four 500-gallon tanks above the school. Hughie put the finishing touches to his 'memorial' septic tank, the largest in Sutherland, he claimed. At the same time he built six two-man sailing dinghies and six double canoes from kits in the breakfast room of the main timber building. Dunrobin boys worked away to build two more dinghies and two more canoes in their castle at Golspie on the east coast.

Dick Shuff, who was due to join the staff after a six-month visit to the jungle of South-East Asia, helped work on the track from Skerricha at the road end, along the south shores of Loch a Chadh-fi to the school itself.

That track had become a nightmare. Old Bill Ross and Donald Hugh, his son, were both quite rightly upset at the state the new track had got into after a winter of hauling heavy materials in the Land-Rover. We had improved it sufficiently to allow the weak ewes to pass at lambing time, but all the same there was much work to be done.

The cost of hiring earth-moving equipment was expensive and our money was done. We decided to turn to Marie Christine for a loan.

On my return from Brazil, after the failure of the sailing venture, Marie Christine told me she had been left some money in an effort to cheer me up. It seemed that while I was at sea a distant relation, Aunt Ina, had died leaving £33,000. On hearing this I cheered up really quite quickly, thinking I might yet salvage something from the wreck of my life.

'Thirty thousand pounds went to the Salvation Army, of course, but I was left two hundred and fifty pounds.' Marie Christine's green eyes actually looked pleased. I closed my own eyes and fervently wished she had never told me the story, at the same time forcing myself to reflect on all the good work done by the Salvation Army, and to remember with gratitude the 'Sally Ann' mobile canteens which had visited us on the coldest days, on the Aldershot rifle ranges.

Now it seemed that Aunt Ina was to be remembered for all time through the Aunt Ina Memorial Track. We were more grateful for the £250 at that time than we ever could have been for the £30,000.

Towards the middle of June, Niel McNair, Dick Howell and John Coates arrived. The pace grew ever faster as the opening day grew nearer.

We were nearly fully booked, and the team was determined to ensure that all five two-week courses of boys and girls, from as far away as the Ivory Coast and America, enjoyed themselves to the full.

In the latter days our one spell of relief from the work was a trip up the coast one evening to the Kinlochbervie Sheep Club Annual Dance. Every one of the crofters seemed to have a half bottle of whisky in his hip pocket. Rod and I picked the Shepherd's Queen from the galaxy of assembled talent and the night was a huge success. Three o'clock in the morning found us towing a car out of the ditch, on a steep hill half a mile from the scene of the revelry. It was broad daylight and no one could get home until we cleared the road. Next morning, after breakfast, we were back at work carting rations.

At last Saturday, 5th July, dawned, grey and wet. It cleared during the middle of the morning. Rod and I waited at the Skerricha Mailbox for the bus to arrive, bringing us our first students.

Index